What People Are Saying About Soul Connection with Horses:

Soul Connection with Horses is inspiring, spiritual, and insightful. This book is a must-have for any Equine Assisted Worker who wants to truly journey alongside their client and horse, with awareness, authenticity and an open heart. Sharing her own experiences and knowledge, Suzanne Court captures the very essence of this work and the amazing, triangulated relationship with these beautiful sentient creatures.
Brenda Tanner, Founder of Equine Encounters Australia, www.equine-encounters-au.com

Suzanne Court's new book *Soul Connection with Horses* challenges us to expand and deepen our understanding of the dynamic, complex, and powerful relationship between horses and humans. She masterfully and elegantly explores concepts very near and dear to my heart — expanded awareness, presence, spaciousness, honest connection, and so much more. I am over-the-moon excited that this book exists. Thank you, Suzanne, for helping to advance the practices of all those who include horses in their human services.
Leif Hallberg, M.A., LPC, LCPC, author of *Walking the Way of the Horse and The Clinical Practice of Equine-Assisted Therapy*

Soul Connection with Horses

Healing the Mind and Awakening the Spirit through Equine Assisted Practices

Soul Connection with Horses

Healing the Mind and Awakening the
Spirit through Equine Assisted Practices

By Suzanne E. Court

BOOKS

London, UK
Washington, DC, USA

CollectiveInk

First published by O-Books, 2024
O-Books is an imprint of Collective Ink Ltd.,
Unit 11, Shepperton House, 89 Shepperton Road, London N1 3DF
office@collectiveinkbooks.com
www.collectiveinkbooks.com
www.o-books.com

For distributor details and how to order please visit the 'Ordering' section on our website.

Text copyright: Suzanne E. Court 2023

ISBN: 978 1 80341 566 6
978 1 80341 582 6 (ebook)
Library of Congress Control Number: 2023937983

A CIP catalogue record for this book is available from the British Library.

Design: Lapiz Digital Services

UK: Printed and bound by CPI Group (UK) Ltd, Croydon, CR0 4YY
Printed in North America by CPI GPS partners

The author of this book does not dispense medical advice or prescribe the use of any technique as a form of treatment for physical, emotional, or medical problems without the advice of a physician, either directly or indirectly. The intent of the author is only to offer information of a general nature to help you in your quest for emotional and spiritual well-being. In the event you use any of the information in this book for yourself, which is your constitutional right, the author and the publisher assume no responsibility for your actions.

We operate a distinctive and ethical publishing philosophy in all areas of our business, from our global network of authors to production and worldwide distribution.

Contents

With immense gratitude I dedicate this book to the horses with whom I have had the pleasure of sharing my life and from whom I have learned more than I could possibly say: Sydney James, Bertha, Jesse James, Jim the Eagle, Hawk, Marnie, Goldie, Sandy, Jaz, Riley, Tara, Romeo, Jake, Chipper, Randolph, Bounce, Gypsy, Pippin, and Johnny. I love you all and owe you so much.

Equally, I dedicate the book to all my clients, present and past, who have willingly and honestly participated in the work with horses, giving me as much of value as I could possibly have given them. In particular I dedicate the book to Hazel and Briar for their enduring openhearted work through their abiding love for horses.

Acknowledgements

I give heartfelt thanks to my family for their support and help in making our equine farm a great working space, and for patiently putting up with me placing major attention onto a laptop for several years. My wife Sarah has shared so many of the trials and joys of working in the equine assisted space, and I thank her not only for her professionalism, but also for drawing my attention many years ago to the existence of equine assisted therapy and encouraging my involvement. Without the training I undertook with the Equine Psychotherapy Institute (EPI) in Victoria, Australia, I would not have started in this work with such a firm foundation. To Megan and Noël and students of EPI, I am truly grateful for your wisdom and dedication to teaching equine assisted psychotherapy and learning. I also thank my other teachers, mainly authors whom I have never met, but who are represented in my bibliography.

I extend particular thanks to Sarah, Violet, and Patte, for valuable assistance with proofreading and for providing useful suggestions regarding content. I am also extremely grateful for the invaluable editorial suggestions of my publisher, John Hunt Publishing, and their skilled editors. However, any remaining misunderstandings or inaccuracies belong to me alone.

Above all I owe huge gratitude to the very best teachers there could possibly be: horses and clients who have put their trust in me. To all the openhearted people who have walked through the gateways of Earthhorse Aotearoa to gain personal insight through working with horses, and who have asked just the right questions to extend my own vision, I thank you.

Foreword

As a reader who has very little personal experience of being with horses, I found on every page of this inspiring book a respectful, compassionate reflection on the human condition and our place on planet earth. The author returns again and again to guided mindfulness practices such that reading the book itself creates a context for mindful awareness—reminding us how to be present here and now, and that we are all one. Suzanne Court, PhD, masterfully demonstrates that when we learn to view the world through the eyes of another being—in this case a horse—and observe how they make sense of their world, we can put aside prior assumptions not only of who they are, but also of who we are. This book helps us to begin to be aware of a bigger dimension of existence, and to fathom the meaning of soul and spirit. Written as an outgrowth of her own experiential learning with horses, the author makes clear that all that is required from the reader is respect for animals, interest in psycho-spiritual enquiry, and curiosity towards the transformative presence of horses. The scientific underpinning for the effectiveness of equine assisted (or facilitated) therapeutic practices is growing and the book believably shows that learning and therapy with horses works. By transcending outgrown personal stories, people learn through their interaction with horses to step out of old ineffective ways of thinking and being, and to step into connection and wholeness. As the author asserts, modern humans (especially Westerners) have come to believe in the myth that we and nature (our environment) are separate things that can somehow operate independently. The book is a timely reminder of how nature can lead us back to who we really are, our true selves. By detailing inspiring examples of working with people who have suffered trauma or are experiencing life crises and difficulties, we learn how healing ensues from inviting horses to be spiritual guides, leading us to a place of peace and contentment that is innate to all beings on this planet. Horses invite us to find wholeness in the very depth of our humanity. I would recommend this book to anyone who is seeking meaning and harmony within ourselves and within our communities in these troubled times.

Dr. Patte Randal LRCP MRCS DPhil, coauthor of *Finding Hope in the Lived Experience of Psychosis: Reflections on Trauma, Use of Power, and Re-visioning Psychiatry* (P. Randal, J. Stanton, Routledge, 2022)

Preface

Following an academic career spanning thirty years, I was able to follow my first loves of psychology and horses, undertaking professional training from the Australian Institute of Professional Counsellors (AIPC) and the Equine Psychotherapy Institute (EPI) in Australia. After qualifying, I practiced under the name Earthhorse Australia, then in 2013 moved back to New Zealand and started the Earthhorse Aotearoa[1] equine assisted counseling practice with my wife, Sarah. I applied the inspiring EPI model while also incorporating my own authentic voice to the work, including understandings from spiritual traditions.

I stand on the shoulders of all the pioneers in the relatively new equine assisted therapeutic and learning practices, most notably, Megan Kirby, Ariana Strozzi, Leif Hallberg and Linda Kohanov, whose insights I have integrated with those who I choose to call my spiritual teachers (Ram Dass, Eckhart Tolle, Alan Watts, the Buddha, Jesus of Nazareth, Thomas Merton, Thomas Moore, Richard Rohr, Jack Kornfield, Marshall Davis and Carl Jung, to name but a few) whose wisdom has enriched my life. In this book I acknowledge wisdom, points of view, and direct quotations from the above sources wherever possible, but due to familiarity with their work, some modes of expression assimilated into my language may be unwittingly claimed as my own.

Throughout this writing I provide some examples from my professional practice with clients. In the interests of maintaining client confidentiality I do not use real names and I disguise details that might otherwise identify a client. What I retell is factual but, of necessity, comprises brief snippets of what are usually long periods of involvement with a client. Although I describe some insights coming to clients through the work with horses, I do not mean to imply that through our interactions anyone was relieved of their presenting issues and problems in any single session. This work is not about quick fixes, although reading short case studies can erroneously give such an impression.

I do not use the names of the current horses we work with either. I sense that given the option, they too would opt for anonymity. Throughout the book, where I need to refer to a horse as he or she, I alternate genders among chapters.

Footnote

1. Aotearoa is the indigenous name for New Zealand, and Earthhorse is the seventh animal of the Chinese Zodiac. https://www.earthhorse.co.nz

Part I: A Meeting of Souls

Chapter 1

Introduction

Ancestral inheritance

Asking horses and other animals to work alongside humans in personal learning, emotional healing and spiritual spaces appears to have started at the beginning of the 21st century. However, these kinds of relationships with animals go back millennia to the period when our ancestors ventured out from the forests and onto the plains. In that environment all animals were potential and actual sources of sustenance, however, the remembered histories of indigenous peoples tell us that human regard for animals (and in this case, horses), as sentient beings with whom we share many perspectives, had its beginnings eons ago.

Early human contact with horses and other large animals is evidenced visually by a set of beautiful rock paintings on a cave wall in Pech Merle, France, known as the Chauvet cave paintings.[1] These paleolithic rock paintings of white horses with dark spots (not unlike the modern appaloosa leopard pattern) rendered in unprecedented detail show no hint of being hunted, although horses were certainly a food source at this time. What makes these drawings stand out in significance is their accuracy and precise detail, suggesting that the artists had observed horses over long periods of time and, importantly, that they valued them aesthetically. The Chauvet cave paintings are estimated to be between 25,000 and 35,000 years old, although according to fossil evidence it wasn't until 6000 years ago in Ukraine that humans first domesticated horses.[2]

The earliest known written account in the Western world showing appreciation and respect towards the horse comes from the Greek writer Xenophon, 2300 years ago. He expressed an understanding of the horse's point of view, much of which remains relevant today:

> One great precept and practice in using a horse is this — never deal with him when you are in a fit of passion. A fit of passion is a thing that has no foresight in it, and so we often must rue the day when we gave way to it. Consequently, when your horse shies at an object and is unwilling to go up to it, he should be shown that there is nothing fearful in it, least of all to a courageous horse like him; but if this fails, touch the object yourself that seems so dreadful to him, and lead him up to it with gentleness.[3]

It is a given that humans didn't develop independently of animals but that we coevolved with them. If we ever question how much we owe animals in terms of mutual development and evolution, it is worth considering the work of Dr. Robert Wayne.[4] He and his colleagues from UCLA found that around the time that Homo sapiens evolved from Homo erectus, wolves and humans cooperated in ways that hugely affected the futures of both species. Homo sapiens had initially lived in small nomadic groups, had hardly any tools and probably not much in the way of language, and before they teamed up with wolves they had little in the way of social skills. What's more, the earliest humans living on the plains had hunted alone rather than in groups, and according to Robert Wayne it was wolves who taught humans their complex social skills, pack-hunting traditions and establishment of non-kin friendships. Animal scientist Dr. Temple Grandin in reference to Wayne's work writes that, "By the time these early people became truly modern, they had learned to do all these wolfie things [and] when you think about how different we are from other primates, you see how dog-like we are."[5] Sharing our living spaces and hunting together with wolves (and later with dogs) was mutually beneficial: just as they brought strategies and protection to the human group we, in turn, nurtured them. Furthermore, anthropologist Dr. Pat Shipman makes the claim in her book, *Our Oldest Companions*, that if it weren't for dogs, humans would be extinct by now. She bases this on the relatively inferior capacities of our olfactory and hearing senses, arguing that they didn't evolve further because we learned to rely on dogs for their superior ability to detect sounds and smells. She writes, "People learned to work with other species so that we could borrow their exceptional abilities without having to evolve them ourselves."[6] The common saying "why have a dog and bark yourself" uncannily expresses what happened through evolution. This kind of research supports the concept that we are *communities of beings* and that on our own we are neither complete nor sufficient to maintain life. We need nature to complete us, or to put it another way, human beings and their environment are one single entity.

We have much to learn from indigenous cultures who have shared their lives with horses, some of whom regarded specific animal species as semi-gods and guides, and many relying on them for survival in ways other than as food sources. Native Americans, for instance, made meaningful connections with horses whom they regarded as sacred beings with special powers from which they could draw. Wendy Baker in her book, *Healing Power of Horses*, says that, "Horse medicine men had dreams or visions in which they gained knowledge about herbs and roots from wild horses or stallions. With this knowledge they could not only cure sick horses but people as well."[7] The extent to which interspecies learning occurred in the remote past we are now coming to understand from writers such as Meg Daley Olmert, who in her book, *Made for Each Other*, effectively presents scientific evidence of how interspecies relationships have helped shape human evolution.[8]

It seems odd to realize now that the history of the predator-prey connection between horse and human is very much longer than the history of cooperation and domestication. Fossil records indicate that horses were on the menu for 20 to 30 thousand years before humans realized how beneficial they could be to us alive. In turn, we have been of value to the horse: without human veneration and utilization of the horse's fidelity, strength, speed and stamina, it is doubtful they would have survived as a species into the present day. However, let's not forget that equines of all varieties have paid a considerable price for their survival as they have been coerced into taking on heavy burdens through agricultural labor, warfare, competitive sports and major forms of cartage and transport.

Ever since humans domesticated horses we relied on them to ease our burdens. The horses' lot might have improved overall within the human world since the invention of the combustion engine, but their subservience to humanity has changed only in detail as they continue in so many ways to be treated as extensions of the human ego. But there is something special about horses that predisposes them to choose cooperation with human beings, for which we are indebted. The horse, like the dog, is prepared to share space with humans despite our differences (or maybe because of them), and through their willingness and generosity they have endeared themselves to us. But although horses today are rarely asked to work in agriculture and warfare, all too often they are treated no better than sporting equipment or commodities with which to advance human wealth or status. Humans have an unfortunate habit of objectifying horses (along with most animals) from the underlying assumption of human superiority, forgetting that we too are animals and that ongoing species diversity is essential for the longevity of planet Earth and humankind. Even the kindest of horse owners can unwittingly fall into behaviors that objectify horses, something which in ignorance I have done myself. Often we don't realize we have such an underlying bias of superiority until retrospectively we learn more cooperative ways of relating to our mammalian brothers and sisters. If we are not careful, working with horses within mental, spiritual, learning and healing spaces can become yet another way of objectifying the horse, although I like to think that we are moving beyond that and are increasingly appreciating the uniqueness of horse nature.

Equine assisted practices

Half a century ago equine assisted (or facilitated) learning, coaching and therapy practices were unknown in a formal sense, but in recent decades learning resources with varying approaches to the subject have emerged, and with them, experienced practitioners and authors. The first writing on Equine Assisted Learning that I came across was Linda Kohanov's groundbreaking 2007 book, *The Tao of Equus*,[9] that introduced me to a fascinating new world. At that stage, had I already known the modality existed, I would have said it was the book I'd been waiting for. And it seems that it is what the world had been waiting for too, if the explosion of interest in healing and spiritual work with horses is anything to go by.

Today many people are discovering that as they work in collaboration with horses, either in a therapeutic or learning capacity, they also become more self-compassionate, accepting and awake. Once people open themselves to equine wisdom through the guidance of an experienced practitioner they may rediscover their own innate wisdom as they become grounded and connected with such a beautiful manifestation of nature. This capacity for healing and awakening through specific equine assisted approaches has been enabled to a large extent by the increasing utilization of less exploitative horsemanship techniques.

The "natural horsemanship" movement (which owes considerably to traditional indigenous knowledge), through its emphasis on learning the language of the horse, treats them more compassionately than had been the predominant practice. However, "natural horsemanship" is a misleading term since we are dealing with domesticated horses rather than free and wild animals in their natural environment, and that includes unnatural practices such as confinement to paddocks or stables and being sat upon by human beings. To have predator-like beings ride on a prey animal's back and take command of his or her movements can hardly be regarded as natural. But despite my misgivings about the term "natural horsemanship", without having been a devoted disciple of the modality for several decades I would not have seen the possibilities of working in equine assisted learning and therapy.

Today I take "natural" to signify the intent to communicate honestly with horses by learning to read their nonverbal language and by determining to see their point of view. But even though willingness to learn their nature and language is a good start, it is not sufficient to ensure truly noncoercive partnerships (as numerous indigenous human cultures can attest to in the wake of colonization). I have learned valuable skills and understandings from natural horsemanship, although much of what I considered to be natural horse handling methods twenty or thirty years ago, I have since revised. All too often back then I witnessed overpowering approaches bordering on cruelty from trainers in the name of "showing leadership" or "being the alpha horse", but because they usually got the promised results I put my doubts to one side. I remember with shame how wholeheartedly I adopted and practiced some of those domineering attitudes, but I suppose we must start somewhere. Even the language I used around horses then such as calling him or her an "it" or talking of "using" and "catching" a horse, and "making" a horse do something is cringeworthy to me today. Obviously, horses don't appreciate the finer points of human verbal language, although it is inevitable that they detect our intentions behind the language we use.

The foundation stone of my equine assisted work is to establish honest, non-objectifying relationships with the horses regardless of the healing or learning discipline with which it is approached. Whatever the background and discipline, it is essential to consider that communication between horse and human flows in both directions. We are not working with a useful animated tool, but with a sentient and sensitive being worthy of respect and compassion, that is, with our equal. For any equine assisted work to be effective the fundamental relationship of practitioner and horse must be questioned and assessed constantly. Therefore, this book starts by focusing on the practitioner-horse relationship as the fundamental value underlying equine assisted learning and therapy, without which the work would be much less effective and meaningful. I have become convinced through working with horses in the therapy and learning space that it is essential to open oneself to inner transformation before attempting to facilitate the same with other people. This book attempts to give some advice in this regard, as well as offer ideas for working with clients to help them traverse from mental discomfort to inner peace and acceptance.

The professional arena

There are several avenues into equine assisted work. A quick browse through the Internet demonstrates just how many varieties of practices and training modes there are currently in the equine assisted and facilitated space, along with a profusion of different names for the work.[10] There are any number of different styles, philosophies and theoretical underpinnings for which there is currently no standard global practice, although inevitably some organizations and practitioners claim to offer the primary model. In my opinion, standardization within the equine assisted learning and therapy space is both unrealistic and unnecessary given that practices have emerged from diverse professional fields such as psychology, psychotherapy, counseling, leadership, personal growth, coaching, goal setting and physical therapy. What I consider far more important than standardization is maintaining sound ethical and professional practices, with certification and supervision grounded in the therapy or learning discipline from which the equine assisted work emerges for practitioners.

The various equine assisted modalities which have arisen worldwide fall into the three broad categories of learning, therapy and coaching, none of which in my opinion is superior to any other. Rather than be competitive with each other, I see a potential for these modalities to offer mutual enhancement across their presumed boundaries and to benefit from a spiritual perspective (Example 1). Since my training and practice is in the counseling profession I naturally lean towards the language of talk therapy but for a reader whose expertise is otherwise, I trust that you will see relevant applications for yourself in this book. My objective is to present a sound ethical basis for the work and to provide an environment where spiritual enquiry may arise naturally with clients within all varieties of equine assisted therapy and learning practices.

On a practical level there appear to be two predominant modes of practice in the equine assisted space. One is for an individual to take the joint roles of horse handler and practitioner while under the umbrella of a particular mental health, coaching or learning profession. This requires practitioners to be equally well versed in therapy, learning or coaching (according to specific experience and qualifications) as they are in horsemanship. The other approach is for a specialist teacher or mental health practitioner, along with someone well versed with horses, to work together as a pair. Working in pairs, an equine specialist with a mental health specialist, is not my preferred mode of working but I accept that it is for some. My misgivings are that working in pairs could potentially blur the lines of confidentiality for clients, present trust challenges and make sessions prohibitively expensive since two professionals are engaged per session.

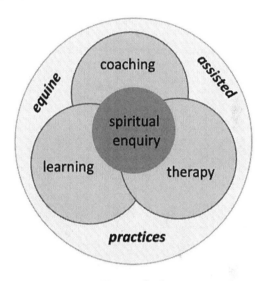

Example 1

Currently, while there is little uniformity within equine assisted (or facilitated) practices, nonetheless, an emerging body of scientific research is gradually adding credibility to the work. Scientific underpinning grows as research students in various disciplines continue to produce doctoral and masters theses on equine assisted/facilitated therapies and learning, and as tertiary institutions open to supporting research in animal assisted therapy.[11] However, while it is encouraging to see some verification of the effectiveness of equine assisted work we can't afford to wait for science to confirm definitively what we already know: that learning and therapy with horses is highly effective. The scientific method doesn't give us the full picture since it always follows behind experiential knowledge, and scientific tools are developed in accordance with perceived need. As Dr. Paul Holman suggests in his book, *Living Space*, "the scientific method plods along, often light years behind intuition, but gets there in the end; like doubting Thomas it has to experience the truth in a very direct and sensual/consensual way."[12]

Knowing as intuition

We live at a time when it is increasingly important for humans to trust the world of experience from both intuitive and intellectual perspectives and to realize that these two ways of knowing are not in conflict. Intellect and intuition need each other if we are to live in balance and harmony, but historically the intuitive abilities of humanity have been increasingly ignored as we have become more "civilized". We are at a stage now in human development where establishing meaningful connections between the intellect and intuition (i.e. between the left and right hemispheres of the brain) is an imperative for survival.[13]

Equine assisted therapy and learning is an invitation to horses to work with us to reestablish natural bonds and intuitive ways of knowing that have become buried beneath layers of conceptualization. The conceptually dominated way of life, despite the many successes and benefits it has brought to human society, has contributed enormously to the psycho-spiritual ills of humanity. We are now realizing that human beings are incapable of living contented lives through the exercise of intellect alone; we also need to trust our intuition and turn to nature in its many manifestations to rediscover the wholeness that is our birthright. Intelligence alone will not get humanity out of the dilemmas currently being experienced worldwide. Albert Einstein is supposed to have said something along the lines of it not being possible to solve a problem from the same state of consciousness that created it, but this is a message slow in being adopted. Thought, intelligence and concepts will not by themselves simplify what they have so effectively complicated. Since we humans *en masse* are no longer the grounded and interconnected beings we once were, we will continue to complicate our lives until we learn how to access the True Self, which we might also choose to call Soul, Atman, Spirit, Tao, Great Mystery, God or Higher Being.

Losing touch with the wholeness of human nature is a direct result of forgetting that we are part of nature. Not only do the majority of modern humans have very little interaction with nature, we also fail to see that we are not just *in* nature, we *are* nature. In the Western world especially we have become disconnected from natural sources of health and knowledge that were once naturally acquired through the beneficial sharing of space and resources with other manifestations of life. What we have lost above all, is connection with each other, with animals, with the natural environment and therefore with ourselves. When we ask and are open enough we learn from horses, through their willingness to share their candid honesty, and how to awaken our innate capacity to live in harmony within ourselves and in community.

There are three ways of knowing ourselves: through cognitive activity (the predominant model in Western cultures), somatically through the body-mind[14] and non-conceptually through the soul (or spirit). Ideally all three should work together in balance but it's the last two ways of knowing that Western society largely disregards and devalues. It is the premise of this book that the horse willingly leads us back to the non-conceptual spaces of knowing that we knew and trusted in previous generations. This writing itself emerges from that space as an outgrowth of my own experiential learning with horses who continue to offer meaningful connection.

Focus and readership

In equine assisted work it makes sense to only bring horses into the work who are emotionally balanced and comfortable in the company of humans. Both horses and practitioners should be familiar "speaking" to each other in horse language, however, this book doesn't focus on the training of horses other than what is necessary to "read" them while working with clients. Neither is this a manual on "how to do" equine assisted work with clients. Rather, it assumes that readers either have, or are heading towards, their own practice within a bona fide mental health or personal development discipline and are curious to consider exploring the underlying spiritual dimension within the work.

The writing is directed towards three groups of readers: equine assisted (or facilitated) practitioners wishing to explore a spiritual dimension within their practice; equestrians with a desire to deepen their relationships with horses; and anyone awakening to their own inherent spirituality by accessing the wisdom of the natural world. All that is required from a reader is respect for animals, an interest in the psycho-spiritual enquiry and curiosity towards the transformative presence of horses.

There are two sections: the first part, "A Meeting of Souls", is an appreciation of the commonalities and differences between humans and horses by comparing how both species make sense of their phenomenological world. We discuss making meaningful connection with nature, ourselves and other beings, through centering techniques and practices originating from several thousands of years of human philosophical and spiritual enquiry. By considering how horses experience the world through their senses, how they process emotion, and how they express their needs we view the world through equine eyes. This provides insight into how they live through similar social, psychological and spiritual paradigms as humans. We get a feel for who horses really are, and with that, we approach an understanding of who we really are. When we learn to view the world through the eyes of another being, in this case a horse, and observe how they make sense of their world we can put aside prior assumptions of who they are. At the same time, we learn to put aside assumptions of who we are. The first part, then, introduces the essential physical and nonphysical (psycho-spiritual) ways of being of both horses and humans while introducing philosophical and spiritual perspectives in preparation to leading clients through their spiritual enquiry.

The second part, "The Horse as Teacher and Therapist", explores lines of communication among practitioner, client and horse, and demonstrates how the horse teaches and heals. This discussion is directed primarily towards practitioners but remains highly relevant to horse lovers and anyone wishing to deepen their connection with nature and animals. Counseling techniques such as Narrative Therapy are adapted to the equine assisted space because they draw on the natural human tendency to project meaning onto others and to live through personal story-making. This is an approach to which horses respond readily. Through simple practices, clients' personal narratives are identified, questioned, externalized and, in the end, rewritten. Learning through their interaction with horses to step out of ineffective ways of thinking and being, clients transcend their outgrown personal stories and step into connection and wholeness.

There are two underlining premises of this book, firstly, that it is human conditioned thinking that separates us from the innate peace and wisdom of our birthright. The initial approach with a client, therefore, will usually occur on a psychological level as mental discomfort resulting from lived experience is addressed through psychology, psychotherapy, counseling and other professional underpinnings. However, equine assisted work, regardless the theoretical approach, naturally leads to questions of spirituality if we allow it. In my experience, clients at any stage of the work are likely to question *who they really are* and *what life is supposed to be about*. This link is not surprising given that psychology and spirituality coexist within the single continuum of psycho-spirituality and it is actually difficult to know where one ends and the other starts. Within a few years of full-time practice I experienced most long-term clients take their own enquiry towards the spiritual end of the continuum, teaching me that there are few limits to where the enquiry may lead. In terms of introducing spiritual matters, my advice is to follow the lead from clients rather than to bring in your own perspectives. It is also advisable to use the language around spirituality that your clients introduce (which may well include none at all). This work can't help but approach questions of spirituality, the point being that work with horses will occur on a spiritual plane whether or not we recognize it, and whether or not we name it. The invitation of this book is to allow yourself to support the existential enquiry of clients in the presence of a very talented Zen master, a horse. Our job is not to supply the answers, but to be open to client enquiry, setting the scene in the presence of horses to enable individual inner discoveries.

Secondly, it is only through honest connection that we can possibly make real change, whether we are considering inner enquiry or human interaction. As practitioners we can start to make honest connections ourselves by putting aside our ideas of what a horse is. If we avoid regarding the horse as an object, i.e. as an animal that *works for us*, the horse is much more likely to react honestly, enabling us and our clients to derive individual meaning from the interaction. Drs. Adele and

Marlena McCormick in *Horse Sense and the Human Heart* express it this way: "Horses teach us to expand our consciousness by going beyond the human realm. They connect us with divine mind. Working with horses makes this experience tangible. To be in tune with a horse is to be in divine attunement, or at one with nature."[15]

I invite you as equestrian, equine assisted practitioner, and/ or seeker of spiritual connection, to walk in the hooves of the horse, to experience their worldview and to access their soulful wisdom. May you be as comfortable living from the heart and soul as from the head and may you know yourself to be as free as a horse running wild with the wind blowing through your mane.

Footnotes

1. "Pech Merle" [online]. Available at: https://en.wikipedia. org/w/index.php?title=Pech_Merle&oldid=1150349574 (Accessed 1 October 2022).
2. Budiansky (1997) p. 35.
3. Morgan (1962) p. 37.
4. As quoted in Grandin (2006) pp. 304–5.
5. Grandin (2006) pp. 304–5.
6. Shipman (2021) p. ix.
7. Baker (2004) p. 26.
8. Olmert (2009).
9. Kohanov (2007).
10. The varieties and permutations of equine assisted and facilitated practices are too numerous to discuss here, but Leif Hallberg in *Walking the Way of the Horse* (2008) gives a comprehensive summary of worldwide practices. In *The Clinical Practice of Equine-Assisted Therapy* (2017) Hallberg assesses and summarizes best practice in equine assisted fields. I highly recommend both books as offering solid foundation to any equine assisted practice.

11. For a comprehensive assessment of current research, theory and practice see Leif Hallberg (2017).
12. Holman (2018) p. 202.
13. For an illuminating in-depth discussion of the left and right hemispheres of the human brain with particular focus on contemporary neglect of the insightful right side of the brain, see McGilchrist (2009).
14. The term "body-mind" comes from understanding that the body is inseparable from the mind. It is now established in scientific fields that body and mind work together within a complex network and that the mind does not dominate the body as has been presumed for centuries. See Candice Pert in *Molecules of Emotion* (1997) p. 187.
15. McCormick (1997) p. 111.

Chapter 2

Who Am I?

As a child I dreamed day and night of horses as I continually begged my parents for a pony. Sadly, there were neither the funds nor room in our backyard for a massive grass-eating animal. In due course I stopped thinking about horses, but in adulthood something woke me up to the memory of that old yearning as I began to take weekend trips into the country simply to look at horses. Eventually I figured during one holiday period that I could, at the very least, go on a couple of gentle guided trail rides. These were such a delight that I felt like the child whose wildest dreams had finally been realized and in a short time I bought my first horse and learned to ride. Wanting to do this with some rigor (while making up for lost time), I took lessons in both "English" methods and "natural horsemanship". To study both systems at once was confusing to say the least, but eventually I made some sense of it as I came to see that they both headed in the direction of harmony of communication with horses.

My life with horses has been a truly fascinating journey, full of joy and love for this amazing being, and although riding has brought some uncomfortable encounters with the solid ground, nothing could dampen my desire to spend all available time with horses. For three decades now I have loved every aspect of being with horses but above all I relish simply *being* with a horse. I have always been astounded by how a prey animal, far exceeding the size, weight and athleticism of any human, so graciously shares space with a cumbersome predatory animal that walks on its back legs. What's more, horses allow humans to sit on their backs and make decisions on their behalf; both are unnatural and potentially uncomfortable. But riding aside, it is pretty obvious that horses just like hanging out with those humans who regard them with kindness and respect.

My first horse, Sydney James (Syd), opened a whole new world for me. When I adopted him, he was a skinny eighteen-year-old retired racehorse with significant wins to his name who at first seemed very calm and quiet. But all that changed once he got good nutrition into him (a familiar story to many first-horse owners) and that's where the real learning started. Initially, learning to ride felt entirely natural and relatively easy as I enjoyed twelve months or so of beginner's luck. But this was to be followed by testing years of tumbles and hard slog as my horses showed me in no uncertain terms that it was not as easy as I had assumed. It became clear that the physical challenges of riding can be met with study and practice, but that the emotional and spiritual challenges are less well known and much more demanding. Having horses has brought many joys and benefits, but the ones I value the most are those that have required me to dig deep.

I adored riding, but what especially fascinated me about Syd was his inner life. What did it mean to be a horse, and what did it mean that he was a horse while I was a human being? Who was behind those lovely big brown eyes? "Who are you?" I would inquire mentally as I stared into his soulful eyes, not really expecting an answer but longing to know. I needed Syd to speak for all horses to explain the mystery of what it is to be a horse and, by extension, what it is to be human. He did not answer my existential inquiry directly other than to stand there solidly confident in his own equine nature which, I now realize, *was* the answer. He taught me that there is a knowing beyond words, beyond conceptualization, and that the most profound wisdom and peace comes from becoming confident with *just being*.

Decades later, I now feel that if horses could speak they would say, "We are all made of the same stuff; we are all one in nature." Exploring the mystery of who horses are helps us understand who we are through the non-conceptual dimensions of being. This is the journey I invite you into, as we ask horses (through various means) who we really are, and as we rediscover our ancient connection with nature. I invite you to come to know on an experiential level that your life, as well as that of a horse and any other living being, is an expression of the one singular life force. I want you to be able to look into the eyes of a horse and know from the essence of your being (which you might choose to call "soul") that you share the same life force, and to know that thinking of ourselves as entirely separate beings is not only illusory, it is the root of all psycho-spiritual pain. We are no more separate beings than the waves are separate from the ocean or the hills and mountains are separate from the earth.

If we ask a horse who he is, by extension we must also ask who *we* are. All humans at some stage wonder who they really are and why they are here. These are questions around which every culture has built its own religious beliefs and mythology to account for the mystery of existence. During my teens and early twenties, I was mesmerized by the question of who I was and why I was on planet Earth, but not finding a satisfying answer in formal religion I allowed the hustle and bustle of life to occupy that space. But the hunger of the soul so often calls us back. The question of who we really are is central to all spiritual inquiry and has occupied theologians and philosophers of mind for thousands of years. It is a fundamental question to which human beings are naturally drawn and to which the world's religious traditions have all pointed. "Who am I?" was the central question that the great Indian guru Ramana Maharshi posed to his disciples to lead them to enlightenment. But there really can be no sensible intellectual response to that question.

If there were, it would be wrong, because the question of who you are can't be answered on a conceptual level. The statement "I AM" of the Jewish scriptures is equally non-conceptual, and the closest we might get to an interpretation is "beingness". The whole point of asking the question, "Who am I?", is to draw us deeper within our being to the place (for want of a better term) where we feel the *essence* of life, the seat of the soul.

An essential awareness of being brings with it a sense of belonging to everything—an inner knowing of interconnectedness. This is a dimension of being we have probably all experienced when something arrests our attention and we stop for a moment to take in a sunset, feel the power of the ocean or observe an eagle soaring. In those moments thinking stops for a second or two as we look in awe and know at a deep level that all creatures share the same life force. What stops us from knowing this in other moments of our lives are domination of the ego, a sense of separateness as individuals and incessant busyness. What helps us out of the bind of ego and into experiencing interconnection is to spend time with beings who are *not* dominated by work and ego: horses! And why would we want to do that? What is special about horses?

Horses show us who we can be. Our ego-driven mind represents the most significant difference between us and other animals, and is a major source of human psychological dysfunction. But most of the time (until a crisis of spirit or mind arises) we are not aware of that. Often it is not until we see ourselves reflected in another being that we begin to know who we really are. Horses become clear mirrors by showing us how our egotistical view of life dominates. Once we are confronted by the ego sitting in the driver's seat we might wish to get rid of it, but that's not the aim. Neither is it possible. We can't eradicate ego (besides, it does serve a purpose), but we can *observe it in action*. By noticing our ego at work, and by holding

26

back on making judgments, ego begins to take second place in our lives and that gives us tremendous choice and agency. For most of us, this happens gradually but for some it occurs as a blinding realization (as it was for Saint Paul, Eckhart Tolle, and Ramana Maharshi among others). But most of us grow gradually through a daily practice of bearing witness to the ego's desire for control.

All spiritual traditions (through a variety of techniques, ideas, and rituals) point to the need to step outside of ego and disidentify with the stream of thought. This can happen spontaneously through an arresting sensory experience, but it can also be sought through regular spiritual practices such as meditation, contemplation and prayer, depending on one's religious and cultural background. Through such practices we see ourselves as the *subject* rather than the *object* of experience. When we know ourselves as the subject of experience, we see that we are not what happens to us or what we think about, but that we are that which knows what we think and experience.[1] If we live as though we *are* our thoughts, experiences, feelings, emotions and sensations (which is the norm for most modern humans), we have very little agency in our lives and might feel as though we are swept along by a river of mental constructs over which we have little control. If we are *attached* to our thoughts (as Buddhism puts it) then we are entirely made up of thought. Believing our thoughts to be true simply because they arise within our own heads leads to an assumption that we *are* our thoughts. At that point there is no space between the thought and the thinker, which can lead to the sensation of life being out of control. If you have experienced this, then you will know that exerting mental effort to gain control is likely to make the situation worse.

All too readily, thought becomes a source of self-torture for humans, but most of our thoughts do not actually belong to us.

They occur randomly as a result of many years of conditioning from our family of origin, from the beliefs and values of the society in which we were raised, from ancestral history and from our own accumulated personal histories. Not only are our thoughts not what we would necessarily choose ourselves, it is also very hard to stop random and useless thought from playing incessantly in our heads. You might have tried and discovered that willpower is useless for controlling thought since the more we try not to think a certain way the more solid and habitual the unwanted thoughts become. We can, however, lessen the stream of thought by becoming the conscious witness or observer of the mind to take us out of identification with thought. The thoughts are not the problem, it is identifying with them and believing them to be *who we are* that is the issue. But there is an immediate and simple remedy to being trapped in thought: thinking stops when we fully appreciate what is coming to us through our senses, such as when breathing in the nutty smell of a healthy horse, looking deeply into their soulful eyes, or watching a herd prance with delight at the end of a storm. We free ourselves from the constant stream of useless thought by giving our full attention to whatever is happening *right now*.

A daily practice

Ensure every day that you are in nature for a few minutes or, at the very least, that you can see some aspect of the natural world through a window. Even a treetop or the sky is good for this. Make a point of looking at something in nature for a few seconds without thinking or making up a story about it. Simply stop, look and absorb. If it helps, imagine that it is the first time you have seen this thing (and in a sense that is true) or that you might never see it again (which one day will be true).

Horses model for us what it is like *not* to be controlled by streams of thought. They don't think about themselves in terms of past or future (a favorite obsession of the human ego) because they don't have grammatically constructed language with which to do so. Neither do they make up ego-driven stories about who they are, since they have no need to exist on the level of personal image. Quite possibly this is one reason that humans are so attracted to animals in general and horses in particular: we know instinctively that they show us at a fundamental level how we too can inhabit a peaceful inner space free from the tyranny of random and pointless thought activity.

Accessing our true self, which we might choose to call the soul, can occur naturally in any equine assisted modality whether that be goal setting, coaching, therapy or learning. If we are open to the possibility of discovering our true selves, horses will lead us there effortlessly because they naturally live from their true selves, unencumbered by ego. If you are an equine assisted practitioner, an important part of the job is to connect with your own true self before trying to lead others to do the same.

We are not really dealing with two separate things when considering psychology and spirituality since they form a continuum, with both ends depending upon the other. To a large extent, differences between mind and spirit boil down to a choice of language, to ways of labelling experience. After all, "psychology" originally meant "the study of the soul or spirit", hence in its inception the concept fully embraced spirituality. Psychology and spirituality are neither separate concepts nor antithetical to each other, however, for those who work in mental health professions it takes some degree of bravery to admit to working within a spiritual paradigm. This is not an issue for horses though, who bring their whole psycho-spiritual being into the healing and learning space. Ultimately they show us who we really are by revealing who they really are. My invitation to you is to continue to ask, "Who are you?" while looking into the eyes of a horse; and my promise is that eventually an answer will arise if you let it. The important part of that sentence is "let it". Such existential questions resist efforts of "trying hard" and by and large they elude conceptual explanation because spiritual enquiry exceeds the limits of human language. In the journey of this book our enquiry begins on a conceptual level as we compare the characteristics of horse and human, starting with the question of why we would choose this animal above all others to teach and heal.

Footnote
1. Rupert Spira, "I Am That Which Knows" [online]. Available at: https://www.youtube.com/watch?v=Thl6kNVBiio (Accessed 1 October 2022).

Chapter 3

The Horse as Spiritual Teacher

Some truths simply cannot be demonstrated. But if we open our hearts to other creatures and allow ourselves to sympathize with their joys and struggles, we will find they have the power to touch and transform us. There is an inwardness in other creatures that awakens what is innermost in ourselves.

Gary Kowalski

All animals can teach us on a spiritual level, as can any aspect of nature. Sitting on the banks of a river and watching the water flow by teaches us patience and perseverance through modelling the power of letting go and allowing life to flow. Looking at a flower teaches us that nature employs and values design and color in aid of the perpetuation of other species. Dogs teach us about loyalty, affection and how to have fun with simple things. Job of the Bible knew these things about three millennia ago when he is reported to have said: "Ask the animals, and they will teach you, or the birds in the sky, and they will tell you, or speak to the earth, and it will teach you, or let the fish in the sea inform you."[1]

As regards animals, to derive great benefit from their company we need do very little other than have an attitude of openness. It is well known scientifically, for instance, that being with animals (especially pets) increases our dopamine, serotonin and oxytocin levels. Dopamine supplies the sense of pleasure we feel when we have achieved something; serotonin is the neurotransmitter that makes us feel focused, calm and happy; and oxytocin, known as the love hormone, is especially present in the development of bonds with our babies. Animals also have been found to bring cardiovascular and behavioral benefits to people who perceive their pets as important and supportive aspects of their lives.[2]

While the therapeutic value of relationships between humans and their cats and dogs are well documented, information on the benefits of therapy in the presence of horses is mostly anecdotal; that seems to be gradually changing as scientific attention is increasingly directed towards the effects of Equine Assisted Therapy on humans.[3] A 2019 study by Saan Ecker and Amy Lykins, for instance, finds that interaction with the horses can have a stress-moderating effect in the therapeutic context.[4] Their findings also support evidence of human stress arousal when near horses, which is not surprising when people find themselves in the company of a large mammal. An increase in stress in the EAP context can be useful, as we will discover later.

Both physical and psychological benefits derived from the presence of horses in the Equine Assisted context have become more available to scientific study, whereas evidence for soul-to-soul connection with animals effectively remains anecdotal. However, the same applies between people who feel they have a soul connection with each other, and that shouldn't deter people from valuing and acknowledging such human connections. I view considerations of "soul" or "spirituality" as a natural continuation of psychological phenomenon, best expressed by the term "psycho-spiritual" as discussed in the previous chapter. While psychology concerns itself with the workings of the mind, embedded within mental activity and experience is that which emerges from philosophical questions such as "Who am I?" and "What is life all about?" Who has not asked these sorts of questions at different times in their lives?

The terms "soul" and "spirituality" are subject to misunderstandings and multiple applications, but by using these terms I do not infer religious belief systems, and neither do I think of the soul as a separate and definable entity. The soul is not a *thing* but, rather, a *spaciousness* with which we have our being. It is a formlessness within which we experience the fundamental life force in common with all living creatures. One of the difficulties of trying to define soul is that it is *subject* rather than *object*, hence efforts to define it as a "something" contradict its non-conceptual nature. One way I do *not* think of soul, at least not for the purposes of this book, is as a separate part of us that survives the inevitable culling from the Reaper's scythe. That aspect of spirituality is for each one of us to decide, or I should say, to feel our way through. Dr. Gary Kowalski in his book, *The Souls of Animals*, puts this beautifully:

> *Many people think of soul as an element of personality that survives bodily death, but for me it refers to something much more down-to-earth. Soul is the marrow of our existence as sentient, sensitive beings. It's soul that's revealed in great works of art, and soul that's lifted up in awe when we stand in silence under a night sky burning with billions of stars ... Soul is what makes each of our lives a microcosm — not merely a meaningless fragment of the universe, but at some level a reflection of the whole.*[5]

Traditionally, the soul is defined in binary terms such as a division between time-bound humanity and its divine and immortal origins. Donald Kalsched in his book *Trauma and the Soul* elaborates on the meaning of "soul" in this manner, saying that it originates as *oneness* with the divine, but that during the process of human development, divinity empties out into our particularity, limitation and alienation. Kalsched writes that, "Such alienation from our essential nature seems to be the necessary and inevitable price for becoming conscious, and yet there remains within us a part of the original oneness that longs to return to that great spiritual reality from which we came and about which we have forgotten."[6] I agree with Kalsched's understanding, while at the same time believing that spirituality and soul defy definition and, for the purposes of this book at least, are best couched in analogies such as the soul is:

- that which is experienced *beyond thought*
- the depth of being within us that is *constant*
- the very *foundation of our being* that we are usually unaware of but can experience
- an ever-present *dimension without form* (like the air we breathe, which we don't see and seldom consider)
- the knowing of our *innate nature*
- the sense of aliveness, of understanding ourselves and the world *beyond concepts*
- the inner recognition that we are *one with all beings*
- a place inside, where *personal truth* resides
- a longing for *oneness*
- that which is experienced *beyond thought*

We should all feel free to choose our own analogies. Albert Einstein, who had a profound understanding of spiritual life, encapsulated it in a series of analogies. He valued the concept of oneness of human experience unlimited by time and space, not confined by mental concepts and not separated from other living beings. He emphasized that our task is to free ourselves from a mental prison by widening our circle of compassion to embrace all living creatures and the whole of nature in its beauty.[7]

Horses live from the soul space, which they invite us into. They know no other way of being since the soul is where they reside. When we make soul-to-soul connections with horses we open ourselves to ancient equine wisdom and to a deep connection with nature. When we make meaningful connections with horses, we build willing and generous partnerships and, in turn, have more to offer our human herd.

The attributes of horses as fully realized, spiritually awake beings align with primary Buddhist definitions of spiritual realization as follows:

- *Mindfulness as being engaged fully in what is happening right now.* One way to express this is *living in the moment,* a clearly observable trait of horses. Mindfulness is a product of observation, something that all prey animals practice in abundance to ensure survival.
- *Investigation and awareness of what is happening in one's environment.* Everyone with horse experience knows that horses are sensitive to change in their environment, such as seeing a new object in a place not previously witnessed.
- *Energy, or right effort.* From a horse's perspective this means to find the perfect balance between activity and rest. Unless a horse is stressed by unnatural living conditions they get this one right daily.
- *Joy of being alive.* We see this constantly such as when horses are moved into a new paddock as they run around joyfully kicking and rearing while emitting loud farts.
- *Tranquility, relaxation and contentment.* This attribute pretty much defines most of a horse's day if he is left to his own devices.
- *Concentration.* Doing one thing at a time without distraction is demonstrated in the way horses graze with great discernment and single-mindedness.
- *Equanimity.* Being calm and consistent without getting caught up in suffering is a key message from both the Buddha and Jesus. Suffering results from our own neurotic thinking, but horses don't experience this since they don't have the language necessary to attach mental concepts to events and things.

Horses are self-aware. They are very clear about their likes and dislikes, comfort and discomfort, and are secure in the interpretation of their reality. They don't doubt themselves and they don't suffer from lack of self-esteem; indeed, the concept of self-esteem would be entirely foreign to them. There are quite a few emotionally messed up horses around of course, and you might know of some, but they are the result of thoughtless human intervention. One kind of messed up horse is one who has been weaned too early with no chance for his dam to teach him all the things he needs to know about being a horse. Similarly, a horse who has lived without the company of others for a good stretch of time (especially in their first five years) is likely not to have formed meaningful attachments with other horses. All sorts of neurotic behaviors result from such needless neglect (just as it does for young humans).

A characteristic of horses I have noticed over the decades, which I attribute to their being such good role models and teachers, is that *they expect us to be like them*. When they notice a significant difference between us and them, they let us know through their subtle reactions. This is not so weird when you consider that humans do the same. We expect other people to hold views and values that reflect our own, and we actively seek out people who are likely to agree with us. We choose to spend time with friends, partners and family who reflect much the same values and beliefs as our own. When we meet someone significantly different we can feel threatened, but we love it when we meet someone who echoes all that we hold dear. Horses are no different in this respect. They appreciate us when we share their concerns for the things they value. They invite us to view the world through their eyes and they expect us to be on the same plane as them, much as humans expect (or at least wish) of each other. Known as *confirmation bias*, this is common to most species, since being surrounded by similar interpretations of the phenomenological world provides a mutual sense of safety. Naturally, horses and humans have different attitudes and reactions from each other, but it is the horses' honest reactions to our differences that provides fodder for learning. Their expectation for us to behave as they do provides the cutting edge of equine therapy and learning. A simple example of this is when a horse detects a person's emotional state while he or she pretends to be in another. When these situations occur we can read the horse's reactions (often very subtle), and learn something about ourselves. I recall in my early days of having horses during a period when I had a stressful full-time job that if I'd had a fraught meeting before going out to my horse in the evening he would very smartly let me know that my state of mind was not to his liking. So often he let me know about stresses I was carrying, of which I had been largely unaware.

One obvious difference in how human and horse species experience the world is that horses' thoughts are not rendered into words, whereas ours mostly are. As far as we can tell, horses mentally conjure up images but they are not so good at logical thinking or planning. However, this does not mean that they are unintelligent. Their brains are perfectly suited to their needs and physiology, but for us to understand them it is advantageous to put ourselves in their hooves (so to speak) and find out as much as possible about their habits, personalities and characteristics. We need to know who we are dealing with, but equally, when we are with horses we need to *know who we are* through awareness of our own thoughts, attitudes and feelings. When we experience an emotion but pretend that we are feeling some other way, for instance appearing confident when we are afraid, it can be quite disturbing to a horse. They are uncomfortable with incongruence and tend to respond, not to the person on the surface but to the authentic person inside that they know by reading physiological cues. Through their reactions to our incongruence, horses hold up an exacting emotional mirror.

Authenticity is such an important concept that Dr. Gabor Maté defines it in *The Myth of Normal* as a *core need* rooted in survival instincts that simply means "knowing our gut feelings when they arise and honoring them." He adds that, "Authenticity's only dictate is that we, [rather than having] externally imposed expectations, be the true author of, and authority on, our own life."[8]

Practicing authenticity

Enter a horse's paddock, asking permission to be in her space. Ground yourself and ask your body-mind how it feels to be there. If you identify some discomfort, tension, pain, anxiety etc., be fully aware of how it feels. Move closer to your horse (if she accepts it) and "tell" her how you are feeling. Be brutally honest with yourself and see how she reacts. What does her reaction mean to you?

Unless they have been cruelly treated, horses don't hold on to fear any longer than is necessary. Our habit of holding on to fear from the past and projecting fearfully into the future confuses horses. Unlike us, they generally don't project into the future and imagine all the things that could possibly go wrong. An exception is when a horse has been conditioned to anticipate pleasure, pain or danger. When a horse sees a snake on the trail for instance, he is likely to have a big reaction since he instinctively knows how lethal they can be, but as soon as the snake disappears or is seen to be benign (e.g. the snake turns out to be a stick) most horses will return to a position of homeostasis after a few minutes as their fear dissipates.

Humans, on the other hand, are expert at holding on to fear and building stories around events. If I as a rider hold on to my fear, my horse may assume that I'm anticipating a whole family of snakes further up the trail. We might assume it is the memory of the first snake that keeps him in a nervous state but, more likely, the possibility of further threat is what we have put into our horse's mind.

Practicing relaxed breathing

Whenever you think of it throughout your day, take one deep and relaxing breath. Maybe do it again a few times. Allow your stomach muscles to fully let go for the exhale. To establish a habit, connect the breathing consciousness to something you do a few times a day, such as having a drink of coffee or tea. Once this becomes a daily habit you will want to access a conscious relaxing breath whenever you feel slightly concerned, worried or anxious.

Most of our communication issues with horses come from our own inconsistent behavior, fears and need to get things done, but once we respect behavioral differences between us and them the interspecies relationship blossoms. Eventually we learn how to think of a horse *as a horse*, not as a differently shaped human. Clearly there are differences in the way they perceive the world, in the assumptions they make, and in how they process their emotions, but if we want to know what a horse is really like, we simply need to "ask" the horse.

A young Native American horse trainer, Gawani Pony Boy, reported in his beautifully illustrated book, *Horse, Follow Closely*, that he got this kind of advice from an elder when he was having difficulty teaching people about horse behavior. He realized that most people weren't seeing a horse as a horse but as a sort of four-legged human. He said, "If we can understand what it means to be a horse, react like a horse, and relate to other things like a horse, then we can have a more productive relationship with a horse."[9] This is the basis for empathy, whether we are considering it in relation to animals or other people. As reported in his book *Kinship with all Life*, Allen Boone got similar advice from an elder regarding a famous movie actor dog he was looking after for a year with whom he wanted to forge a deeper connection: "There's facts about dogs ... and there's opinions about them. The dogs have the facts, and the humans have the opinions. If you want facts about a dog, always get them straight from the dog, if you want opinions, get them from the human."[10] This turns out to be good advice, but how do we "ask" a dog or a horse who they are? It turns out that we do it outside of human language and the best place to start is to observe deeply.

As horse people, how often do we freely receive and give advice about horses such as what they need to eat, how to train them, what their character is like and so on? If we followed all received advice from friends and other horse people we would end up with quite a few mixed-up ideas. I've certainly allowed myself to be confused by well-intentioned advice regarding diet, health and care, but eventually if we want honest and meaningful relationships with our horses we must reference reputable sources of knowledge ourselves and, equally importantly, learn to "listen" to horses. They are constantly trying to communicate with us, but how do you ask a horse about themselves? Human language is not much good for this purpose, while spending time with them without expectations, agenda, or time constraints is how to listen to them. When interacting directly with horses we find that they "ask questions". It's relatively easy to see this in a dog as they ask for a game, a ride in the car, bones or a cuddle on the sofa, but it is less obvious with horses until you learn to read their very finely tuned expressions. I first consciously experienced a horse questioning me when as a novice rider the young horse I was working with reached a position of trust. While trekking out alone we came to a fork in the track and I felt him hesitate for a split second. This was a definite question: "Which way do you want me to go?" It was a beautiful moment and from then on I purposefully set up situations where my horse would ask questions. It is essential to allow the horse to pose questions if we wish to work with them within an environment of trust.

The horse has many attributes that we humans could do with ourselves. Take the way they communicate with each other, which is mostly nonverbally.[11] Humans rely heavily on verbal language, conceptual symbols and mental constructs for communication. Of course, our large brains and developed technologies are extremely useful but as a species we have pretty much forgotten how to communicate on somatic and energetic levels. Although, this isn't strictly correct either since humans *do* still communicate somatically and energetically. We constantly communicate nonverbally but are generally unaware of doing so. By spending time looking for the nonverbal signals when we are with horses we can learn a great deal about them, and ultimately, about ourselves. The horse *expects* to communicate with us nonverbally and tries to do so through body language, even if we don't know how to listen. It's natural for the horse, so he doesn't understand why it's not natural for us too.

Horses have amazing memories. Even though they live in the moment with little concern for past or future, that doesn't mean they forget everything that happens to them. The opposite is the case. If you've ever tried to retrain a horse who's been badly treated, you will know how well they remember. And there is much anecdotal evidence of horses remembering their dam or siblings many years after being separated from them. They remember cruelty and injuries, both as body sensations and as fear when the same stimulus that once hurt them represents itself. The big difference between them and us though is that they don't dwell all day long on the unpleasant thing that happened to them.

One of our therapy horses has a history of being beaten with farrier tools, so every time I trim her hooves I need to take the time to reassure her from a calm presence while reintroducing her to the tools as though she is seeing them for the first time. She has improved hugely, but her fear can be resurrected so easily with the wrong kind of move or attitude on my part. We get the same pattern arising from people who have been abused. Horses, however, don't replay the story of their abuse, which as image-thinkers rather than word-thinkers they can't do unless directly stimulated (but that doesn't mean they can't be permanently damaged). Most humans think in words, making personal story invention a natural ability, although thinking in visual images is natural for some, especially those on the autism spectrum. We can all utilize and develop the ability to think in images though. I have noticed that when I deliberately form a picture in my head of what I would like my horses to do, they respond much more readily than if I had merely formed a sentence in my head or had spoken out loud. For this reason, I recommend mostly working in silence with horses, using imagery rather than words. This works beautifully as horses readily respond to us being more like them.

Horses read emotional states as if they belong to the *present* (which is the case, of course). I can't emphasize enough how important this is to remember: if a horse picks up on somebody's anxiety about an imaginary future scenario or a past event, they assume the tension arises from the present moment, that there is something wrong *right now*. In terms of human physiology it is also true that our bodies don't know the difference between a scary thing we are afraid might happen, and the thing itself.

Our bodies react to dwelling on past or future pain as if it is happening in the moment.

Horses know us better emotionally than we know ourselves, and uncannily they so often know what we need at any given time. They show us how to reclaim parts of our humanity that have been lost through unnecessary thinking. They demonstrate that it is possible to rediscover our true selves. If we are looking to reclaim the direct experience of that which underlies all of life; if we are looking to reclaim our soul identity (the unconditioned true self), we couldn't do better than to ask a mammal such as a horse to show the way. The soul is what we were born with and what we will die with. It is the *essence of our being*, but we can become so caught up in the busy material world that we lose this awareness. Without access to that deeper part of ourselves we experience niggling feelings of being incomplete and dissatisfied with ourselves. But we don't need to live like that. I lived for almost two decades so engrossed in my career that I became convinced that I had no soul. I remember the heaviness of feeling dead inside and it was not a pleasant way to be.

How can we become self-aware like a horse? The big difference physiologically between our two brains gives us a clue to that. Dr. Janet Jones in *Horse Brain, Human Brain* points out that horses have very little prefrontal cortex, whereas ours takes up 41% of the space in our skulls.[12] This gives us the capacity for useful higher-order thinking, but this very capacity screws us up if we fail to distinguish between useful and useless thought. In addition, many of our stories undermine aspects of ourselves and make us miserable. We don't do this on purpose, it comes from our conditioning, but the key to being free from negative thinking is to recognize thought without identifying with it, i.e. without believing that we *are* our thoughts. Horses model this for us in the way they accept what is. They show us that it is possible to live a healthier life not driven by old thought patterns. To make a start with this enquiry, first we need to consider how horses and humans make sense of the world.

Footnotes
1. The book of Job 12:7–8, New International Version of the Bible.
2. Glenn Levine et al. (2013) "Pet Ownership and Cardiovascular Risk", *Circulation*, Vol. 127, Issue 23, 11 June 2013.
3. See for instance, Hallie Sheade (2021) *Equine-Assisted Counseling and Psychotherapy*; Leif Hallberg (2017) *The Clinical Practice of Equine-Assisted Therapy*; Andreas Liefooghe (2020) *Equine-Assisted Psychotherapy and Coaching: An Evidence-Based Framework*.
4. Ecker, Saan and Lykins, Amy (2019) "Effects of Short-Term Human-Horse Interactions on Human Heart Rate Variability: A Multiple Single Case Study", *People and Animals: The International Journal of Research and Practice*, Vol. 2, Issue 1, Article 2. Available at: https://docs.lib.purdue.edu/paij/vol2/iss1/2 (Accessed 10 October 2022).
5. Kowalski (1999) p. 23.
6. Kalsched (2013) p. 17.
7. Walter Sullivan (1972), "The Einstein Papers. A Man of Many Parts". *The New York Times*, March 29, 1972.
8. Maté (2022) pp. 106–7.
9. Pony Boy (1998) p. 19.
10. Boone (1954) pp. 47–48. This a good read for anyone wishing to forge a closer bond with animals and, although published almost 70 years ago, is still insightful.

11. Horses are not entirely nonverbal since they have four basic sound signals (nicker, blow, squeal and whinny) with graded nuances within each. See Budiansky (1997) p. 105.
12. Jones (2020) p. 183.

Chapter 4

Making Sense of Senses

Horses know us better than we imagine. They know us well on physical, energetic and emotional levels. They are expert at reading the inner states of other animals (including humans) by cueing into information through their primary senses. They have relied for thousands of years on this ability as their finely tuned senses have enabled their survival as a species of prey animal. Most horse senses are more acute than ours: they are aware of human heart rates, they detect our levels of adrenalin and they very effectively pick up on nonverbal physical cues. It's impossible to fool them more than once or twice. If you have ever walked into a paddock to "catch" a difficult horse while holding the rope and halter behind your back to disguise your intention, you will know the futility of such deception. Horses are so adept at detecting our inner states that it is no surprise to learn that a horse's neurons fire in direct response to human neurons and *vice versa*, "as if the synaptic gap crosses skin," as neuroscientist Dr. Janet Jones puts it.[1] This is known as neuron mirroring, and it happens between people, between animals of the same species and across species. It accounts for the feeling between two people of truly "getting" each other. Jones adds that when we attune to horses we "become part of the horse's brain when working together, and he becomes part of our human brain."[2] This partly accounts for the very close connections that can and do occur between horses and people, as well as between us and any other animal with whom we spend a significant amount of time.

While the horse's sensitivity to human physical and emotional states might seem astounding, humans have this ability with each other also. We are generally not consciously aware of it, but when you or someone else picks up on good or bad "vibes" from a person or a group of people, what is likely to be happening (provided it is not a case of projection) is an exchange of information from one human body to another. Humans do this all the time with each other, for instance when in peaceful proximity we are known to match our heartbeats, and it is well known that women who live together are likely to menstruate at the same time. Neuroscientist Dr. Lisa Feldman Barrett points out in her book, *Seven and a Half Lessons About the Brain*, that when we are with someone we care about, not only do we match our body positioning, our breathing and heart rates are likely to synchronize, a phenomenon also known to occur between therapists and clients.[3] I find it beautiful, but no longer surprising, when I notice someone (or myself) unintentionally breathing in time with a horse.[4]

Although humans share the same five primary senses with horses (sight, hearing, taste, smell, touch) we experience the world quite differently due to the way both species detect and evaluate data. This is due in part to the sensory organs that do the hearing, seeing, smelling, tasting and touching (for which there are clear differences between species), but more especially it is how the data is interpreted by various specialist centers of the brain that is responsible for sensory experiences. For all human senses other than smell the neural pathways are complex, each engaging different sections of the brain. The most direct neural pathway for human sensory processing is reserved for the sense of smell as it bypasses the thalamus and travels directly to the cerebral cortex.[5] Horses have even faster processing times because, as Janet Jones points out, they are more stimuli driven than we are and unlike us their cerebral cortex is primarily devoted to sensation and movement. Their sensory sensitivity evolved to the species' advantage for reacting at lightning speed to unpredictable events and they just don't have time for the tenth of a second required to evaluate a stimulus before acting.[6] Many an equestrian will have experienced being with or on a horse as she spooks at a bird in the grass, does a lightning speed take off, then spins around to figure out what just happened. Only an experienced and confident rider manages to sit through such a scenario. When a horse "spooks" like that the tendency is for people to think that she is overreactive, whereas she is simply doing what horses have done for millennia to keep themselves safe. Clearly, it is a strategy that has worked.[7]

Practicing awareness

As you groom, lead, ride, or simply stand next to your horse, work on experiencing your environment through the five primary senses, one at a time. What can you smell (that lovely horse smell?), what can you hear, taste, see, and feel on your skin? There is no need to name all these things, all you need is to draw your attention to them. If you notice a tendency to name them and perhaps go further by inventing a story about them, simply move on to noticing what you can experience through a different sense to refresh your awareness.

In terms of the primary five senses (and, by the way, there are more than five), horses and humans experience the world differently. To paraphrase Dr. Jeffrey Masson from *When Elephants Weep*, although the range of hearing for a horse is quite close to that of humans, they miss out on some of the lower tones and have more sensitivity in the higher tonal range. What horses miss in the lower range they feel transmitted through their teeth and jaws as they graze. They also transmit lower tones into the ground through their legs and feet (as elephants do, but to a much greater extent).[8] Anyone who spends time with horses will tell you that they take much more notice of sounds than we do, especially small sounds. In part, that's because they don't have the interference of the thinking brain distracting them from sensory input. Surprisingly, humans are better than horses at locating the precise location of a sound, although the ability of horses to hear sounds is greater than ours.[9]

It is generally understood that horses have an almost perfect 360° range of vision, with binocular vision at the front (a blending of information from both eyes) and monocular vision on both sides and towards the rear. The small blind spots in front of their nose and behind their hindquarters are readily included within a 360° range of vision by a slight turn of the head for the rear and a sideways glance for the front. What is perhaps less well known is that horses don't perceive detail equally well throughout their visual range. They might have to move their heads up and down, for instance, to see objects in sharp detail. This can be a hazard for riders as a horse might poorly perceive an object in her vision for some time, then when it suddenly comes into sharp focus it can cause an unwanted reaction.[10]

The differences between human and horse in terms of color vision are worth considering. Humans and most primates have trichromat vision made available from three kinds of cone in the eye responding to the wavelengths of blue, green and red, giving us what we might think of as full color vision. But this ability is surpassed by birds who see in four colors: ultraviolet, blue, green and red. Unfortunately, we can't imagine what the world looks like to birds, since the fourth set of cones doesn't simply add another color to the palette, it adds a whole other dimension that amounts to a multiplicity of different color mixes.

In their evolution, horses have had no need for tricolor vision. Their vision is dichromatic, meaning they have only red-blue color perception, so they can't tell the difference between green and grey, or white and grey, and it's likely that red, orange, and green look much the same.[11] They see similarly to dogs, with yellow, blues and greys dominating. The colors that dichromatic animals see best are yellowish-green and bluish-purple. The Pulitzer Prize winning science writer Ed Yong in *An Immense World* notes that the color used most often as markers at racecourses (orange) ironically blends into the background instead providing the stark contrast that trichromatic humans perceive.[12] And animal scientist Dr. Temple Grandin points out in *Animals in Translation* that yellow is a high-contrast color which will really pop out at horses, so it's clearly not the best color choice for a human to wear as a vest or raincoat or to apply to jumping equipment and the like.[13] If you do have yellow things in your horse environment, it's a good idea to take the time to introduce them consciously to avoid overreaction.

An important thing for horse people to know (and most do) is that equines have poor depth perception. Asking a horse to walk through a puddle or a shallow stream can be a major issue until she has accepted that it is not actually a bottomless well of water. Some years ago my partner Sarah adopted an eighteen-year-old warmblood who was the biggest-hearted well-behaved horse imaginable, but trying to coax him over a tiny dribble of water on the beach was a major challenge. This sort of training needs to happen when horses are young (which the warmblood did not have), otherwise we end up fighting against the hundreds of times that a particular fear has been reinforced.

Temple Grandin highlights an important difference between human and horse perception namely that, unlike us, animals don't have to be paying attention to notice something new. They are simply hardwired to notice *anything* new in their environment, whereas humans usually don't notice anything different unless they pay conscious attention to it. As she puts it, *"humans are built to see what they are expecting to see,* and it's hard to expect to see something you've never seen."[14] The difference in this respect between the two species has much to do with horses' near-360° vision giving them *wide vision* in every sense of the term. Humans, however, probably due to being hunters historically, are best at *single-pointed vision*. This difference has huge ramifications for how we live and experience our environments, as we will discuss later.

Where humans and horses differ immensely is in their sense of smell. Our abilities are minimal in comparison with horses, and as Stephen Budiansky suggests, "our vestigial sense of smell has left us blind to a whole world of animal communication."[15] It is likely that our primate ancestors had much more powerful olfactory abilities than we do, but as trichromatic vision evolved in humans through natural selection, sight became the primary means to seek food so our sense of smell declined (or never developed to that extent). Horses, on the other hand, with their dichromatic vision have continued to need an enhanced sense of smell to discriminate within their environment. We can witness how horses utilize their sense of smell constantly. Stallions mark their territory with dung piles, but even domesticated geldings and mares become preoccupied with sniffing each other's dung to discover who has recently passed by. The scent from dung also indicates whether there are any nearby mares in season. We all know how obsessive dung smelling can be from experiences of coaxing a horse past a new pile of dung as they pick up a cocktail of personal and herd information.

The amount of information horses detect through their olfactory sense is huge. It includes the location of water, whether there are other horses around, where the nearest predator is, which is the tastiest clump of grass to munch, emotional states of other horses and whether they have met a particular horse before. Reportedly, some nomadic groups of humans can smell water from many miles away, whereas modern urban-living humans have lost that ability. Water has no scent though, so for an animal (including human) to detect water, they must learn to smell the plants, minerals or algae associated with a water source.[16] When horses are confronted by humans they know whether we are vegetarian or meat eaters, how much adrenaline we have currently running around in our system, whether we are wearing perfume (not a good idea as it can be confused with pheromones), whether we are pregnant and possibly whether or not we have an illness. When horses meet each other they exchange a massive amount of information as they "share breath" in an intimate exchange.

How much more sensitive the equine sense of smell is as compared with that of humans is difficult to measure, but it is deemed to be at least as effective as the smelling capacity of a dog, which is potentially a staggering 40 times greater than our ability. Horses and dogs must therefore be privy to much more information through smell than we can possibly know and, as Jones points out in *Horse Brain, Human Brain*, it's likely that smell is "more important to equine functioning than either vision or hearing."[17]

One sense where horses and humans share similar sensitivity is touch. The horse's sense of touch is exquisite, and ours is pretty good too. With a twitch muscle lying directly beneath the skin they can detect and twitch off a small fly with precision as tactile sensitivity all over their bodies matches the sensitivity we have in our fingertips. They are especially sensitive around their mouths, and given that their big long nose gets in the way of seeing what they are eating, a heightened ability to feel and smell grasses beneath their noses is essential. When you look at them eating you can see just how adept they are at selecting one blade of grass over another, yet they do not see it. Given how sensitive they are to touch, I believe we could afford to be more mindful of how hard or soft our touch is with each horse we groom, as some horses are more sensitive than others. There can be so much more to grooming than simply removing mud and loose hair; it is an opportunity to express empathy and to communicate, being to being. I have a mare who is reluctant to be brushed or touched, so we have had illuminating sessions whereby I ask for her permission for where, how, and at what intensity I may use a brush on her. She so appreciates being asked that after ten minutes she usually begs me not to stop.

Differences in the way human beings and horses experience the world through the five primary senses of touch, sight, taste, smell and hearing begs the question of what "reality" is. This is a word that is often tossed around without really questioning what it means. I am reminded of a politician who routinely answered media questions put to him with the annoying response, "The reality is..." but of course it was only his version of reality. Since reality is constructed from sensation there is no way of knowing whether my experience of color, or any other sensation, is the same as yours, hence we can only talk of relative reality. Through sensory experience, every species of bird, insect and animal (including the human animal) experiences a different reality. These differences have been determined by evolutionary adaptation since nature never maintains for long anything that is surplus to requirements.

The senses that evolve for each animal species are perfectly adapted to their survival needs. Human senses also operate within a definite spectrum that is defined by, and limited to, what we need to survive and thrive. Different species experience different realities according to the relative capabilities of their senses, hence there is no such thing as the experience of a single unified reality. Or putting it another way, if we assume a single universal reality, an individual human can only ever experience a tiny slither of the totality. Not only is our reality partial due to our limited spectra of sensory capacities, but we also *construct* reality through the brain's interpretation of sensory signals. For every animal, there are several processes that occur between what a sense organ detects and the brain's eventual interpretation of the signals, which are further refined by the accumulated memories of similar sensations. Imagination and experience play major roles too. Neuroscientist Dr. Anil Seth in his book, *Being You*, goes so far as to refer to human perception as "controlled hallucination". He explains that the brain makes predictions about the causes of a particular sensation, then incoming sensory signals are assessed according to how similar or different they are to the prediction. In Seth's words, "We never experience sensory signals themselves; we only ever experience interpretations of them." What we perceive, he says, is a "neuronal fantasy that is reined in by reality, not a transparent window onto whatever that reality may be."[18] All sensory information the brain receives effectively updates, or controls, the brain's hallucination.

Another blow to the assumption that what we see, hear, touch, taste and smell constitutes universal reality, is that we don't even take notice of everything around us. Humans become oblivious to their environment in a way that animals do not, possibly because we are at the top of the food chain and don't need to be as vigilant as other mammals. We stop seeing the detail whereas, as Dr. Temple Grandin points out in *Animals in Translation*, animals take in all the tiny details that make up the big picture.[19] Anyone who has ridden a trail in a forest and has "enjoyed" their horse's fascination with every individual moving leaf will know what I mean about horses' fascination with detail. Paradoxically though, we humans perceive a whole lot more than we are aware of consciously. Grandin describes sensory experience thus: "In a normal human brain sensory data comes in, your brain figures out what it is, and only then does it decide whether to tell you about it or not, depending on how important it is."[20] In other words, we are not always conscious of what is around us, and this can be a serious disadvantage at times. What is more, as Dr. Lisa Feldman Barrett indicates in *Seven and a Half Lessons About the Brain*, a certain amount of sensory data is lost as it is transmitted from the sense organs to the brain.[21] Exercises with horses in which we practice a mindful approach to all we see, smell and hear, attempting to take note of detail but within a wider view of the surroundings, gives us a window into horse perception and extends our limited visual experience.

Try being a horse

Stand with a horse and remind yourself of how they experience their world through their senses. Follow the horse's every movement and make note of where she is putting her attention. Imagine yourself to be a horse, feeling what it is like to be her in this moment. You might only "get it" it for a second or two, but this is enough.

Then there are suggestions from numerous philosophers and scientists that there is more to the way we know our world than through the five primary senses, with some proposing that humans possess more than five senses. For instance, we have an awareness of our inner bodily states (somatic awareness) that is referred to by some as a *sixth sense*. This can be experienced as awareness of a quickening heart rate, tension in the stomach, adrenaline and other chemicals flowing around, along with tense muscle groups. Such a "gut feeling" or "heartfelt" sense helps us make decisions based on something in addition to cognitive evaluation. Unfortunately, so many of us dismiss somatic (bodily) information, which is a pity since this way of knowing is supported by scientific findings such as those reported by

Dr. Frans de Waal in *Mama's Last Hug* that we have as many neurons in our gut as in our brains and that they supply vital information.[22] Sometimes gut feelings keep us alive. Famously, Lt. Col. Stanislav Petrov of the Soviet Union saved the world from nuclear annihilation in 1983 by acting on a gut feeling. The Soviet nuclear early warning computer screen indicated that the US had launched five intercontinental ballistic missiles, and Petrov was instructed to retaliate. But it didn't *feel* right to him, so he chose not to launch. It turned out that the sun's reflection was bouncing off a cloud, giving a wrong reading![23] If Petrov hadn't responded viscerally you wouldn't be reading this book today.

Many a good decision has been made according to gut feelings and I can think of several occasions in my own life when I ignored them only to regret the consequences. Eckhart Tolle calls the sixth sense, *inner body awareness*, which is a useful concept since it is relatively easy to access with the conscious mind.[24] We can become aware of the inner body when there is little or no stress (like sitting in a chair or lying down before sleeping), by asking ourselves whether we can feel the aliveness in different parts of the body. This sense of aliveness might come as a sensation of warmth, tingling, pulsating or something nameless that nonetheless feels real. To do this as a conscious practice is beautifully relaxing and helps us to be more fully present. Mindfulness expert Dr. Daniel Siegel in *Mindsight* also recognizes a sixth sense that he describes as the ability to perceive our internal bodily states.

Siegal also posits a seventh sense that he defines as "the ability to look within to the content of our mind and to reflect upon experience as it is unfolding". He calls this "mindsight".[25] Others might call it meta-awareness, meaning being aware of awareness or being aware of being. I like to think of it as being conscious of the one who is aware, or putting it more simply, conscious awareness. Here I seem to be describing three internal entities: sensory experience through the five senses; awareness of somatic being (inner body); and conscious awareness of both experience and the experiencer (also called the observer). These are not delineated and separate from each other but are embraced within the fluid totality of experience (Example 2).

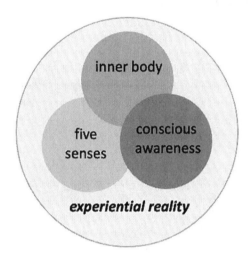

Example 2

The task of conscious awareness (observer) is also to take note of what is going on in the mind without bringing judgment into the situation. As soon as we criticize our thinking, talking and actions, judging them as good or bad, desirable or undesirable, we are captured by our thoughts. All is not lost when that happens, however, since we can simply notice it and return to observing our thinking, talking and actions without adding further judgment. If we practice not adding to our thoughts by criticizing them or getting carried away by the story, they soften and move into the background. This gives us a sense of *presence* embraced within a field of experience or spaciousness which we can call the totality of being. This is the canvas upon which the painting of our lives is manifest. We might choose to call this the totality, or the soul.

What is it that equips horses so well to work with us in the equine assisted space? They communicate honestly through subtle and highly effective body language; they are sentient beings just as we are, sensitive, patient and kind; and through their authenticity and honesty they help us become aware of our own inauthenticity (incongruence) when it occurs. They are grounded so they readily reconnect us with the natural laws of life; they live in a web of connection and relationship just as we do and model for us how to live in the present moment without complicating our thinking with concern for past or future. In short, they are soulful beings.

In the interests of creating a fuller picture, next we look at the brains of horses and humans for their similarities and differences.

Footnotes

1. Jones (2020) p. 263.
2. Jones (2020) p. 263.
3. Barrett (2020) p. 8.
4. Matching heart rates with a horse is most likely to occur in a ratio of 2:1. A normal heart rate for an adult horse ranges from 28 to 40 beats per minute. The ratio of equine heartbeats to breaths is 4:1. For every four heart beats, the horse takes one breath. See Brett Scott & Mike Martin, "Understanding vital life signs in horses" [online]. Available at: https://texashelp.tamu.edu/wp-content/uploads/2016/02/understanding-vital-life-signs-in-horses.pdf (Accessed 1 December 2022).
5. Barrett (2020) pp. 163–164.
6. Jones (2020) p. 194.

7. See McBane (2012) for an in-depth consideration of the differences between horse and human in relation to equestrian sports.
8. Masson (1995) p. 195.
9. Jones (2020) p. 61.
10. Jones (2020) p. 45.
11. Budiansky (1997) pp. 94–97.
12. Yong (2022) p. 88.
13. Grandin (2006) p. 44.
14. Grandin (2006) p. 51.
15. Budiansky (1997) p. 115.
16. Jesslyn Shields, "Why Didn't Evolution Give Us the Ability to Smell Fresh Water?" *How Stuff Works* [online]. Available at: https://science.howstuffworks.com/life/evolution/humans-smell-fresh-water-evolution.htm?srch_tag=cl35wo6ghmuwvtk7zo7bkuanzwvc3ebs (Accessed 10 December 2021).
17. Jones (2020) p. 79.
18. Seth (2021) pp. 82–83.
19. Temple Grandin, who herself is on the autism spectrum, makes a distinction between neurotypical people favoring the big picture over detail, and many autistic people who view their environment similarly to animals, as masses of tiny bits of data. (2006) p. 57.
20. Grandin (2006) p. 66.
21. Barrett (2020) p. 153, fn. 66.
22. de Waal (2019) p. 84.
23. "Stanislav Petrov" [online]: https://en.wikipedia.org/wiki/Stanislav_Petrov (Accessed 1 February 2023).
24. Tolle (2005) pp. 248–253.
25. Siegel (2011) p. xi.

Chapter 5

The Brain, Emotion and Empathy

Horse and human brains have many similarities but the most significant difference comes from the relative size of the cerebral cortex, specifically the front part called the prefrontal cortex, which in humans is enormous by comparison. As mentioned earlier, horses have very little prefrontal cortex, whereas ours takes up 41% of the space in our skulls. The largest part of the horse brain consists of the cerebellum at the rear of the brain, and that is tasked with controlling horses' highly developed athletic abilities. Our brains differ according to how we function: equines as grass-and foliage-eating animals are designed for fast and effective escape from threat, while we are omnivore animals designed primarily for gathering and hunting. A horse has little need for the higher-order thinking of the cerebral cortex to survive in her world, and we don't need the highly evolved athletic abilities of the equine cerebellum (although, wouldn't that be great!). Under threat we are used to thinking our way out of situations more than running away as a horse is want to do. For us humans there are many more predators who can outrun us at a short distance, so if survival had relied on our athletic ability alone we would be extinct by now. As a species we have learned to make tools, shelters and traps, and to devise plans so that we don't always have to rely on fleeing from predators. We outsmart them instead. Horses, by contrast, have evolved to devote as much brain as possible to managing fast getaways. They have no need for a massive prefrontal cortex, just as humans have no need for a large cerebellum designed to control the fine movement of four legs coordinating at great speed.

The common model of the human brain is of three distinct main sections: the large outer layer of the *cerebral cortex* (rational brain), the inner section comprising the *limbic system* (mammalian emotional brain), and the section at the back of the head, the *cerebellum* (primitive lizard brain). It has long been assumed that each part has built upon the other evolutionarily as our ancient ancestors developed from having a lizard brain through to a mammalian brain, then to a human rational brain. This three-part brain model, commonly called the "triune brain", neatly distinguishes the human brain from other mammalian brains by emphasizing the superior size of the human prefrontal cortex. However, neuroscientist Dr. Lisa Feldman Barrett and others challenge aspects of the triune model, especially the long-held assumption that, "One part of your neocortex, called the prefrontal cortex, supposedly regulates your emotional brain and your lizard brain to keep your irrational, animalistic self in check."[1] The assumption that is now discredited is that our brain's three sections represent the evolutionary development from reptile, to mammal to human. Since the 1990s, neuroscientists have learned that not only did the brain not evolve in such sections or layers, but it is not the role of the prefrontal cortex to keep emotions and animalistic urges in check. Perhaps the most important aspect of the misinterpretation of the triune model is the assumption that we humans have transcended our brutal animalistic nature through applying intelligence, logic and objectivity. Until very recently, rationality and emotionality have been thought of as competitive with each other, a misconception reinforced by the triune model that assumes human superiority and supremacy over all other animals as possessors of a superior brain. There is no foundation in thinking it is the role of one part of the brain to control another as though they are, as Barrett put it, "in an epic battle with each other."[2]

Neuroscientists now consider the brain as functioning not as three major sections in competition, but as a "network of 128 billion neurons connected as a single, massive and flexible structure."[3] What's more, there is no justification in thinking of human brains as more evolved than that of other species. They are just differently evolved. Our brain is built for purpose according to the evolutionary challenges humans have confronted, as it is for any creature's brain. To think otherwise is to assume the supremacy of humans over all other species.[4]

Another common misconception about the brain (readily adopted in some natural horsemanship methods) is that there is a left brain responsible for rationality and a right brain for creativity. While true, it is a fantasy to assume that individual people and horses are ruled by one or the other hemisphere unless there has been a physical rupture such as a stroke. Although the left and right sides of the brain clearly do serve a multitude of different functions, the idea of hemispheric predominance in a normal brain is an urban myth. However, it does no harm to think mythologically or even to add further typologies to such a construct, so long as it is not taken literally and applied categorically. Mythology and metaphor are valuable tools both in inspiring creativity and in making mental associations, but it is self-limiting to take metaphor and myth literally and to apply predetermined attributes to people and animals by calling them a left-brain or right-brain human or horse. One thing we can unequivocally say about the left and right hemispheres of the brain though is that the right side, which is more reliable at making value judgments, has been hugely neglected in modern human life in favor of the more logical left hemisphere.[5]

Like us and other mammals, horses have autonomic nervous systems and neural networks throughout their bodies that are responsible for arousal and calming. When they come down from high arousal (from the sympathetic to the parasympathetic[6] nervous system), horses typically blink, yawn, lick and chew. This is often referred to as the horse "thinking" or "processing", an interpretation that is not strictly correct although it is true that it's a sign that the horse is coming to a point of deeper relaxation. The physiological reason for licking and chewing is that their mouths have dried up somewhat from a flow of adrenaline through their bodies, so when they come down a notch or two emotionally they lubricate their mouths. This action gives us two opportunities for learning from the horse: firstly, when we see licking and chewing it is a sign that what we asked them to do immediately prior has put them in a heightened state of alertness and activated their sympathetic nervous system. We should question ourselves each time we do that if we don't want to make a habit of tipping the horse into a state of fear. If we ask our horse to walk backwards away from us for instance, and if she raises her head high and moves reactively, we have put her into a fear zone and what we think we achieved in that situation is not at all what we achieved from the horse's point of view. If we have significantly heightened her fear, it's highly likely that the lesson she learns from the exercise is that it's a relief when humans stop harassing her. And it's worth remembering that no human or animal learns well while in a state of fear! The second opportunity arising from a horse licking and chewing is that it indicates a deeper level of relaxation, and this is an indication to give the horse time to relax given that she did what we asked of her. She needs to know that she responded in the right way by having a rest.

Do horses and humans experience the same emotions, and if they do are they expressed in the same way? I think we can safely say no to the second half of the question. Horses do not express emotions in the same way that humans do, which I suspect is the main reason people have assumed that horses don't have emotions. Not only are horses' expressions very subtle, but we forget that it is possible to feel emotion without expressing anything overtly. As for whether horse have emotions, here is what the animal scientist Dr. Temple Grandin has to say:

> *All animals and people have the same core emotion systems in the brain ... Unless you are an expert, when you dissect a pig's brain it's difficult to tell the difference between the lower-down parts of the animal's brain and the lower-down parts of the human brain. Human beings have a much larger neocortex, but the core emotions aren't located in the neocortex. They're in the lower-down part of the brain.*[7]

The influential neuroscientist Dr. Jaak Panksepp in his book *Affective Neuroscience* reports that he is confident that the basic emotions that we share with all mammalian species are fear, anger, sorrow, anticipatory eagerness, play, sexual lust and maternal nurturance.[8] Horses and other equines are emotional creatures, as are all mammals, even if their expression of emotion is not identical to ours. There's good reason for this of course since humans at the top of the food chain can afford to express emotion overtly, whereas for a prey animal such as a horse it would be unwise to draw attention to themselves. According to Dr. Frans de Waal in his book *Mama's Last Hug* it is becoming clear that horses have much the same emotional range as humans that they show through a wide variety of expressions in their faces as a product of seventeen distinct muscle movements occurring in countless combinations.[9] Their expressions are very subtle, nevertheless it is possible for us to learn to read them. The big difference between us and other mammals emotionally is that our prefrontal cortex enables the mental analysis of whatever we experience. This can be to some advantage, but unfortunately it is also the conceptualization of emotion, i.e. the story we wrap around our emotions, that adds complexity to our emotional lives and is a major source of misery. The Buddha referred to the pain we cause ourselves in this way as "second order thinking" or the "second arrow". In other words "bad" stuff (pain) is what happens to us, while misery or suffering comes from our *thinking* around the pain. Scientists such as Dr. Lisa Feldman Barrett have proposed that emotions are themselves mental constructs in that they originate as bodily reactions to specific thoughts, for which the expression of them is largely culturally defined.[10]

Horses don't add thoughts and stories to their emotional reactions and they don't hold on to emotion as we do, so we might assume that a horse is sulking or harboring anger when it is just as likely to be our projection. They let go of their emotions quickly because they need to return to a state of body balance (homeostasis) to be ready for what might come at them next from behind a tree or from over a hill. If a horse has a bad experience, let's say while entering a trailer (bumping her head, or feeling claustrophobic) and she subsequently shows fear the next time, she has not held on to resentment or fear in the interim. It is simply that when she sees the trailer again it reminds her of prior events and she predicts a repetition of the bad experience. The horse is simply looking after herself in that situation, whereas when we experience problems we are inclined to build up a story of "this unjust thing that happened to me" and expect it to happen again as we continue to talk about it for the rest of the week (if not for the rest of our lives).

It's the horse's ability to *go back to grazing*[11] almost immediately after an emotionally arousing event that offers us a vision of how we too can be. Horses save their energy for what they consider to be vital and don't waste it by holding on to emotion, or worse, by amplifying it. (I give examples in Part II of how beautifully the image of going back to grazing models behavior for us.)

I have already mentioned the horse's astounding ability to detect the emotional states of people, especially through the sense of smell, but let's consider what the horse does with the knowledge of a person's emotional state. They have a choice: they can walk away from someone experiencing pain or disturbing emotions, or they can choose to show empathy towards individuals. Domesticated horses are just as capable of caring for us as they are for each other, staying present in empathy with both people and other horses. Primatologist Frans de Waal argues convincingly that the concept of empathy in animals is well established, although during his career he has certainly encountered professional pushback to the idea that mammals and humans share the same emotional world.[12] Kindness, an action arising out of empathy, can be witnessed every day in a herd of horses. I have more than once seen a horse lead an equine friend over to a bunch of hay or to share a bucket of feed, although they won't do this with every horse. But the most moving evidence of kindness and empathy I have witnessed has been with horses concerned for sick and dying members of their herd, and subsequently going through what we would call a grieving process.

Domestic horses often show empathy towards people, don't they? How many times has a horse offered his warm neck for an adolescent to sob into as she seeks solace from interpersonal problems? Perhaps less well known is how horses express empathy and grief for each other. Since we have been on the Earthhorse Aotearoa farm, we have lost two horses to sickness and old age. The herd's reaction in both cases has been astounding.

Both horses who died were in their early thirties and had medical issues that were growing more and more evident, so we reluctantly called our veterinary surgeon. The first horse to go was an old pony we had adopted three years earlier. He did beautiful therapy work for us, as he knew better than most what suffering was. He especially showed empathy for troubled children. He had recurring laminitis as well as Cushing's disease, both of which we had been managing for him. But in his last few days he stood in one place on the side of a tree-covered hill, calling out to the herd as each horse answered him back or came to "share breath" with him. It looked very much like a farewell party.

After the vet's visit, we leave the euthanized pony on the ground for a few hours for the other horses to sniff him and fully comprehend that he had gone. We observe from a distance as one at a time they come to visit him. In the evening we have a digger make a deep hole to put his body to rest. The herd isn't particularly interested in that process, but in the morning, we see something extraordinary: all the horses are standing together beside the mound as the lead mare takes each of her herd members over it one at a time. They sniff for a while, then move off as the mare then picks up another horse to do the same thing. The last horse to walk over the mound lies down on it, not for a roll in the newly turned soil, but simply to lie there with his ear to the ground. The herd respects the burial site for three days, pausing whenever they pass, after which time the area returns to being the same piece of dirt as anywhere else.

The second elderly horse we had to euthanize had developed an invasive cancer on his hindquarters. As we monitored how much it was bothering him, one day we noticed him standing next to a tree with his forehead leaning heavily onto the trunk. He stayed in this position for an hour while another horse stood motionless beside him. It is the sign we needed to call our vet. After the lethal injection we see the same grieving behavior from the herd as we had for the old pony. This was also followed by a funeral ritual from the herd. I don't recall seeing a horse lying on the mound this time, but each horse "hoofed" the earth mound and for the next three nights they hung about the gravesite, whinnying softly.

The capacity for horses to recognize grief in people never fails to astound us in our work with clients. It seems that all horses are sensitive to human grief, but we have one mare who suffered the loss of a foal in unfortunate circumstances and she is the one who invariably chooses to be with a client experiencing loss. The influence this mare has had on people in grief is profound.

Stephanie, a woman in her forties, arrives with a sense of psychological heaviness she had been carrying around for months. After a grounding session and a brief discussion I invite her to take her sense of heaviness to the herd to see what the horses bring to it. Meantime, the horses who have been waiting in the nearby arena line up in a row while looking towards the cabin as they intuitively do when we work in there with clients. Stephanie walks into an arena where a young mare and an elderly gelding, who have both experienced grief, are hanging out. After a while those two horses come up and form a triangle with her, their rumps nearly touching each other while their heads position to either side of her. Each horse is only about half a meter away from her head. There is no talking but there is a great deal going on: Stephanie has tears in her eyes, and the horses have soft eyes and lowered heads in states of total relaxation. She talks to me about how she feels an enormous sense of release and acceptance while recognizing the feeling as one of unresolved grief from an abortion she had in her twenties. She chooses to stay for about fifteen minutes in the horses' embrace and later talks about what a hurtful period it had been and how she still suffers. What we do not discuss is that both horses have known intense grief of their own. They know intimately about emotional healing and learning to trust. Stephanie stays for a while longer to soak up the empathy from these beautiful beings. She takes away with her the physical and emotional memory of the horses holding her in empathy and kindness, and the memory of this session becomes a mental talisman to return to when she needs emotional support.

Stephanie revealed that before her first session with the horses she had no conscious awareness that the abortion of twenty years previously had been having an ongoing negative effect on her state of mind. It wasn't the only issue that had been adding to her sense of psychological heaviness but it was a good portion of what unconsciously had been weighing her down.

We are fortunate to work with an animal with the capacity for empathy, but horses are not alone in this. Dogs too are masters at cross-species empathy. Naturally, when working with empathetic animals it is incumbent upon us to return empathy, in fact we naturally want to since bearing witness to empathy in an animal only makes us better humans. We develop greater empathy as we make the effort to see the world from the horse's point of view and to consider her likes, dislikes, comfort and discomfort. It is not a sign of weakness if we respect a horse's likes and dislikes, rather, we have a much better chance of doing meaningful work with them. Knowing the horse's individual characteristics is an advantage when building attachment and empathy between humans and horses, just as it is between people.

Practicing empathy

Spend time showing empathy for your horse by sharing every concern or interest she has. If she looks or listens to something on her right, do the same. If she sighs, sigh also. If she walks off, walk with her. If she stops, sit and be with her. As you sit and observe, tell yourself that you are at the center of the universe. This might seem like an egotistical thought, but it is not. You are the only one who can possibly know life as you do, as experientially everything happens around you as the still point in a turning world.[13] Because we experience life (the world and the universe) from the very center, we can't help but be "self-centered". The horse is equally self-centered. She too is at the center of the universe. She only knows her own horsey reality; she doesn't question her experiences, which to her are the truth, real and meaningful. Feel into what it is like to be a horse at the center of the universe.

The central message of this book is that horses help us access our own souls, so it is time we dealt with the business of discussing the soul. We make a start in this exploration in the next chapter.

Footnotes
1. Barrett (2020) pp. 14–15.
2. Barrett (2020) p. 24.
3. Barrett (2020) p. 31.
4. Barrett (2020) p. 25.
5. This is the thesis of Iain McGilchrist's book, *The Master and his Emissary* (2009).
6. Both the sympathetic and parasympathetic systems are part of the central autonomic nervous system. The sympathetic (SNS) is responsible for high energy reactions such as flight and fight, whereas the parasympathetic (PNS) controls the calming, energy-conserving needs of the organism.
7. Grandin (2009) p. 5.
8. Panksepp (1998) p. 46.

9. de Waal (2019) p. 58.

10. Barrett (2017).

11. This is a useful term that I first came across from Linda Kohanov (2007).

12. de Waal (2019) p. 101.

13. Lilly (1972/2017). Being the still point of a turning world is a prevalent theme in Dr. John Lilly's autobiography, *The Center of the Cyclone*.

Chapter 6

Living from the Soul

What is the soul? It resists definition because it represents a non-conceptual situation or space. A useful metaphor for the soul is that it is the canvas upon which experience is painted. It underlies all of life, independent of the conditioned personality and is the unconditioned natural state of being that we were born with. The soul is the essence that we share with all other animals and humans, but we have been conditioned into thinking of our true selves (or soul) as separate from all others. Not only is the soul generally regarded as a separate individual entity, we experience it as a still and constant situation, so it is easy to overlook it entirely. The journey of awakening is a process whereby we learn how to recognize and experience the still inner presence, not as something we possess as individuals but which we share with all life. As Gary Kowalski puts it, "Soul is what makes each of our lives a microcosm—not merely a meaningless fragment of the universe, but at some level a reflection of the whole."[1] The soul is the *true self*; it is the felt constant that we have within us as the underlying dimension of our being, supporting all our comings and goings. If we look within we see that we don't live *through* our experiences, thoughts and feelings, but that our essence is the still presence within which our experiences, thoughts and feelings occur.

There is also the concept of consciousness to consider. If there was nothing capable of knowing what we experience we would not be conscious of experiencing very much, in fact we wouldn't be conscious at all. Consciousness in a spiritual sense is being aware of the being that is experiencing, thinking and observing. Another way of putting it is that it is *awareness of being aware*. It is the seventh sense that we discussed earlier. Consciousness does not mean the absence of coma as in a medical context, but without it we wouldn't know that we exist as something separate from our thoughts. (Sadly, that is the case for many human beings.) Instead, our identity would be entirely caught up within an endless stream of thoughts, experiences and feelings. These things can't be aware of themselves, so there must be something else that is aware of them. This is consciousness, whereas the soul is the background to all experience, both external and internal. Because experiences and thoughts come and go, arise and die, and can be remembered as concrete events or things, we expect the soul to be the same. But the soul is the eternal presence and therefore is constant and not subject to fluctuation. That's why we fail to take notice of it, just as we don't notice the air we breathe. The soul can be experienced if we look at inner constancy throughout our lives, but not if we are looking for a *thing*. We don't *have* a soul, we *are* a soul in connection with all of life. Soul is itself the life force.

As I refer to the soul in this writing, I am not assuming to know what happens to that aspect of us when we die, and neither am I attaching any religious dogma or belief to the concept. I have a *felt* sense that the soul, or the true unconditioned self, is indestructible but only in the sense that life itself is indestructible. Life on the planet (and in the universe) goes on regardless of the changing seasons, of birth and death of all individual creatures, of extinctions, and of the cycle of death and birth of stars and galaxies. All animals are expressions of the one life force and it makes sense that the same rules apply to us. Humans don't operate under different laws of nature, as much as we might like to think we do. However, exactly how the soul manifests individually or within the collective after the dissolution of the body, I do not pretend to know. I am happy with the non-knowing aspect of death because I trust the life energy operating throughout the universe. Whatever works for the planet and the universe is fine for me.

In Jewish scriptures the individual soul is the expression of "I AM" (*subject* without *object*). This is a concept almost impossible to encapsulate through mental concepts, although spiritual teachers, poets, philosophers and religious mystics have made valiant attempts to describe the soul through words. Rupert Spira puts it this way: "All of life is like a temporary coloring of eternity, of this dimension of presence, of awareness, which shines in each of our minds as the knowledge I AM and which is felt in our hearts as peace, happiness, love, and which shines in our perceptions as beauty."[2]

If you feel your way back to when you were a child, you might notice that essentially you are the same being now that you were as a six-, seven-, or eight-year-old. Your personality has undoubtedly changed and evolved with time, as has your body to the extent that every cell has been replaced more than once, but the essential you as the background to experience remains untouched and unchanged through the years and decades. In other words, you don't become a completely different person every time you have a birthday. Of course, as we age, we look in the mirror and see the effect of time on our body. We can choose to look through the eyes of the conditioned ego and feel shamed by the accumulated wrinkles and atrophied muscles, or we can look through the eyes of consciousness and see that in our essence we remain ageless and untouched by time.

Practicing awareness

As you share space with your horse, how aware are you of being in the moment? Do your thoughts go to the next moment, the next thing you want to do, or back to something you did earlier? Each time that happens, bring your thoughts back to something happening right now, your breath. There's no need to count it or alter it in any way; just be aware of it, then put your awareness back onto your horse. While you are doing something with your horse (or doing anything for that matter) remind yourself from time to time to be conscious that you are breathing. You don't need to change your breathing or to control it, but simply remind yourself to be conscious of the air going in and out for several breaths. Enjoy the deep full-bodied relaxation of the out-breath. At some point, you could put your hands on the side of your horse's chest and be one with his breathing.

In everyday life we experience pure moments of soul awareness when our mind naturally gets out of the way, even if we don't express it quite that way. This can happen, for instance, during moments of wide focus. When we are in a relaxed state of observation that doesn't engage self-talk, we are as close to our equine brothers and sisters as we can possibly be. In addition to such serendipitous moments, we can actively develop soul awareness through regular practices of meditation, mindfulness, chanting, contemplation or prayer, all of which have the potential to lead to stillness of mind. Such practices might take place in purposeful daily sessions, but equally, they may be daily micro-practices in which aspects of nature (including horses) become the object of attention. The choice of which spiritual practice to use is likely to depend on one's cultural and religious background, but it's of little consequence since in common to all religions is the desire to attain peace, tranquility and knowledge of the unconditioned self as a sacred space.

I enter the paddock where our horses are quietly enjoying fresh hay while soaking up the warmth from the new spring sun. I want to do something useful with one horse but I succumb to an urge to sit under a tree and watch them for a while. Several of the horses come near and stand peacefully still, making their soft snuffling noises by way of greeting, but seemingly wanting nothing. It occurs to me that I, too, want nothing in that moment. I can hear birds singing, I feel the sun on my skin, I hear the horses gently snuffling and chewing, and I smell the heady mix of grass, hay and horse. Why would I want to be anywhere else? Why would I want to do anything else? Everything in this moment is sufficient in its fullness. My mind becomes still as I put my attention on sensory experience and on my breath, feeling part of the herd and everything around. A thought comes in that horses know everything they need to know to be successful horses. By successful, I mean that they know exactly how to be healthy, contented, relaxed, peaceful and supported within their herd; they know how to be fully functioning horses. And with delightful simplicity, for this moment, I realize that I know everything I need to know to be fully human.

Why do we even need to consider the soul? Haven't humans always known how to be human? We must have done something right over the 315,000 or so years of the history of Homo sapiens or we wouldn't still be here, so why is it that so many of us today lead disturbed, unhappy, insecure and dysfunctional lives? Why is it we don't trust ourselves simply to be any more? I believe it is because we have layered so much of a material nature over our true selves that we have become lost. We have also accepted the untruth that we need to be "doing" something constantly as justification for existence. Look at any animal, and provided they aren't in a ridiculously confined and unhealthy situation they know perfectly well how to be. A dog knows how to be a dog, and a duck knows how to be a duck. But most of us don't believe it is enough to simply know what it is to be human. The modern human generally does not trust her innate human knowledge or inner state of being. This occurs because we lose touch with our innate nature as we take on layer upon layer of conditioning and materialism[3] and forget that our best spiritual teachers are animals, plants, trees, the elements and our inner essence. We substitute for our inner wisdom, a sense of urgency as we hurry from one thing to another, leaving no space for contemplation of inner truth. The subject of the next chapter, being in a hurry, is a modern human obsession that contrasts vividly with the natural mental state of a horse.

Footnotes

1. Kowalski (2007) p. 23.
2. Rupert Spira, "Our Unborn, Undying Nature" [online]. Available at: https://www.scienceandnonduality.com/video/our-unborn-undying-nature (Accessed 10 October 2022).
3. Materialism doesn't only mean the practice of gathering up more and more things, objects, and money. In its essence it refers to the habit most modern humans have (some more than others) of being mentally attached to things, objects, possessions, ways of being, and other people. Mental attachment to material things, or we could say, to form, implies deriving one's own existential meaning from them while at the same time denying or fearing the impermanence of all we hold dear—a perfect recipe for unhappiness.

Chapter 7

Hurry Up and Slow Down

Horses are one of the fastest animals on the planet, which is undoubtedly one of the reasons we love them and have found them useful in so many ways. However, whether they are in the wild or in a paddock as a herd, they don't seem to move very much at all. In part, this is because of the 18 hours a day they need to devote to eating, but also because they know to conserve energy. Unless a horse sees a good reason to move in a hurry, he just doesn't bother. If they ever express a sense of urgency, it is because they believe their lives could depend upon being on the move. Or they may go for a gallop sometimes for the sheer joy of it.

The sense of urgency that humans experience is very rarely existential. It is more likely to be habitual and conforming to the lie that we must achieve as much as possible, as quickly as possible. The haste we bring to situations not only colors our experience, but it also determines the quality of experience. Unfortunately, millions of humans feel dictated to by time and live at such a fast pace that we convince ourselves there's not enough time to truly live. Have you ever called yourself "time poor"? I have, often. But it's a crazy thing to think, given that we all have the same amount of time in any given day. It's how we choose to *experience* time that makes it feel either eternal or scarce.

As human life speeds up, some people deliberately choose a slower pace of living, not necessarily by deciding to move to a small town or live rurally (you can still be very busy in the country!), but simply by living at a slower pace. In Europe in the 1980s a groundswell of people saw how profoundly they missed out on a peaceful inner life through living at an exaggerated pace physically and mentally, so they started a "slowness movement". As reported by Carl Honoré in his book, *In Praise of Slowness*, this began in 1986 with a protest against fast food when a McDonald's restaurant opened in Piazza di Spagna, Rome, sparking the "slow food movement".[1] It's appropriate that it was in Italy where this awareness emerged, for Italians love their food and treat it with great respect. An Italian family or group of friends taking hours over a meal, while enjoying several courses and convivial conversation, is a beautiful and natural part of their culture. Over time, the slowness movement developed into further subcultures in other areas such as the "Cittaslow" organization for slow cities. It's not obvious what impact this movement has had on city life worldwide, but the idea of slower living has filtered down to the level of individuals and many have taken it to heart. Carl Honoré's 2005 addendum to his book *In Praise of Slowness* documents the impact of the slow movement while offering cautious optimism that the human world is getting the message:

> *Everywhere, people are waking up to the fact that the cult of speed is a bad thing. And now growing numbers of us are defying convention to embrace slowness. Speed still has the upper hand but the pressure for change is building.*[2]

I wonder what Honoré would think since the world has been shaped by the Covid-19 pandemic. Much of the world population has lived through extensive shutdowns in which people have been confined to their homes and, as a result, huge numbers of people now choose to work from home when they can. There seems to be a reluctance to return to the fast lane with the same intensity as in pre-pandemic days. Add to that the emerging impact of climate change, and humans undoubtedly have little choice but to slow down. At this time (2023), it remains to be seen just how deep a change these two major disruptions are likely to bring to human life.

The phenomenon of people living in constant haste has so many origins and influences, but one factor surely stems from our desire to outsmart change; to move faster than change in the hope that we will beat it and, if we're lucky, negate it altogether. Certainly, that's how I remember life in the fast lane, but living in a continuous climate of urgency brings with it uncomfortable physical sensations of tension leading to negative impacts on our health. Within such tension we are essentially living under the pressure of the adrenalin-driven *flight or fight* state for which the Norwegian philosopher Guttorm Floistad assigns the term "hurry-sickness":

> *The only thing for certain is that everything changes. The rate of change increases. If you want to hang on, you better speed up. That is the message of today. It could however be useful to remind everyone that our basic needs never change. The need to be seen and appreciated! It is the need to belong. The need for nearness and care, and for a little love! This is given only through slowness in human relations. To master changes, we have to recover slowness, reflection and togetherness. There we will find real renewal.*[3]

Ironically, as soon as we slow down to consciously enjoy the *process* of doing, rather than focusing exclusively on the end result, the more time itself seems to slow down. The faster we go in a day, especially if our activities arise from a sense of urgency, the less we feel we are achieving and the sooner the day vanishes, often leaving us quite dissatisfied. The more we want to achieve through what we are doing, the less enjoyable our doing becomes. I proved this to myself repeatedly while working in an academic environment but I had no idea of how to get out of the habit back then since it was so ubiquitous. Universities used to be quiet, peaceful institutions supportive of idea-driven and colleague-supported intellectual and creative inquiry but through excessive political control they have become stressful environments worldwide as every outcome requires disruptive justification and assessment. From my observations in academic management, it was clear that the quality of work decreased in direct proportion to increased compliance. The sense of working against the clock to achieve what is expected, rather than following creative and intellectual processes according to the time they deserve, is not only counterproductive, it is also stressful. Work created under the stress of performance anxiety is a special form of human craziness and is unlikely to produce much of high quality. But we don't have to be employed by an organization to experience this; we do it to ourselves easily enough!

Eckhart Tolle in *A New Earth* makes a useful distinction between two kinds of time that he calls "clock time" and "psychological time". He acknowledges that we can't avoid living in clock time in modern human society since we have obligations to meet appointments and deadlines, but if we allow ourselves to be driven by clock time as a taskmaster we experience what he calls psychological time: "[This] is the egoic mind's endless preoccupation with past and future and its unwillingness to be one with life in alignment with the inevitable *isness* of the present moment."[4] In his earlier book, *The Power of Now*, Tolle suggests that when we give attention to our body-mind it has the capacity to let us know how compulsively we identify with past and future. When you become conscious of being trapped in psychological time you might notice that it is accompanied by a sense of urgency and restlessness in the body. You might have a feeling of dissatisfaction "as your life's journey is no longer an adventure, just an obsessive need to arrive, to attain, to 'make it.'"[5]

How can we live in the modern world without feeling trapped in psychological time? Tolle's remedy is to train our minds to constantly return to present-moment awareness as soon as practical time-bound matters are dealt with. This is excellent advice; the difficulty is remembering to do it. Another Tolle practice is to retain the focus of attention in the present moment even while working within deadlines, remaining only peripherally aware of time. One thing I used when in stressful employment was a manual egg timer. To take a break, I would turn it over and meditate on the sand passing through it for the whole three minutes that it took. It was a lifesaver some days.

Since horses continuously live in the present moment, they have much to teach us about time. Spending time with a horse shows us how easy it is for hours to pass when doing something as simple as grooming and just hanging out with our equine friend. In my equine assisted practice I endeavor to provide an environment of calm spaciousness without time pressures, regardless of what we are doing. On a practical level this is established by allowing two hours for each one-hour booking so that neither I nor the client are anxious about going over time. (Clearly, this is not a recipe for becoming rich.) Another consideration is to avoid transmitting a sense of urgency to the horses. This is important because at times we can be in a crucial process with horse and client and need spaciousness to allow the situation to play out fully.

Taking the time it takes is normal and natural for horses. They are never in a hurry unless they are running from perceived danger or anticipating feed time (an artificial situation created by domestication). It is incredibly easy to provide a spacious atmosphere around horses because they automatically default to relaxed states whenever they can. Relaxing is their place of balance (homeostasis)[6] as they are hardwired not to waste their energy. Provided nobody bursts into their space carrying buckets of feed, and so long as we are calm and unhurried, horses typically will be too.

Of course, the calming effect works in both directions. Horses, like pets such as cats and dogs, are known to have a calming effect on people simply by being, by doing nothing and by allowing touch. Provided people are not fearful, it has been discovered that when they are with their pet dogs, their oxytocin blood levels almost double, and their beta endorphins and dopamine levels also increase.[7] I wouldn't be at all surprised if it is the same for horses and humans. I have had friends and clients who simply wish to spend time with horses, and leave feeling calmer and better in themselves. You undoubtedly will have noticed that horses are adept at detecting when we are in a hurry and fixated on getting a task done! Anyone who has ever worked within a limited timeframe to halter their horses and load them on to a trailer before an event will know how readily they pick up on our urgency and perceive it as a threat. Horses are not being "naughty" or "willful" if they refuse to be haltered or loaded, they are doing what they would do naturally if they thought there was a threat within their immediate environment. So, it is our responsibility to prepare a slow peaceful space by making sure that we ourselves are in a calm state. The preparation might include making sure that the horses are in place long before they meet someone, and by doing a brief meditation or breathing exercise. Better still, share space with a horse for a few minutes while doing absolutely nothing.

Noticing the spaces

As you observe horses you might notice that there is usually a small gap between them doing one thing and another. I have a bad habit of finishing a job and going straight on to another without a break, but I've noticed that horses will finish eating their hay or patch of grass and take a couple or more seconds to look up, look around and stand still before they move on to the next thing they want to do. I took this lesson from them, and now remind myself every day to take a breath and look around, listen to the environment, feel how the air touches my skin, smell the grass and flowers (and horses) around me. To do this between every task, as well as in the middle of a task, takes no time at all and is very refreshing. Take the time to notice that you are alive.

An excellent strategy to break the tyranny of time is to literally practice doing nothing a couple of times a day. Strangely enough, doing nothing, if "done" in the right way, doesn't feel like nothing. There are two kinds of doing nothing. Firstly, there is the frustration of being stuck somewhere (e.g. a doctor's waiting room) while feeling trapped by the situation and wishing you were somewhere else. "I am too busy to be wasting my time sitting here," we might say to ourselves as we clench our jaw and tap our fingers. Secondly, there is doing nothing while deciding not to be frustrated, and resisting the temptation to label it as "wasting time". In this nothingness you can choose to be open to being fully present, taking in everything around you in an attitude of acceptance of what is happening right now. In this state I am reminded of the beautiful Italian phrase, *il dolce fa niente* ("the sweetness of doing nothing").

Spending "nothing time" with a horse is a wonderful practice, as we will see later. It helps us realize that time does not need to be our enemy. Philosopher Alan Watts puts this sentiment beautifully:

Although the rhythm of the waves beats a kind of time, it is not clock or calendar time. It has no urgency. It happens to be timeless time. I know that I am listening to a rhythm which has been just the same for millions of years, and it takes me out of a world of relentlessly ticking clocks. Clocks for some reason or other always seem to be marching, and, as with armies, marching is never to anything but doom. But in the motion of waves there is no marching rhythm. It harmonizes with our very breathing. It does not count our days. Its pulse is not in the stingy spirit of measuring, of marking out how much remains. It is the breathing of eternity, like the God Brahma of Indian mythology inhaling and exhaling, manifesting and dissolving the worlds, forever. As a mere conception this might sound appallingly monotonous, until you come to listen to the breaking and washing of waves.[8]

Horses model for us how to live with others with minimal stress, how to ignore clock time when we can, and how to be present-moment focused. Most of the time horses look as though they are doing nothing, which is an image at odds with documentaries portraying them as highly active graceful creatures galloping across vast spaces, with stallions fighting for supremacy, mares giving birth and foals joyfully leaping about. All those things are true of course, but a film of real-time horse life would be far too boring to watch since mostly they simply stand quietly, taking in their environment, sleeping, grooming each other, mooching around, foraging and walking leisurely to new pastures and water.[9] Although we admire horses for their athleticism (and exploit them for it too), most of the time they simply chill out and eat while subtly communicating with each other. They keep their vital energy for when they really need it.

What can horses teach us about time? Although they move slowly much of the time (as well as fast when they need to) that's not necessarily the lesson we need to take, although experimenting with doing everything 10% slower for a day is a rewarding practice. When I remind myself of the present moment and decide to slow down I am much more likely to achieve something of value than when I'm in a hurry. I believe this is because I am giving everything quality attention. Horses are masters at teaching us how to be in the moment because they treat the present as though that's all they ever have (which is the case for all of us). Horses appear to have all the time in the world because they don't invent "psychological time", that is they don't tell themselves the story of all the things they have to do next, and they don't live in an environment of assumed scarcity.

Doing nothing

One way to learn about time from horses is to be in their presence doing absolutely nothing for an hour or more. Observe everything and share their space. There is nothing to do, nothing to achieve and only something to *be*. Allow the essential being of the horse and your own essential being to share space. Ask them to show you a peaceful place where there is no need to fill your mind with concerns for past or present. Time will do its own thing without any help from us.

When we are mindful we are not rushing against the clock trying to get as much done as quickly as possible so that we can get to the next more important thing. When we are in a hurried frame of mind we are not fully aware of where we are or what we are doing because a good portion of our mind is taken up with concern for getting to the result. This is regarded as a normal state of mind in modern life but, sadly, it means that much of the time we are not fully aware of the life we are living. If we are not living in the present, then we really aren't experiencing life in anything like its fullness. If we keep wishing we were in the next moment, closer to finishing whatever it is we are doing, we do not know or respect the life we are currently having. In fact, to be projecting constantly into the next moment means we literally have forgotten how to live.

In my last management job, I received anything from 50 to 100 emails a day. Most were notices of what someone else in the top-heavy management machine was planning, or were suggestions of how managers could get more productivity out of staff. If I read each one fully and carefully and follow up with whatever reply is required, it takes up my entire day's work. I have other things to do such as attending and running meetings, planning innovative strategies, trouble shooting, budgeting, mentoring staff, and so on. The way I cope on a personal level is to do everything at speed. I read emails at speed, I write them at speed, I walk quickly, I have working lunches, I keep phone calls short, and I work into the night from home. As a result, I resemble a hamster on a wheel and I don't have much sense of completion at the end of the day. I am powerless to change the culture of the institution and I feel as though I achieve very little of meaning. At times I feel guilty spending time with horses after work, but they keep me sane and alive. Without horses asking, "What's the hurry?" I might just deconstruct.

In early 2020 we had no choice but to slow down as every nation dealt with the challenges of the Covid-19 pandemic. For us at Earthhorse Aotearoa, "lock down" became a perfect time to work at leisure with the horses. We had no clients, and the horses' willingness to offer their calm presence felt ever more spacious, deeper and peaceful. There was no traffic passing by, no visitors, and the birds sang louder than ever as human noise subsided and time slowed down. We gave away expectations of achieving anything as we groomed, trimmed hooves, worked horses on the ground and rode around the farm. We stopped caring about whether a job took five minutes or five hours. We became more aligned with the horses' concept of time; the edges of their attention defined by changes around them as they lifted their heads or turned their ears to listen to a bird, a snapping twig or another horse moving. Sometimes they made the subtlest of movements that demanded close attention to notice. Slowing down to the pace of horse awareness while being mindful of the slightest change in their attention has enriched my relationship with them and given me a different perspective on time generally. Whatever level of communication we seek with them, it is worth spending time getting to know our best four-legged friends without time constraints, and we just might discover a spacious mind bringing us into deeper connection with nature and with ourselves. In the next chapter I explore how by putting time concerns to one side we become able to discover inner spaciousness through which awareness can arise.

Footnotes
1. Honoré (2004) p. 59.
2. Honoré (2004) p. 321.
3. Vincenzo di Nicola (2018) "Take your time: The seven pillars of a Slow Thought manifesto". *Aeon Magazine* [online]. Available at: https://www.academia.edu/36033149/_Take_Your_Time_The_Seven_Pillars_of_a_Slow_Thought_Manifesto (Accessed 1 April 2023).
4. Tolle (2005) p. 207.
5. Tolle (2004) pp. 56–60.
6. Homeostasis is defined as the physiological maintained state of relatively stable equilibrium. Allostasis is a predictive balancing process over time, defined as an equilibrium maintained in response to change within an organism's environment. Barrett (2020) p. 137, fn. 8.

7. Oxytocin is an important hormone that, along with other functions, assists with bonding, recognition, and trust. See studies cited by Olmert (2009) p. 191.

8. Alan Watts, "Love of Waters" radio transcript [online]. Available at: https://alanwatts.org/transcripts/love-of-waters/ (Accessed 10 October 2022).

9. This is not my original idea. I believe I first came across it in one of Carolyn Resnick's talks.

Chapter 8

Awareness and Awakening

What horses give us spiritually is an opportunity to get to know a fellow animal whose being resides outside of the stream of thought. It's not that horses don't think; they clearly do, but their thinking is through visualization rather than verbalization, hence they don't create narratives about who they are. If we are open to seeing how horses view their world, they show us that it is possible to experience life in ways other than through a constant stream of words in the mind. Horses freely take us beyond mental concepts and into a realization of our shared spiritual nature. There is nothing wrong with thinking. It's a great asset when we need it but we seem to have forgotten how to handle our incredible mental abilities in everyday life. We don't know how to ignore thinking when it's not needed. It's as though we are driving a Ford Prefect with a Ferrari engine and have forgotten how pleasant it is to take a slow relaxing drive, using the Ferrari engine only when needed.

The slow peaceful pace that horses model for us, whereby we take in our surroundings and understand them without creating unnecessary stories about ourselves, is accessible to everyone. Our fundamental state of being is already embedded within but most of us have forgotten how to access it, so we need generous-hearted animals such as horses to lead us back there. An equine assisted environment is one where we can begin the process of opening to the space of our innate human knowing. Horses don't indulge in complicated mind games, not through having a higher moral compass or because they are intellectually inferior, but because they have not needed to evolve the same way as humans. As horses evolved over millions of years, the challenges that their natural living environment presented were met through the refinement of their physical and mental capacities. Humans evolved within their environment in the same manner but learned how to outthink physical challenges through becoming more cognition focused. But we misuse this ability because we have turned our cognitive attention onto ourselves in ways that aren't beneficial. We use our brain to do wasteful things such as worrying about what people think of us, wondering how we measure up against others, worrying about whether we are successful now or ever will be in the future, and the list goes on. These things have their origins in the natural human need to be accepted within a community but in modern life in which community is fractured it has become a form of mental self-torture. We can be so caught up in self-preoccupation that to varying degrees we are unaware of what we are doing and equally unaware of our surroundings.

Horses don't care about what people or other horses think of them, other than needing to be included in the herd. They are concerned about comfort and discomfort of course but they don't filter things into categories of good and bad. They certainly don't invent narratives about who they are going to be, who they are now or who they once were. If they have egos, which they clearly do to some extent, they are not dominated by them. For humans, developing an ego is essential for learning to live within complex societies. We can see ego development clearly in toddlers as they develop possessiveness over their toys, as they express their wishes with dogged persistence and as they resist parental instruction. A young human's ego development serves the purpose of developing an individual identity that is vital for humans but not nearly so much for horses. From my observations there is an important difference where egoism is expressed by horses, not individually, but as a whole herd.[1] The same applies to human tribal groups, in which the ego of the individual is absorbed into the identity of the group.

Practicing spaciousness

Being aware of the moment is less about the moment itself and more about *what happens* in the present moment. It is about focusing on what you are doing and experiencing as awareness brings you back into the present moment. There is another, deeper kind of awareness, and that is *awareness of awareness* itself. This is the seventh sense mentioned previously. It's being aware of the spaciousness within which everything of this moment occurs. Or it can be thought of as *the observer of whoever is aware*. This spaciousness can be described through words to a very limited extent, but if you put your awareness on spaciousness without the need for thought, you will realize that it has always been there like the air you breathe. How can we practice this awareness? Look for the spaces between things, between spoken words, between horses in a herd, between people, above the horizon, between buildings and within your own being. If you practice this way of looking you will see life in terms of *pattern* in which everything belongs to everything else and to which you belong. The world we experience is not a collection of a million separate things.

Opening to the foundation of one's being where ego doesn't rule is often called *awakening*. It is given other lofty names too such as *enlightenment* or *nirvana* in Buddhist traditions and *salvation* in Christian traditions. But these words are never fully accurate or sufficient so we must use them carefully. "Enlightenment", for instance, can give an erroneous impression of a saintly person in a strangely altered state of mind, and "salvation" that is usually associated with earning the right to eternity through good works is a mistranslation from the Greek "sozo" with its primary meaning of "to heal". A definition of awakening that I like comes from the American spiritual teacher Adyashanti who says, "Awakening is a moment of expanded awareness and true interconnectedness with the world."[2] I would alter that slightly to: "Awakening is a moment of expanded awareness *as* true interconnectedness with the world." In other words, it is through real connection with our environment that we bypass complete identification with individual concerns. Putting it another way, awareness is choosing to experience our environment fully, unaccompanied by an ongoing personal story, without exercising judgments of good or bad and without taking personally that which happens.

For most of us, awakening doesn't come from outside ourselves as a blinding flash but gradually arises as we use our senses to observe and experience our world in the absence of judgment and grasping. With practice, by becoming more aware of the world through our senses than through the endless stream of mental activity, the ego lessens its influence over our lives. To aid the awakening process we can observe how "awake" beings live: horses, dogs, cats, birds, cows and pretty much any animal. All we need do to receive their lessons is to observe without an agenda, taking the time it takes. Perhaps rather than "taking" time, which betrays an attitude of stealing, it is preferable to *ignore measured time* as we take in every aspect of what we are observing. We can't live this way continually in the modern world of course, but we can make a point of looking around spaciously several times during a day.

We can also awaken through specific spiritual practices that lead us to view the world in ways other than cognitively. Through such practices we see how everything is connected to everything else. A teaching in Buddhism called "dependent origination" emphasizes how all things are connected by a mass of contributing origins and causations, a concept that is the foundation of Zen Master Thich Nhat Hanh's *"Letter to Mother Earth"*:

> *Dear Mother, wherever there is soil, water, rock or air, you are there, nourishing me and giving me life. You are present in every cell of my body. My physical body is your physical body, and just as the sun and stars are present in you, they are also present in me. You are not outside of me and I am not outside of you. You are more than just my environment. You are nothing less than myself.*[3]

Ironically, if we actively seek awakening it can prove elusive because through applying effort we use focused intention (as a product of ego). But if we open ourselves up to nature through the senses while retaining an innocent mind, awareness is given freely. If we learn to become as unselfconscious as horses by putting our attention on everything around us, we can touch the space of awareness that is always with us and always has been. All we need do is divide the curtain of ego and re-dis-cover (uncover) the life of the soul. But if we *strive* for a different state of being, we are unlikely to find it since the very act of trying involves self-rejection. That is, if we try to be a better self we are essentially saying that our current self is insufficient and not worthy, and if we follow that line of thinking we set one part of ourselves in conflict with another.

I stand in the winter breeze next to our warm, nutty-smelling mare and ask to experience her world with her. It seems she could just as well be praying to Mother Earth as she feels solidly grounded and connected to the earth. She moves her ears discreetly in response to rustling leaves of the forest trees while her herd mates amble nearby. She embraces me with her strong neck, and I have a sense of interconnectedness of two quiet minds as we stand together, asking for nothing but to share experience. I look into her beautiful soft eyes and sense an incredible depth within. There is no judgment of me; there is no neediness or desire; there is no restlessness; no projection of her will upon mine. In short, there is no ego. She is my Zen master.

How does awareness or awakening arise within humans? To a few people it comes through something happening without willing it to happen, such as an event that forces us to reconsider what we have taken for granted as meaningful. It can come as a sudden sense of knowing through a painful situation that forces the ego to let in the light, allowing the mind-derived entity to fall away for a while. But for most people the change is undramatic, more like a slowly emerging recognition in the form of a gentle nudge to one's perception when immersed in a natural environment.

Awareness is usually not accompanied by flashing lights, nor is it a drastically altered state of mind; rather, it is a subtle yet profound sense of connection with the non-conceptual experience of being alive. It is what comes when we experience the world through our primary senses, unaccompanied by an internal running commentary about what the experiential world means to us as individual entities. Every one of us has experienced spacious awareness; we just might not have recognized it for what it is. It is not a mysterious state of being but is a quietly felt peace beyond the realm of thinking. It is "the peace that transcends all understanding", as Saint Paul expressed it, and it is something that belongs to us all.[4]

We all know this state. Allow your mind to drift back into childhood. What moments do you remember clearly? Putting aside childhood trauma for now (which we all have experienced in different ways), does your recollection seem alive to you? I have random memories of things happening as a child, some of which are baffling, painful, and alienating, but there are also many that are beautifully spacious and peaceful. Those childhood memories are rich in sensations of sight, touch, hearing, taste and smell unencumbered by self-talk. Today they can be rekindled through specific smells, birdsong and sights. They are spacious memories that do not include any sense of doing, hurrying or worrying, but instead are enveloped in quiet wonder. These memories are as simple as making daisy chains while sitting on the grass at my aunt's farm, sitting up a tree in my grandmother's orchard while eating juicy red plums, and being scooped up by a relative in a hug of unconditional love. I occasionally revisit these moments (as much as one *can* revisit the past) not to kindle nostalgia or to feel good, but as simple inquiry. I want to know why such memories are so different from the incomplete, muddled memories of the more ordinary things. It seems they have one thing in common: a sense of being fully supported by nature or another person, and of being so engrossed in the sensory experience of the situation that there is no room for thought; there is only still spaciousness. These are moments of true aliveness.

Awareness arises not only from being conscious of our immediate environment through the primary senses, but also from observing our thoughts and accessing a deeper sense of being that is beyond conceptualization (the sixth and seventh senses). When noticing our thoughts we need to know the nature of them, what they are and when they arise, without being hijacked by them. It's worth repeating that the thoughts themselves are not the problem, it is identifying with them that's the problem. The more we believe that thoughts are self-generated and always true, the less we are aware, the more confused we are likely to be and the less inner spaciousness we experience. In the conviction that they accurately represent who we are we become sucked into thought processes as we identify with them. Let's face it, most of our thoughts are not worth listening to. They are repetitive and tedious unless we are genuinely trying to solve a problem or make a plan.

Is it possible to stop the constant stream of thoughts? Yes, but only for short periods such as during meditation practices or when we witness something of intense beauty. One thing's for sure, we can't stop thoughts by *trying*. The more we tell ourselves to stop a thought, the more thought we add to our minds. "Stop thinking" is a thought, and what's more it's a disturbing one because it's obvious that it's impossible to dismiss thought by exercising willpower, and that makes us feel even more powerless. The way to reduce the stream of thinking is to notice it, observe it as it's happening, then to put our attention onto something else. In other words, we acknowledge the presence of randomly arising thought patterns, but we choose not to identify with them. Once we get into the habit of observing our thoughts without identification or judgment, our mind becomes freer to take in information through our senses and the more awake we become.

It helps to have a conscious practice to take us out of habitual ways of conditioned thinking, whether that be yoga, meditation or devotional practices. Whatever you choose is of little concern since there is no single "right way". Such practices simply offer us a way towards awareness of that place that never changes, providing the background for all experience. Awareness can be likened to the playing of a movie on a screen in which the constantly shifting image is the *stuff that happens* in our life, while the screen that we are normally unaware of is the *essence of who we are*.[5] Of course, we have difficulty seeing that which is constant and unchanging because it fails to attract our attention. It is said, for instance, that a fish has no awareness of water because it is her constant environment and she is only aware of what is *in* the water, not the water itself. In a similar example, Eckhart Tolle writes in *The Power of Now* that what we think of as consisting of a room is constituting its walls, ceiling, furniture and floor. We fail to notice the space without which there would be no room.[6] This analogy illustrates the habit of modern humans to be mentally captured by material things and by what happens. We might think we *are* what happens to us and assume it will take us somewhere meaningful. The seventeenth-century philosopher René Descartes famously argued that we consist of our thoughts and experiences: "I think, therefore I am," and most people still believe this to be true even though it is a dysfunctional idea.[7] Very few thoughts are self-generated, and if we believe we *are* our thoughts life never feels as though it is in our control. What we think of as meaningful (education, relationship, career, possessions) never fully satisfies us.

What is the problem if we are taken on endless journeys by our thoughts? There are two problems: one is where thoughts come from; the other is what they say. The endless stream of thought activity arises from a lifetime of conditioning and the accumulation of past experiences. Conceptually, we are largely what we have been taught by prior experience, formal and informal education (from school, family, society), and what the culture continues to reinforce in us (through other people, television and social media). Most thoughts are repetitive, useless, unconsciously arising and (all too often) personally undermining. Much of what we think involuntarily tells us that we are not good enough, not adequate, not talented enough, not good-looking enough and so on, and the worst thing is that usually we believe them. If our negative thoughts were to come in verbal statements from someone else, most certainly we would not tolerate that person's company, yet we are expected in Western society to constantly measure ourselves against others.

There is always someone better. Or we might be convinced that we are better than everyone else, brighter than anyone else, or richer than anyone else. Either way, it is an illusion and a major cause of suffering.

Freeing yourself from thought

A simple four-part practice can free us from habitual, useless and harmful thoughts.

1. Simply *notice* thoughts without adding judgment to them: *"Ah there's that thought again."*
2. Ask the question, *"Is this true?"* Frequently thoughts about ourselves are not true, and simply asking this question will cause them to shrink.
3. Turn your *sensory awareness* onto something else. This could be something attractive in your environment, or awareness of your breath.
4. Remind yourself of what you are currently doing, whether it be walking, driving a car, listening to conversations or riding a horse, etc., then choose to do it more consciously.

Here I use the terms awareness and awakening interchangeably, essentially meaning the ability to place one's attention and center of being onto something other than the stream of thought. There's a fine distinction between the two terms though, in that awareness is the engagement of attention, and awakening is what that engagement does to the essence of our being. There is only one way to know what this means, and that is to experience it by directing our attention away from thoughts that serve no useful purpose.

Spacious awareness arises naturally from being with horses without holding onto a mental agenda. As we grow in awareness we are able to react effectively in the moment, protecting ourselves and others from sudden movements from a horse when necessary. This is not the same thing as anticipating problems, being fearful or imagining injuries. Spacious awareness is turning down the volume of the inner movie soundtrack, ignoring its attempt to draw us into dramas and worries, while being awake to what is happening in the moment. The ability to do this is acquired through constant self-reminders to be present, one of the most basic prerequisites for working with horses in a learning or healing capacity. So too is the ability to be honest with ourselves so that we can truly say that our attitude towards horses does not objectify them, that we do not treat them as mere commodities in the service of our superior humanity. Attitudes and values set us up for what we experience and how we interpret experience, which is what we will consider in the next chapter.

Footnotes

1. Egoism, meaning the development of individuality, is not to be confused with egotism, meaning excessive conceit and self-absorption.
2. https://www.soundstrue.com/collections/shop?q=adyashanti (Accessed 15 May 2023).
3. https://plumvillage.org/articles/love-letter-to-the-earth-2 (Accessed 1 October 2021).
4. Philippians 4:7, New International Version of the Bible.
5. This is an often-quoted analogy from present-day spiritual teachers that is supposed to have originated from Ramana Maharshi.
6. Tolle (2004) p. 138.
7. *Cogito, ergo sum* ("I think, therefore I am") comes from philosopher René Descartes' *Discourse on Method* (1637).

Chapter 9

Attitudes and Values

Attitude means everything in a horse-human relationship, just as it does in any relationship. We set the tone for whether we work with our horse in a cooperative partnership or whether the relationship is shaped by fear and coercion; whether we hold the horse in high regard or think of her as a commodity; and whether she is merely an extension of our ego. The use of force is unfortunately still prevalent in the human-horse world. There are still some who believe they must "show the horse who's boss", and to that end use tools and techniques of intimidation to "make" the horse do what they want. But fortunately, the horse world is evolving gradually and the fact that you are reading this indicates that you expect a lot more from your own horse relationship than tradition might dictate. Working for mutual trust with horses is fun, exciting, rewarding and mind-heart expanding, so for a start let's examine the verbal language we rely on around horses. Do you think, do, or say:

It *or* he/she?
Tell *or* ask?
Make *or* suggest?
Insist *or* offer a way?
Catch *or* invite?
Get angry *or* quietly assert?
Yell *or* whisper?
Slap *or* rub?

You may wonder, given that horses don't understand the finer nuances of human languages, why it would matter what words we use. It matters for two reasons: firstly, through our choice of words we are normalizing values for others around us to absorb and, secondly, the way we talk affects how we think and feel, which is transmitted to animals much more readily than we might believe. This is a process that also operates in prejudicial thinking towards fellow humans. If we constantly think badly towards a particular group of people our attitudes will eventually burst forth in words and actions. If we think our horse is an "it" we will feel more justified in "telling it what it must do" as a subservient being, or even in "punishing it".

Human beings can say the oddest things to horses. One behavior that I see persisting is people yelling "stand up" to a horse already standing. It makes no sense, but what they want of course is for the horse to stand quietly (be still). But demanding stillness through a tone of frustration without accessing that still place within ourselves only leads to further frustration. I suspect there is an element, too, of people wanting to demonstrate to others within earshot that they are in full command of their horse. We see this also with dog owners, something of which I have been guilty many times with my own dog. When he runs after another dog on the beach, I have been known to shout vigorously for him to return even though I know that to a dog my noisemaking tells him that I'm joining in on his immense fun. What actual sense horses make of being shouted at is anybody's guess, but for sure they would be far more aware of the anger and frustration in the tone of voice of the human than in the meaning of the words. More often than not horses respond to human anger by standing still, reinforcing the belief that superior forcefulness gets the desired result. However, what forcefulness really results in is an emotionally shut-down and disassociating horse.

I have proved to myself time and time again that when working with horses it is consistency and transparency based on values of respect that achieve lasting results. It might take longer to get there initially, but once a horse learns what we are asking for from a place of stillness and respect, we are more likely to get into a good space with her.

To find out what our underlying (and possibly unconscious) values are, we can question ourselves along the lines of whether we:

- respect horses as beings *equal* to humans
- work with sustained *patience*, allowing the time it takes
- value *process* more than results (means before ends)
- *avoid blaming* a horse when things go wrong
- ensure that we are *fully present* before we work with a horse
- work with a horse in such a way that he is *nonreactive*
- work with a horse in such a way that *we* are *nonreactive*
- *leave our emotional business* out of the process
- put *meaningful relationship* before everything else

When working on my own with a horse, if my usual approaches don't work so well I find it useful to drop my habitual ways and experiment with doing something quite different before losing patience. Changing the task and/or the approach can refresh both the horse's and my minds. It seems we so easily can be trapped by the way we do things without questioning how effective they are. It can be worth even experimenting with doing something the *opposite* of our usual way. Many traditional horse-handling techniques and habits have come from hundreds of years of military practice and no longer serve the purpose for which they were devised, so it is worth questioning traditional ways. For instance, the habit of mounting from the horse's left side was to avoid a soldier's sword getting in the way when mounting alongside others and accidently impaling a horse or fellow soldier. So why don't we also mount from the right side these days? Some horsemanship teachers recommend this, and it certainly can be useful when out in the middle of nowhere you injure your left ankle or knee (as I have discovered). That is not an ideal time to try a maneuver such as mounting from the "off" side with your horse for the very first time!

We need to constantly question our values and ask how the horse would be interpreting what we are asking for. Below are three simple examples of how we can question normative values, and I'm sure you will be able to come up with many more ideas of your own. It's an experimental process that can yield interesting results:

1. With the aim of establishing a warm trusting relationship with a horse most horse lovers like hugging and cuddling up to them, as do I. I'm not suggesting we shouldn't express affection physically to our horses, but we might look inside ourselves to see if we have an element of wanting to bribe them with affection to win their good behavior. It really is worth questioning our motives. Our horses are looking for a leader, not a dependent, and loving on them will not win their loyalty. Hug your horse if you want to, but a horse will love you more if you prove to him that you are trustworthy, consistent and fair. It is more important to make a habit of *giving space*, remembering that it is a highly valuable commodity to a horse. When a horse chooses to move towards you after giving space it is much more rewarding than demanding affection. The same principle applies in the human world, of course.

2. Instead of "catching" your horse, learn to *invite* her to follow you. This is what the Native Americans learned to do with wild horses and it works because it uses the

horse's own language. If you want your horse to follow you, after a greeting ask her to move her hindquarters then simply walk away from her. This feels contrary to our nature because we are used to reaching out and *grasping* what we want rather than walking away and *allowing* something to happen. Eventually she will simply follow you, but equally importantly, you will have learned how powerful *letting go* can be and you might be inspired to try it in the human world.

3. Practice silent communication. To build a strong relationship it helps to remain silent as you work with your horse. Talking to a horse doesn't do any harm, but it can give you the impression that you are communicating when you are not. If you deliberately turn off your voice, you will become much more aware of the actual messages you give out through your energy, body language and focus. Silence also encourages us to be more aware generally of both our outer and inner environments, meaning that we are more likely to keep ourselves safe. When we learn to communicate silently it demonstrates how powerful our body language and intention can be and, again, we start to notice how they work in human interactions.

The take-home message from this chapter is to never be tempted to skip the step of establishing a respectful relationship with your horse before inviting a client to work with her. By being in a hurry and skipping the step of questioning your attitudes and wondering how the horse regards your actions and demeaner, you might inadvertently sabotage the session with your client. How you feel at the end of the session is an indicator of how well you have held space for both you and your client.

Chapter 10

Meaningful Connection

We are interconnected beings and therefore do not learn about ourselves and what it means to be human by leading lives isolated from other humans and being separate from nature. We live and learn through connection.

How do modern humans connect meaningfully with each other? We are generally aware of how we communicate verbally, but long before we say anything to another person we unknowingly take in, and give out, loads of other information. We exchange vital information through touch, by how we stand and hold ourselves, by the angle of our gaze, by our facial expression and through movement. What we are not always aware of, but which communicates even more directly than verbal language, is the level of our energy, our intentions and unconscious physiological information (heart rate, levels of adrenaline, blood pressure, rates of breathing, smell, etc.). An influential psychological study by Albert Mehrabian and Susan Ferris reports that only 7% of human communication is verbal, the remaining 93% being transmitted through physiology.[1] This is an astounding statistic, but I don't think you would find horses arguing with it, so in our communication with horses we must rely on nonverbal modes as we experience the power of our own body language. This is a great thing to realize, because the more we consciously employ nonverbal modes of communication with horses, the more meaningful and effective our relationships with them become. It also affects our relationships with people. I recall when I first started to learn how horses communicate nonverbally and how to replicate it (in my clumsy human manner), that I saw how I also communicated through body language with my students. It was an awareness that changed my teaching for the better.

Questioning what we do habitually is a fruitful way of deepening our communication with horses. I once had a horsemanship teacher who used to say that whenever we are with our horse, we are either training or untraining him. This is true, but we forget too that whenever we are with a horse we are either communicating (empathizing) or un-communicating (objectifying). The normal way for humans to treat a horse is to "catch" him with a halter and rope, pull him from the front, tie him up to a rail, groom quickly and efficiently then put on a saddle and ride. In these and other habitual ways of interacting we are in danger of regarding and treating the horse as either a piece of sporting equipment, or as a non-sentient being whose role is to obey our wishes as if he were a slave or servant. In other words, we so often *objectify* the horse in our subtle and unconscious assumptions of superiority. Even in the equine assisted space we can fall into an objectifying mode by a simple thing such as thinking of *using* a horse rather than *inviting* him to work with us. To have horses willingly work with us in partnership is an essential basis for any work with horses to do with therapy, learning or coaching for the benefit of humans.

The horse doesn't know our language apart from understanding a few select commands and possibly responding to their own name, so instructing them verbally is of limited use. If we turn off our chatter, we discover there is another way to communicate with horses: silence provides an opening for other forms of information to come into consciousness. As Dr. Allan Hamilton points out in *Zen Mind, Zen Horse*, horses are mostly silent creatures who have learned to "make sense from being, *not* thinking".[2] They don't have the problem of inner or outer chatter because their verbal language doesn't go beyond a few vocal greetings and alarms.

The way we walk with our horses tells them a lot about us. If we do just one thing as simple as treating the halter and rope as a safety tool to be activated when needed rather than for dragging our horse along, the relationship changes profoundly. Walking beside your horse's head without any pressure on the rope emulates being at liberty with him. You only need to put light pressure on the rope if he gets distracted. Too many traditional and habitual ways of managing horses are based on the premise that they are too stupid or too dangerous to cooperate fully with us and that we need to hold physical power over them and pull them around. This arises partly from a misinterpretation of what being a leader means to a horse; it too easily becomes confused with dominance. Dominant leadership doesn't work for horses any more than it does in human society; it's called totalitarianism.

For so long, humans have gotten away with forceful dominance while handling horses simply because domesticated horses learn to respond with indifference through habituation. Called "shut-down" it is simply another survival mechanism, not to be confused with calm willingness. Employing modern horsemanship approaches (which owe a great deal to indigenous knowledge) we can find out how to treat horses with the kind of respect that *asks* for their cooperation. Over thousands of years, horses have given us so much service by adapting to our weird attempts to communicate, so it is surely time for us to communicate through their language, not ours. Equine language is a subtle form of communication that has helped them survive in wild herds, and what we need to do is respect that and learn enough of their language through observation and personal research. Horses love it when we make the effort to make real connection.

There are some general guidelines for doing this, but the best horsemen/horsewomen who have described and taught horse language have arrived at what they know through observation of herds, both wild and domesticated. As in learning a human verbal language, books and teachers can only take you so far. In the end you need to get out there with the native speakers and soak it up.

Utilizing space

One learning method I have found effective is to observe a single horse within a group for an hour or so to *practice viewing the world from the perspective of one individual horse*. It takes some doing not to be distracted by the others, but with practice it can become a form of meditation as well as a way of yielding good information.

On another day, try this: *concentrate on the space between horses* within a group. Look at that space as a shape. What would fit in that space? How much space do the horses like to maintain? What purpose do you think that space serves to a horse? What does one horse do when another one walks into her space? How does she invite another horse to be physically close? Which horses does she allow into her space and which ones does she not allow in? Which horses mutually groom? How do they indicate that they want to be left alone? It can be revealing to create a "dossier" on individual horses over a period of weeks according to how they communicate through managing their space.

Some horsemanship teachers suggest that space is the most important commodity to horses beyond food and water, and I would have to agree since horses negotiate space constantly. Once you recognize how horses value space, I guarantee that from then on you will see them continually in action negotiating space.

Effective communication with horses comes from a combination of listening and talking in their native language.

You might not be discussing philosophy together (or will you?) but at the very least you will want to learn how to ask them to work willingly with you. Conversations with horses require one thing first and foremost, our presence. The more present we are as handlers and partners, the more present the horses are with us, and in turn, with others. Presence builds trust, without which very little of value may occur.

Our horses are our learning partners and colleagues. How well that relationship works depends in part on how willing we are to adopt nonverbal communication as our primary mode. If you are in a role as the facilitator of learning or therapy sessions it is essential to be on the same page with horses before inviting anyone else into the dynamic. Regardless of how many years of experience we have had with horses, we need to question our underlying values by asking whether the horses work *for* us, or *with* us. If our horses work for us, then I strongly believe we have some relearning to do before working with them in therapy or learning capacities. If you find yourself using terminology such as "catching" your horse and "using" him, it is time to reconsider the ethical basis of your relationship. But don't feel bad if you find yourself doing this, it's an ingrained habit and we all have done it. All we need do is notice what we are doing and thinking, and change will follow over time.

As we learn horse language it can seem as though we are training our horse, but we're not. Our horses already know their own language, so we don't need to teach them how to play at their own game. What we are doing is teaching them that *we* know their language (even if with a heavy accent). We are the ones doing the learning, not the horses. There is one exception, however. We usually need to actively teach each horse where our personal boundaries are, because they tend to regard us as herd members that come and go, and they want to know immediately whether we are higher or lower in rank.

Most horses will experiment by trying to push us a little, and if we comply, that push will become stronger before too long. Boundary setting is something to put in place with horses long before we introduce others into the therapy or learning space and is a subject we deal with specifically in a later chapter. Boundary setting is necessary for safety reasons of course, but it also turns out that establishing personal boundaries with horses is a transferable skill since most people have difficulty with boundaries somewhere in their lives. A necessary aspect of making meaningful connection with horses is developing our presence, without which no horse will fully trust or respect us.

Footnotes

1.   Albert Mehrabian and Susan Ferris' widely cited study, "Inference of attitudes from nonverbal communication in two channels", *Journal of Consulting Psychology* (1967), concludes that 7% of meaning is communicated through spoken word, 38% through tone of voice, and 55% through body language. This study has a been widely criticized for being so prescriptive but regardless of the exact percentages, the principle has become widely accepted.
2.   Hamilton (2011) p. 4.

Chapter 11

Being Present

The greatest gift you can give any other being is your focused attention from a still mind, from your *presence*. Presence is the dynamic focal point of therapeutic and spiritual processes. It is through offering our presence that people know that their point of view is respected, that they themselves are valued and that they are being listened to with compassion. This, more than any specific technique or therapeutic practice, is what enables others to arrive at their own answers, their own truth and their own soul. If you are a practitioner it is your job to provide the environment and space for that to happen while resisting the desire to direct people into whatever meaning you consider they should take from a situation. There is power in presence, whether we are in a professional relationship with a person or with a friend listening to their story. Horses do the same for us. They "listen" with compassion within a space of acceptance. By offering their presence to us they support our personal discoveries.

Presence is a concept that, like most spiritual words, also has an ordinary everyday meaning. In its commonplace meaning it denotes "existing" or "being in a specific place". So, we can say that we are present with our horse when we are standing next to him. Equally, a teacher notes her students as being present in the classroom. True presence in the spiritual sense, though, is something deeper. It is being fully *in the present moment* while witnessing what is happening from the position of a quiet mind. It requires giving your full attention, but not the kind of attention synonymous with focusing intently on something. Being fully present with another being means being aware of everything at once including your environment, your body, and your thoughts while listening without judgment and without putting your own interpretation on to what you hear. This is also what Palmer Parker calls *deep listening* in a therapeutic setting.[1] Can you listen to what another person is saying without judging them as right or wrong, without wanting to jump into what they are saying to offer your own opinion or solution? Are you able to listen in a state of stillness while remaining at one in your own body and immediate environment? Are you aware of your own defences, and can you let them go or put them to one side? This is key to being a good healer, therapist or friend, and like anything it requires practice.

One way I find effective in accessing a state of presence when I am with another being is to put my attention into the area of my belly just below the navel so that it feels totally relaxed in both the in-breath and out-breath. Karlfried Dürckheim points out that *hara* is the Japanese word for this part of the belly, and that it denotes much more than a region of the body; to the Japanese it is the physical center of gravity of a human being as well as the primal center of being. "Hara means nothing other than the physical embodiment of the original life center in man."[2] Once you feel strong and at ease in your *hara* it can feel like you are opening the center of your being as if a doorway (maybe double stable doors is an appropriate image), while sending compassion to who you are with, whether human or animal.

If your belly is not where you feel your center of gravity, a similar practice is to feel as though you are taking your center of being down from head space into heart space where you access so much more wisdom than can be generated by the mind. To be in a state of presence we need to be at peace ourselves, not harboring worries, judgments or projections into the future. That includes not wondering what we are going to say once someone stops talking. The very thought process of organizing our response is a projection into the future and is more likely to be about the positioning of our own ego than about what someone needs from us. The right response simply arises on its own if we have been engaged in deep listening within a space of stillness. When the time is right and when we are both ready, the right words are likely to arise. In Buddhism this is called "right action", as it grows naturally out of compassionate nonjudgmental listening and awareness.

Sensing the present moment is necessary for developing presence as it brings awareness directly to what is happening in and around us without the interference of thought. Horses reside in the present almost constantly, so they beautifully model this for us by demonstrating their acceptance of *what is*. Learning to live in the present is recommended by every world religion as a way towards self-knowing, although each has its own terminology for it. Judaic scriptures beautifully encapsulate it in the statement, "Be still, and know that I am God."[3] Jesus also told a parable about wild flowers which in all their splendor do not need to labor or spin, making the point that we are given all we need and that worrying adds nothing more.[4] We do not need to make up stories in our heads about what we think we lack (desiring more) or what we imagine might go wrong (catastrophizing). This is easier said than done, I know, but the place to start is to notice our own thought patterns with compassion, with acceptance and without judgment.

The concept of living in the present moment has become such a familiar trope that too easily it can be taken lightly and its value missed. So, what does it mean to live in the *moment* or in the *present* or the *now*? It's easy enough to describe the opposite, i.e. living at a fast pace without bothering about the consequences within your own being. If you are working on developing presence you wouldn't take such a choice very far in any case because you would be alert to what fast-paced living was doing to your body, your mind and others around you.

Living in the moment (or being present) is making a choice about the quality of the space you wish to inhabit. I first learned about the benefits of living in the moment when I practiced Buddhism in England in the 1970s, but I mistakenly thought that reading about it, thinking about it and listening to talks about it would somehow give it to me. Of course, it didn't do much more than add further mental concepts, and no matter how attractive the concepts were they didn't change me. I could see the value of living from a place other than the ego, but ironically, trying to be egoless does little more than strengthen the ego.[5] If our attempts to live in the present moment are merely *thoughts* about living in the moment, we have simply found another concept with which to clutter the mind, and we will have adopted another ideal to fail to live up to. In due course, life taught me that to know the present moment it needs to be unaccompanied by mental activity, even if only for a few seconds. The meditation that I practiced back then was helpful up to a point, but I didn't really know how to do it since I tried too hard and was overly self-critical.

What is it like *not* to live in the present moment? We do this by being continually attached to past and future. We worry about what we did yesterday or last year, regretting what we see as wrong choices, possibly even wishing we could go back to make changes to bring about a better result for our present situation. Or we might want to return to the glories of past achievements, mentally dwelling on them as reminders of our self-worth. We might also dwell on the past as though it is something that can be changed just by willing it. This is a common human preoccupation. Just listen to the conversations around you and you will notice that they are often about "what I wish hadn't happened to me", "what might happen to me", and "what might, or will, happen to others". The past is a condition of mind through which we waste a huge amount of energy either by trying to relive beautiful moments or by wondering why we were so stupid to make the decisions we did. We might also resent what others did to alter the course of our life to make it less perfect than it should be. Dwelling on the past can be unsettling since it is obvious that no aspect of it can be changed or relived. The past is an illusion in any case, as is the future. We simply can't go into either the past or the future because they don't exist as places to go to. They are simply vague concepts of the mind. They are mental constructs based on incomplete memories and conceptual biases.

There is no harm in thinking about past or future, in fact it is good to learn from the past and we often need to make future plans. What living in the present means is being free from *identifying* with past or future events in the expectation of finding meaning, fulfilment, revenge or whatever we wish to control or change. If I look to the future as the place where I will one day be happy, I will never be happy because I will never get to the future of my imagining. That is because getting to some point in the future is arriving at another now with its own striving for a better place, and even hard-won achievements can feel hollow once we get there. Getting a new job, finishing an apprenticeship, earning a degree, falling in love, buying a house, all are situations that very soon become past events in the memory. If we cling on to those events as if to preserve them, we are likely to breed bitterness, regret and sadness that the time has passed. Essentially, this is telling ourselves that the present moment as it is, is insufficient and not good enough for us. We create in our own minds a gap between what *is* and what we think *should be*. This gap is the root of much human unhappiness.

Practicing awareness

Whatever you share with your horse, how aware are you of being in the moment? Do your thoughts go to the next moment, the next thing you want to do, or back to something you did earlier? Each time that happens, bring your thoughts back to something happening right now: your breath. There's no need to count it or alter it in any way, just be aware of it, then put your awareness back onto your horse. While you are doing something (or nothing) with your horse, remind yourself from time to time to be conscious that you are breathing. You don't need to change your breathing or to control it, but simply remind yourself to be aware of the air going in and out for several breaths. Aim for deep relaxation in your hara during the out-breath. Make sure your shoulders have no physical part to play during the in-breath. At some point, put your hands on the side of your horse's chest and feel how he is breathing.

I was recently reminded of the 1877 book, *Black Beauty*, that my father read to me as a young child. It's quite a brutal book as it focuses on animal maltreatment, and in rereading it I see how much of a heartfelt plea it is from its author, Anna Sewell, on behalf of humane treatment for horses. Black Beauty the horse descends from a life of comfort and care to one of hard labor and cruelty, yet the voice of the horse does not become one of resentment and complaint as it might have done were it the sad story of a human's life. The voices Sewell gives horses in the story could serve for many horses today. For instance, Black Beauty asked a horse friend why she puts up with bad treatment. She said, "I did once [stand up for myself] but it's no use; men are strongest, and if they are cruel and have no feeling, there is nothing we can do, but just bear it, bear it on and on to the end."[6] By giving a horse a voice to describe his sad personal history, Sewell actually speaks for thousands in similar predicaments. The tone of the writing represents the giving nature of horses and their tendency to accept pretty much whatever comes their way. I'm not suggesting that horses should "like" such treatment, but Sewell clearly understood that horses can tolerate a cruel life largely without complaint and without the accompaniment of a "poor me" story. There are plenty of autobiographical human stories too where an author accepts a terrible situation without complaint. One that springs to mind as deeply insightful and astoundingly positive is Austrian psychiatrist Dr. Viktor Frankl's *Man's Search for Meaning*, which emerged from his experience of surviving Auschwitz during World War Two.[7] Through radical acceptance, such people offer beautiful models of strength for us to emulate.

One problem with dwelling on past or future is that our thoughts have neediness attached to them. Neediness (or desire) is accompanied by the bodily sensation of grasping, and if you take notice of it you will realize that the body does not actually like feeling that way. Another emotion that often accompanies looking into the future is the impulse to block something from happening. This occurs out of fear, and again, taking note of how your body reacts will show you that blocking is not a pleasant feeling. The way to deal with it is not to analyze fears and desires (although there's certainly a place for doing so with a qualified psychotherapist) but in the first instance to simply notice them arising. When working with people and horses, the two motivations of grasping and blocking, once acknowledged and seen for what they are, become perfect images for metaphorical work that we discuss in further chapters.

Two highly effective and simple ways to return to the present moment are to engage the sixth and seventh senses: *inner body awareness* and *cognitive awareness*. Inner body awareness brings us back into the present moment because it is immediate, and we can access it at any time by simply giving attention to what it feels like inside our body in the absence of mental commentary. The other portal into present moment awareness is through noticing our thoughts, by becoming the conscious observer of the mind. Some people can do this naturally, but it is not natural for everybody. In fact, many people on the planet are run by their thoughts so much that they do not recognize any space between thought and thinker. They *are* their thoughts, constantly. If we break that pattern every now and then we invite real and lasting change and growth into our lives. Once you notice that you have been lost in thought unrelated to what you are doing, you can increase your awareness by simply noticing that you have been thinking about something else. Then return to something that is always there, your breath. Without changing your breathing in any way, observe yourself taking several breaths in and out. These and other practices such as to look at or listen deeply to one single thing for half a minute brings us back to the present. You will know when you are there because the present moment brings with it a sense of still spaciousness.

Spiritual teachers (past and present) give pointers to still spaciousness while using differing terminology and exploring the variety of ways of expressing and practicing awareness. I have found it helpful to immerse myself in the books and podcasts of spiritual teachers who describe different *portals* (as Tolle would say) into spaciousness.[8] Reading the ancient texts of religious traditions is also inspiring so long as we seek our own meaning through the texts rather than rely entirely on traditional interpretation. In the world religions it is wise to be aware of how dogma can obscure the heart of the message. Equally, we need to be aware of our own dogma as individuals. We all have fundamental beliefs whether we are aware of them or not, and they can limit us if we don't make a practice of recognizing them.

Present moment awareness arises only when judgment is put to one side. As soon as I mentally judge whether I am doing present-moment awareness well or correctly I have lost the moment and lost the point. But just as in formal meditation I can return to it at any time through body awareness or thought awareness. Why would I want to? Because if I live inside worry, regret and a sense of urgency, I have very little time and energy left over to live where I am right *now*, right *here* in the only place where I can possibly experience life in its fullness. Strictly speaking, being aware of the present through noticing our thoughts and somatic states is not actually being aware of the moment, it is being aware of the *content* of the present moment. But the present moment itself is without either content or time. We can become aware of something happening right now, but can we become aware of the now itself as the space within which the objects of experience occur? This second stage arrives all by itself if you let it.

The present moment is the only place where horses invite us to meet them. They only want to know what is going on right now. They don't want to chat about yesterday or discuss future plans. A horse finds just enough fascination in a day filled with eating, dozing, looking around, smelling the air, walking to his water, sniffing dung and such things. If he experiences something unpleasant or threatening he deals with it (flight, fight or freeze), then quickly reaches homeostasis (goes back to grazing). If I need to remind myself of how it feels to experience the moment without the disruption of thought I might choose to sit in a paddock with our herd and simply be with them. Thought can always disrupt inner peace though, just as it does during meditation, but the moments of awareness that arise here and there show me what is possible, and if I observe with openness for long enough I just might see myself mirrored through the horse's being.

Footnotes

1. The concept of "deep listening" or "mindful listening" has been developed by Parker J. Palmer in his *Circle of Trust* approach as a pathway to authentic leadership and trustworthy relationships. See Palmer (2009).

2. Dürckheim (1956) p. 8.

3. Psalm 46:10, Revised International Version of the Bible.

4. Luke 12:27–31, Revised International Version of the Bible. "Consider how the wild flowers grow. They do not labor or spin. Yet I tell you, not even Solomon in all his splendor was dressed like one of these. If that is how God clothes the grass of the field, which is here today, and tomorrow is thrown into the fire, how much more will he clothe you — you of little faith! And do not set your heart on what you will eat or drink; do not worry about it. For the pagan world runs after all such things, and your Father knows that you need them. But seek his kingdom, and these things will be given to you as well."

5. Living in the moment, and presence, are not synonymous with being egoless. Finding a way of living where one is not entirely ego-driven is desirable, but any attempt to be free from ego is both unrealistic and unnecessary.

6. Sewell (1877/1994) pp. 212–213.

7. Frankl (1959/2006).

8. For instance, Eckhart Tolle, Ram Dass, Richard Rohr, Jack Kornfield, Adyashanti, Rupert Spira, and Alan Watts.

Chapter 12

Being the Mirror

The spiritual teacher Ram Dass advises that:

Hanging out with realized beings or saints, with their words and pictures, is a way to inspire and find guidance for your own path. A realized being is like a pure mirror who shows you all of the places where there is dust on your own mirror. Such a being is a clear mirror because he or she doesn't have any attachments, so all you see are your own attachments writ large.[1]

Although Ram Dass is unlikely to have been thinking of horses when he wrote *Polishing the Mirror* (2014) much of his advice applies to equine assisted work in that when we spend quiet time "doing nothing" with horses we are likely to experience a mirror image of ourselves. Eastern spiritual and philosophical traditions apply the term "realized being" to someone who is fully aware of their soul in connection with other souls, who is not driven entirely by ego, who lives predominantly in the moment and who accepts *what is*. By this definition a horse living in a healthy environment is a fully realized being, whereas we humans have learned to obscure our true selves with constant mind activity. The good news is that we can learn how to be a little bit like a horse by sharing space with one without an agenda of "doing something".

Ram Dass suggests that for all human beings the primary job is to understand that we are souls passing through life in which the entire drama is a script for our awakening. He suggests we are much more than the drama. We are spiritual beings having a human experience who access our spiritual heart and watch the drama that is our entire life. He advises that, "One way to get free of attachment is to cultivate the witness consciousness, to become a neutral observer of your own life."[2] The practice is to observe our thoughts and behavior, then to look purposefully at something that can bring us into the moment. This is a different kind of watching where we become aware of our fundamental being. What we choose to look at might be a candle flame, a flower, or a person's face, or for another truly "in the moment" experience we could watch a horse. It is even possible to feel that there is no difference between the horse's soul space and our own. We can even get to the point where we feel in some sense that *we are the horse, and the horse is us*. We can come across this realization with any aspect of nature and with any living being since we are all part of the one soul. We are part of the collective soul, as Carl Jung would put it. As we begin to "see our inner being reflected and projected onto every experience of the outer world … we can bring our external experience into ever closer alignment with our inner being."[3] It is in such moments when the mind is still that we experience oneness and wholeness.

Horses bring to us a special kind of mirror that not only reflects how we are at the soul level but also what we pretend to be and what we think we are projecting out to the world in our minds. Horses are not interested in what we think about ourselves but are expert at letting us know our present inner state, even if we are trying to put forward a different persona to what we feel. For instance, we might try to project an image of being confident as a cover for fear, but a horse will let us know that they can see right through our lack of authenticity. By their honest response, they give us what Leif Hallberg in *Walking the Way of the Horse* calls "reflective feedback", a term that works well in the equine assisted context since it implies a two-way process rather than a straight mirroring phenomenon.[4] It is good to realize that the mirroring works in both directions and that reflection can continue long after time spent with a horse. One of the hidden wonders of equine assisted work is that people can "play back" their visual images and memories of their equine-related activities and sensations. Those takeaway images and memories are so much more enduring than memory of conversations alone.

Maybe you have spent quite a bit of time with horses already and wonder what I mean by "being with a horse". When we are at one with a horse, and our thinking mind is quiet, we can momentarily transcend the ego. This is more achievable than it seems. We don't need to say or think anything special; we merely need to be witnesses of our own minds, thoughts and feelings within a field of compassion and acceptance. In other words, we practice detaching from our personal narratives and learn to put attention onto the life force we notice both within ourselves and in and around horses. This is the basis of unconditional love.

People constantly give reflective feedback to others, both consciously and unconsciously. This is the most valuable aspect of listening, whether we are talking of humans or animals. When listening to another person's story we can paraphrase what they have said, giving them an opportunity for reflection. Deep listening, which offers empathy in a nonjudgmental environment, is a technique that counselors and psychotherapists know well, but with training and practice anyone can do it and it is hugely beneficial within any relationship. As we listen to one another we can choose to be consciously aware, keeping our eyes and ears open while at the same time maintaining a quiet mind and relaxed body.

The responsibility of an equine assisted practitioner is to do what the horse does naturally, that is, to be a clear mirror. It is wise to consciously access our grounded selves before inviting either a horse or a human to interact with us in a learning or therapeutic space. It is our primary responsibility to avoid inadvertently bringing our unfinished business into the therapeutic or learning process. I'm not suggesting that we must be fully enlightened beings before we can even begin work with clients, but I believe it is advantageous to have at least one foot on that path, to have the *intention* of awareness. The only other path is that of the ego. Operating from a place of ego benefits only the ego, not the other person and not horses either. Of course, we are likely to alternate between the two states of awareness and ego but the more conscious we are of doing so, the more likely ego is to take a back seat. Since this is a gradual learning process we need to exercise patience for both ourselves and our clients.

We can practice deep listening daily in our living situations, being present with family members or friends as we listen deeply, allowing the breathing to soften. Scan your body and note points of tension or discomfort, relaxing any tight area. Put your awareness on your hara or your heart and feel your energy opening to the person you are with while maintaining deep listening. This is such a worthwhile practice that when you spend time with people this way you are likely to feel the benefit yourself, and your friends and family will love you for your deep attention. They might not ask you a single thing about yourself within a conversation, but the depth of communication when at least one person is listening deeply is so pleasant that I find it really doesn't matter. When you practice this with clients you are likely to come away from a session feeling as much benefit as they do. If you leave a session feeling tense or agitated it is advisable to review your processes and ask yourself how relaxed, open and present you really were.

In a therapeutic situation there are two reasons to practice deep listening: for people to feel fully accepted and valued, and for us to reflect their thoughts and feelings back to help them gain an objective view. The more we "polish our own mirror" by getting our own inner business resolved, the more helpful we can be to both clients and horses. Horses don't need to polish their mirror though, since being completely honest emotionally is their natural state of being. As Mark Rashid reminds us, horses are incapable of lying.[5] What you get reflected from a horse is always their truth and authenticity since they don't know how to be any other way. This is a special gift for us to emulate, and the more time we spend in nature with plants and animals, the more we realize that we can let go of our defences and just be who we are as part of nature.

Footnotes

1. Ram Dass (2014) p. 7.
2. Ram Dass, "Cultivating the Witness" [online]. Available at: https://www.ramdass.org/cultivating-witness/ (Accessed 1 April 2023).
3. As quoted by Rameshwar Das, in Ram Dass (2014) p. xv.
4. Hallberg (2008) p. 165.
5. Rashid (2015).

Chapter 13

Connection with Nature

Something until now has been absent from the love of nature ...
that there is an ancient bond with the natural world surviving
deep within us, which makes it not a luxury, not an optional
extra, not even just an enchantment, but part of our essence — the
natural home for our psyches where we can find not only joy but
also peace, and to destroy which, is to destroy a fundamental part
of ourselves.[1]

Michael McCarthy

In the above comment, Michael McCarthy in his book *The Moth Snowstorm* reminds us that nature is not exclusively something separate to be admired for its beauty; nor is it entirely something from which to protect ourselves. From our efforts over millennia to find protection from extremes of weather and wild animals we have become so used to living in our watertight insulated bubbles that most modern humans have forgotten what the outside world feels like. Too often our enjoyment of nature is through one sense only, sight, as we watch nature programs on television and look at the countryside from the comfort of a moving car. Of course, nature is not all pretty flowers and delicious forest smells, it also includes tornados, floods, drought, dangerous animals and avalanches. But what we gain through becoming comfortable and protected we lose through alienation from our natural home and from our best teachers. But sometimes nature freely gives us pleasant surprises.

I walk through the horse paddock of our home in the mountains north of Brisbane, Australia, when I notice three kookaburras dancing around at the bottom of a gum tree. They are attacking a featherless baby bird, a rainbow lorikeet, which I quickly gather up and take inside. Sarah is lying on the sofa not feeling very well, so I tell her that keeping this baby bird warm for the day is her job. We call him Phoenix out of hope for his survival and for a while he lives inside the house in a cat cage. He has a "warm bottle" in the straw, and we feed him honey and water from a dripper every two hours. He grows and develops the beautiful colors true to his species. We have no intention of keeping him captive so he graduates to a potted tree on the outside deck where we hang mirrors, bells and birdy things for him to play with. To make sure he knows who he is we show him videos on our smartphones of adult lorikeets, to which he cocks his head sideways and cheeps with excitement. When his wings fully develop we take him outside and teach him to fly by gently throwing him to each other. For most of the summer he perches on our hats and comes with us around the farm as we tend to horse jobs. We take him inside and he runs up and down the neck of my guitar as I play. He loves to lie upside down in my hand for a tummy scratch and I daily share an apple with him. After a few months he manages to fly away for half an hour or more, then returns to the little tree on the deck and squawks for his "porridge" of lorikeet food.

Before Phoenix came into my life I had no idea how beautiful the experience of knowing a bird could be. I had always loved seeing birds and listening to their songs but I didn't realize they had such intelligence and personality and could give such joy. This bird touches a special part of me that I didn't even know existed and to this day I continue to feel a strong bird connection.

We are due to move back to New Zealand and we have good neighbors nearby who are happy to take Phoenix and continue to give him an inside-outside home. But two weeks before leaving he returns with a beautiful friend. They visit together daily, but briefly, then one week before we depart he is gone. We are happy because we know he will be living in his true Australian home in the bush and bringing up a family.

Animals and nature invite us to awaken from our slumbers, from our unconsciousness. They remind us of ancient animal wisdom from which we have lost meaningful connection and they show us how to live in a way that supports both us *and* our environment. Unfortunately, modern humans have come to believe in the myth that we and nature (our environment) are separate things that can somehow operate independently. But this is patently absurd, for when we deny nature we cut off a vital part of ourselves, and today we are seeing quite clearly the effect on the whole planet of our dysfunctional, individualistic thinking.

The good news is that if we ask for it, nature leads us back to our true selves, back to who we really are. That people recognize this is witnessed by a burgeoning interest in learning from animals and nature so it is no coincidence that there is a huge growth worldwide in animal assisted therapies of all kinds. We are also recognizing the perceptive powers of animals such as dogs who can detect with their sensitive noses not only contraband drugs at airports but also acute phases of epilepsy and diabetes in humans, among many other conditions.

If we want to know how to live well all we need do is take a good look at nature and notice the webs of interaction and codependence of all living things. We can recognize the principles upon which everything within nature rests; we see and accept the perpetual decay and renewal in nature, the impermanence and fragility of all life forms, persistence of the life force and the continuous cycles of life. Even a little reflection shows that we are subject to the same principles and processes as all plants, trees and animals. Indigenous cultures have always known the principles of nature as a matter of survival, and so did our ancestors prior to the industrial revolution as they lived out their family, tribal and village lives next to and within natural environments.[2]

Modern humans obviously still belong to the natural world, but billions of people (especially city dwellers) have lost sight of this. We have become so estranged from nature that a term has been invented for the loss of connection: "separation sickness". We are sick because most of us have ceased to look for physical and spiritual sustenance from seas and rivers, forests, deserts, mountains, the sky and the plains. We are sick because we have stopped looking to nature for working evidence of the natural principles of life of which we are an integral part. We are sick because as human beings we have forgotten that we belong to the animal kingdom, that we are one of many mammals that have evolved alongside each other, that we have learned from, and are dependent upon, each other. This is a difficult thing for many humans to admit to because they (Westerners at least) like to imagine themselves as self-sufficient and in control of nature. How often do we stop to think about how we are sustained by all the plants, insects, animals, rivers, air and living soil? We only need to think of the existential threat to the bee as a species to recognize the vulnerability of the whole web of life on Earth as a single entity.

An indication of how far we have strayed and how convincingly we have created the illusion of separateness from the natural world is highlighted by the reactions of many people who are horrified at the suggestion that we are animals or mammals. In fact, in Western society, to call someone an animal can be deeply insulting, but that's exactly what we are.

The way we interpret ancient sacred texts hasn't helped with this perception either: Judeo-Christian thought has unwittingly played a role in sanctifying demotion of nature by assuming human superiority through a misinterpretation of one single statement from the scriptures. According to Genesis 1:26, God said:

Let us make man in our image, after our likeness. And let them have dominion over the fish of the sea and over the birds of the heavens and over the livestock and over all the Earth and over every creeping thing that creeps on the Earth.

I doubt very much that the authors of Genesis meant for humans to assume superiority over all living things, and in any case "dominion" does not mean ruling over and dominating, it means "stewardship" or "taking care of" nature, something we have clearly failed to do on a large scale. Unfortunately, a great portion of humanity has taken this biblical passage as license to conquer mountains, burn forests, drag minerals out of the earth, deplete soils, make living beings extinct, destroy indigenous cultures and treat animals as mere commodities in the service of humans. However, species superiority is not confined to those cultures shaped by Judeo-Christian thought since other cultures are equally culpable. By assuming superiority and habitually objectifying animals (along with all of nature) we have forgotten the principle of stewardship that traditional cultures have lived by for millennia, knowing that their ongoing survival depended on preserving and tending to their environments.[3] Putting misinterpreted religious texts to one side it is patently self-evident that looking after the hut we live in (the planet) equates to our own survival.

The assumption that animals, or I should say *other* animals, are inferior to humans is deeply ingrained. Some would argue that animals are inferior because our brains are bigger, because we have a more fully developed prefrontal cortex than most (but not all) animals, giving us greater thinking and reasoning powers. This powerful and extremely useful brain has enabled us to develop verbal language (although causally, some scientists think it is the other way around)[4] and higher-order thinking. It has enabled mathematics, philosophy, religion, science and the arts, all of which are valuable, practical and illuminating. Our brain is highly useful, and we wouldn't want it otherwise, but in our eagerness to celebrate higher-order thinking we are likely to forget to exercise other attributes such as creativity, somatic awareness and intuitive knowledge, all of which are right-hemisphere attributes. Sacrificing these ways of knowing by putting analytical acumen (left-hemisphere attributes) on a pedestal clearly has not led to sharing the world's resources to the mutual benefit of other living creatures and the planet, let alone to the benefit of individuals or humanity as a whole.

It can come as a surprise to learn that there are ways of knowing in addition to what is processed through the prefrontal cortex. Our education system has for centuries prioritized cognitive knowledge to the exclusion of the nature-based knowledge that indigenous people have valued and lived by, although a few schools today are rectifying this imbalance. We tend to overvalue cognition without realizing that much of the valuable information we process does not involve conscious thought. Recent findings in neuroscience, for instance, show that we can know something and react to it without being consciously engaged. In an emergency, when engaging in a fast-moving sport or when playing a musical instrument, our brain is wired to initiate action *before* we are consciously aware of it, as neuroscientist Lisa Feldman Barrett points out.[5] The human brain is a predicting machine and we can know some things, especially survival-based things, without asking the prefrontal cortex to interpret incoming data for us. We know things in so many more ways than we give ourselves credit for.

Sooner or later the human species will take vital existential lessons from nature whether we want to or not. While our political systems have increasingly prioritized the survival of the richest and most powerful, and as we have indulged our egos through overblown consumption, we have taken a path leading to a cocktail of climate change disasters, pandemics and limited remaining physical resources. We all know this sobering situation and while there yet may be technical and scientific strategies to rectify the damage, in my view, global restoration necessitates a radical change of basic human priorities and values. The good news is that the existential emergencies we currently face globally have the capacity to nudge us collectively into higher consciousness, just as a near-death experience or personal disaster can do on a personal level. For life on the planet to continue, humanity must make a major shift in consciousness and standing right here inviting us to make such a shift is nature herself. All parts of nature can do this job. All living things when approached with respect and willingness to learn can lead us by example out of this mess. One beautiful part of nature, the horse, invites us to make inner change one individual at a time.

The lasting way to create real change for humanity and the planet is to do so individually. The kind of transformation the planet and human society needs won't happen through political will (as history demonstrates), at least not entirely. If we accept that we are collectively responsible for the current state of the world, common sense tells us that first, we must be individually responsible. If the values, beliefs and assumptions upon which civilizations have relied for millennia are questioned on an individual basis, a healthier and more sustainable life within the collective will arise as the sum of individual parts. The world's problems are not "out there", and neither are they entirely the responsibility of "others". Although people habitually look to experts and political movements to fix social and environmental problems, history shows that macro measures do not work for very long. It is at the micro level where we make the most profound change, and to respect all of nature seems the best place to start as Native American horseman Gawani Pony Boy advises in *Horse, Follow Closely*:

> *If we are to understand our relationship with the horse, we must first understand the relationship we have with the entire animal kingdom. The human species, directly or indirectly, affects all other species on the planet, even those species we don't directly encounter. Every one of our actions affects all living things, and therein lies our responsibility to the natural world. Native Americans understood this. They held at their core the belief that all species are related. They also understood that a certain level of awareness must take place before we can truly communicate with that which is all around us.*[6]

Each of us has the capacity to care for the health and well-being of the planet, but only to the extent that we wield any influence, and the most effective way to influence the totality (and it might well be the *only* way) is to become more consciously aware, one human at a time. For me to do this, first I need to take responsibility for my own life to ensure that I don't add to the problems of the world through greed, negativity, destructive behavior, materialism, egotism or neglect. The second thing I must do is learn the forgotten principles that nature knows so well. We already know, just as our ancestors did, to trust in our own intuition and in the patterns of nature, and there is much we can learn from indigenous cultures too before their wisdom is lost.

How are we to do this? It seems a tall order to individually take responsibility for greater awareness and increased consciousness. Fortunately, there are several useful pathways and pointers to show us the way since teachings of numerous spiritual leaders from all traditions are readily available. We don't all have to go to an ashram for ten years or join a monastery to be part of the collective awareness (although both have their attractions). We can start by embracing our interconnectedness with each other and all living things, from which a new Earth will naturally arise. I would not have the confidence to say something predictive like this were it not a recurring theme in the writings of philosophers and spiritual teachers going back thousands of years. The writings of Taoist, Buddhist, Christian, Hindu and Islamic traditions (and others) contain all the gems of wisdom we need, provided we look for their essential meanings unobscured by dogma. Another source of wisdom that is freely available is our own inner knowing as an accumulation of ancestral experience. As philosopher Alan Watts said in *Nature, Man and Woman*, "it is impossible to consider man apart from nature, as an exiled spirit which controls this world by having its roots in another."[7]

Most wisdom of the world's religions and mythologies is presented through the gateway of metaphor for the very good reason that words (which are themselves symbolic) cannot fully encapsulate the meaning of something that by its very nature transcends conceptual thought. However, so many take the religious metaphors literally, which is like mistaking a finger pointing at the moon, for the moon itself.[8] Central to the message of world religions is that we are all interconnected and that it is our responsibility to look after each other, animals, plants and everything in the planet since every living thing is held within a delicate web of interconnectedness.

This is not a book about saving the planet, but yet in a way it is, since every individual action counts, and every meaningful encounter with nature and her principles leads us to a more sustainable place. Connecting with other beings (in this context, horses) *on their terms* teaches us, bit by bit, the valuable truths with which we have lost connection as a species and as individuals. By learning to make meaningful connections with horses on an equal footing, we can step into a healthy spiritual dimension that humans have been encouraged to disregard for so long. As Michael Cohen puts it in his book *Reconnecting With Nature*, "If you are missing the natural joy and wisdom of life, it is because you have been taught to ignore it."[9] But the good news is that anything we have been taught, we can unlearn. Since spirituality is the direct inner experience of that which underlies all of life, it serves us well to part the curtains of ego and consciously merge with life around us. Horses, through their openhearted generosity, willingly become our spiritual teachers in this process and the wonderful thing is that it is simple and easy; we only need to open ourselves to such possibilities of learning to begin an inner transformation and to bring it to others in our equine assisted work.

As we reunite our animal nature with our intellect, we ignite the potential to become the beings we were destined to be. In this journey we invite horses to be our spiritual guides. If we ask them to, they will lead us to a place of peace and contentment that is innate to all beings on the planet. Approached with an open mind and willingness to learn, they can lead us out of the illusion of separateness and into discovering our interconnectedness. Through opening ourselves emotionally and spiritually to animals we have the potential of regaining a true connection with nature, of being completed (i.e. lacking nothing), and of experiencing oneness with all living things.

Horses invite us to find wholeness in the very depth of our humanity.

Footnotes

1. McCarthy (2016) p. 246.
2. For a compelling contemporary account of science and nature within indigenous awareness, see Robin Wall Kimmerer (2013).
3. While we can take many valuable lessons from past indigenous cultures, they did not always make the best decisions for the long-term. In Aotearoa (New Zealand) for instance, the Māori people unwittingly hunted the massive flightless bird, the Moa, to extinction while burning down a large portion of the native forest to flush them out. The Europeans who arrived from the eighteenth century onwards continued the environmental carnage even more efficiently.
4. Iain McGilchrist in *The Master and his Emissary* (2009) pp. 102–3 points out that the neural mechanisms for the emergence of language predated verbal language, and that before the spoken word emerged, humans most likely communicated through music, in some form of song.
5. Barrett (2020) p. 77.
6. Pony Boy (1998) p. 9.
7. Watts (1991) p. 4.
8. This is a well-known Buddhist trope. It comes from the Shurangama Sutra in which the Buddha is reported to have said that the pointing finger is what guides one to the moon, and this saying was intended to indicate the presence of Ananda's True Mind.
9. Cohen (2007) p. 20.

Part II: The Horse as Teacher and Therapist

Chapter 14

The Dynamic Triangle of Trust

The long and varied history of the horse-human connection is dominated by a tilted playing field. It is tilted in favor of humankind as we have asked, demanded and coerced equines to feature in so many aspects of our lives. Today another task is added to the horse's arsenal of responsibility, that of teacher and therapist. We owe it to the horse to build our relationships with them on trust. Building trust has to be the foundation of working with horses and people in learning and therapeutic spaces if we wish to have true and accurate results. As obvious as this might seem, it is worth examining how trust works in this context. When working with horses I believe we should constantly examine ourselves to determine whether or not we are working from a foundation of trust, since therapy and learning depend entirely on the quality of communication. Without a firm basis of trust, we would have no moral justification for introducing anyone into the dynamic triangle of client–practitioner–horse. What's more, the ultimate aim is for the client to trust themselves, to trust their own inner wisdom.

THE SINGLE DIAD

practitioner $\longleftrightarrow$ *dyad 1* $\longrightarrow$ **client**

Example 3

A therapy, coaching or learning session in a traditional client-practitioner situation is a dyadic relationship within which trust flows in two directions: practitioner trusting the client, and the client trusting the practitioner (Example 3). In a dynamic environment trust flows in both directions: the client learns to trust that the practitioner knows what they are doing within a range of safety, and the practitioner learns to trust that the client will engage in processes honestly and respectfully. If trust is not established in both directions, very little of value can come from the relationship. It makes sense that a client comes into this dynamic already trusting the process to some extent, since they are the ones who have made the effort to make an appointment and show up. However, this initial trust from the client must be confirmed and built upon through subsequent sessions.

As practitioners it is obvious that we need to trust our clients since they will be working with our valued horses. We trust that clients are prepared to open themselves sufficiently to what we offer and that they are safe to be around our horses. We need assurance that someone experiencing fear or anger is not likely to hurt or upset a horse, with the other side of the equation being confident that they won't deliberately put themselves in harm's way. If I have doubts about a client's personal safety, or that of the horses, I will seek useful work for them to do at a distance initially. There is always the possibility of being involved in quality observational work from the other side of a fence. The bottom line for me is to trust my gut feelings in the matter of trusting clients. If you have doubts as a practitioner about your client being with horses but go ahead anyway there is a very good chance that your own anxiety will become part of the environment for the horse to deal with. This muddies the whole process.

Naturally enough, people need to trust us in matters of safety, confidentiality, respect and professional competence. Such trust is not static but changes and evolves. The scene for this is set by the practitioner dealing professionally with all practical issues, as well as being fully present and confident. I typically start an equine assisted counseling session with discussion in the rooms where lines of trust are initiated.[1] Some practitioners might choose to start a session straight away in the presence of horses, but I believe in the benefit of touching base with a client first through talk. There are exceptions of course, such as working with a nonverbal person or with children for whom discussing personal matters don't come easily face to face. If they are comfortable in the company of animals we can start right there and allow talk to evolve naturally.

It can take a while for some clients to build trust in a practitioner, especially if the approach differs from what they have previously experienced as therapeutic intervention or personal learning. There is also a significant difference in trust and comfort between adults who seek therapy for themselves, and a child for whom a caregiver or parent has made the decision for her to have equine assisted work. Children don't always understand why they are there or how the horses fit into the process, and they do need to be given some sort of explanation of what to expect. An intellectual explanation of how the process works would not be very helpful, but I do explain at each individual session what they can expect. It is also essential to ask clients (child or adult) whether they are willing to engage in the plan for the session so that they can own the process and find meaning directly relevant to them.

I once had a mother bring an 11-year-old girl for equine assisted counseling. On the phone before they arrived she explained why her daughter needed help with a particular issue, but I was unaware that she hadn't told the girl what it was she was coming to. The session went off to a bad start on two counts: firstly, a presentation of someone's "problem" is far better coming from themselves, whatever their age. If it is presented by a parent, the client has little agency and it's quite possible in any case that the parent won't accurately represent the child's perspective; secondly, pretending that the session was about getting to know horses (or whatever explanation was given) was deceptive, and deception is certainly no basis for therapy. I did my best under the circumstances, but it taught me a lesson to avoid being put in such a position again.

THE TRIPLE DIAD

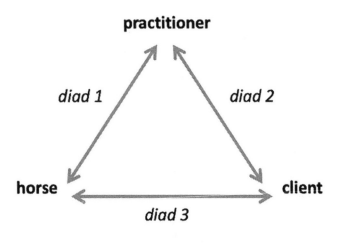

Example 4

When a horse as the third being is introduced into the triangle of trust the lines of communication expand to six (within three dyads), and each one can be consciously worked upon (Example 4). In the second dyad, the practitioner's trust in the horse needs to be firmly established before inviting a client into the arena. Obviously, we wouldn't want to invite horses into this work if we didn't believe they were suited to it and couldn't trust them to work well and safely with clients. But in this dyad we need to put equal emphasis on the horse trusting the practitioner. We need to have worked with our horses sufficiently for them to trust that we know their language sufficiently and are not going to ask anything uncomfortable of them.

Then there is also what I call *everyday trust*, as something to reassess and revisit constantly. This is because both horse and human can come from different emotional places from one day to the next. Reestablishing trust on each occasion is something I have found essential to the preparation of sessions. It takes a few minutes only of being around your horse in a state of presence before the client arrives to make sure he is well disposed to take part. If on any day you have doubts about how balanced and calm your horse is with a client, or if he seems unwilling to engage, it would be wise to invite a different horse (presuming you have the choice).

How can you check in with your horse before your client arrives? The way you approach your horse, halter him and ask him to walk with you is a perfect opportunity to see how willing he is to engage. Did you walk up to him prepared to respect his yes or no? Did you take his concerns into account? Did you give him the time needed to absorb that you were inviting him to come with you, and once haltered, did you walk off together with a loose lead rope between you? As mentioned earlier, the moment we put pressure on the lead rope we objectify our horse. If I feel the need to pull my horse around or to hold the lead rope tightly under his chin, I am giving him the message that I don't trust him! To establish trust, five minutes of walking your horse around objects without tugging the lead rope is worth its weight in gold. It sets the mood for the coming session and doesn't take much time.

The third dyad is where we see the magic happening if the other two dyads are firmly established. Whatever you choose to do with your client and horse it is most likely to relate to issues or themes that have shown up from talking, but let's not forget that we need to consider how our horse shows up. The relationship goes both ways, and deliberately working on encouraging the horse to trust the client can have surprising benefits. If your horse seems aloof or out of sorts for whatever reason, you might want to suggest to your client something like this: "This horse seems unsettled today, so what do you think we can do to help him feel better?" Working a session entirely from the horse's point of view with the aim of helping him feel more comfortable, loved, validated, and so on, deepens the quality of communication and leads to remarkable results for both horse and client. Another likely scenario when a horse is reluctant to engage, is clients projecting a sense of rejection onto the horse's behavior. This can offer an opportunity to explore the assumption of the person being rejected or not likeable, or you could work with your client on relaxation and acceptance techniques while in the arena with the reticent horse. It is a powerful moment when a client recognizes their tension and becomes grounded, then seeing the horse approach freely. Such a response is extremely valuable for building mind-body awareness and for realizing in a direct way that other beings are sensitive to our energy levels.

Focusing on the horse's well-being can be approached by something as simple as grooming while calling the client's attention to how the horse reacts to the brush as it is applied at different speeds, on different parts of the body, and with varying degrees of intensity. All the while, the client is encouraged to give a close reading to the horse's reaction to every touch and movement. As your client works with the brush, ask her to be observant around the horse's head, reading the ears, eyes, mouth and angle of the head. (We go into reading the horse in more detail in a later chapter.) If this ends up being the entire focus of the session that's not a bad thing, as it can lead to your client's awareness of her own capacity for compassion and kindness. It can also be a revelation to some people to directly observe how they affect another sentient being. I have found this work to be particularly effective for people with early attachment pain.

Observation can be extended to inviting a client to be aware of a horse's breathing patterns, and then learning to coordinate with his breathing. For some people, especially the young ones, directly experiencing how effective their kindness and compassion can be is very moving. The last time I did a session like this the young woman, who had her own horses at home and had groomed them thousands of times, declared that she would never again groom a horse mindlessly just to get the job done. She was overwhelmed by the deep state of relaxation the horse went into as she took notice of his reactions, developing a profound empathy for the horse.

It took me a few years in equine assisted work to realize that how the client affects the horse is just as important as how the horse affects the client. Real communication goes both ways! It is too easy to assume in equine assisted work that we have horses for them to do something useful for us. Since humans have objectified horses for thousands of years it's natural to think in terms of "what this horse can do for me" whether we are thinking of competition, carting, ploughing or equine assisted practices, but there is much to discover by putting ourselves in the horse's place. If the focus during this work is exclusively on how clients respond to the horse, we inadvertently make value judgments about the relative worth of horse and human. But even within values of equity, objectifying can drive our behavior without us even knowing. I have caught myself at it numerous times, but it only takes a little imagination to make the relationship work in both directions so that clients can witness their own influence and experience trust and gratitude coming from the horse. When communication works both ways it is magical.

At Earthhorse Aotearoa we have built a wooden pseudo-bridge in the arena for horses to walk over and sometimes we put a pole under the center so that the platform wobbles back and forth as the horse walks on it. This is useful for habituating horses to walk on unstable ground. All members of our herd are now quite familiar with the bridge, but sometimes they are not in the mood for it, or they might be uncertain of a particular client's leadership.

Nathan, a boy of 15, has been in and out of foster homes most of his life and is currently getting into trouble with the law. The only meaningful relationship Nathan has experienced with another person is with his mother who ultimately let him down. During one session I ask Nathan to help our 17-hand gelding over the bridge by showing that he cares about the horse who appears reluctant to approach it. To do this Nathan must juggle the values of kindness (softness) with leadership (taking control). This is a difficult balance for anyone to find but he manages it without much in the way of help from me. After a few tries the gelding goes over the bridge, then Nathan repeats this several times. He is so excited about successfully helping his horse to be, in his words, "brave and strong" that it becomes the focus of several subsequent sessions, leading to fruitful discussions of how he can be brave and strong for himself and how he can identify the resources around that support him.

A few weeks later Nathan moved to another town and wrote to say he fondly remembers having helped his favorite horse to trust him and that the horse has helped him to trust others.

A client's trust in the horse is where therapy and learning processes traditionally take place, but sessions such as Nathan's convince me that horses learning to trust clients is equally important, if not more so. The number and quality of tools or ideas for developing trust within the dynamic triangle are limited only by the imagination. Using whatever images, ideas or concerns a client brings into the process while nurturing mutual trust between them and a horse is deeply affirming. Collaborating with a fellow therapist or teacher (the horse) who encourages people to trust their own intuition brings in an *outsider view* of their influence on another being. Being aware of this mutual line of trust leads to the most extraordinary insights into how a person views themselves within their everyday human environment.

Trust is a process of looking to the future with confidence: I trust that what you can, will or might do will not harm me or let me down. I trust that if certain conditions are in place I will get a particular result. Trust operates on day one in a baby's life (and earlier), without which a baby wouldn't survive. Trust is the foundation of love, which all humans need to thrive and which is a necessary condition for sustaining life. Without experiencing trust, a human will have difficulty trusting another. This is an especially sad predicament for children who grow up without reliable and sustained early attachments. The ideal for healthy emotional development is to reach adulthood with a solid grounding of trust in self and others. The two, trust in self and trust in others, go together.

Trust is so closely related to love that it needs to be established within one's own being for it to be fully extended to other people, animals and situations. It is a fluid and dynamic principle that must keep flowing to be truly supportive of life. When we see how trust in self and trust in others works throughout a lifetime, we also see how it leads to trusting *life*. If we let go of the need to be in control, and trust in the sustaining qualities of life, we realize that we have all the insight and intelligence necessary for a meaningful life. This does not mean that uncomfortable and unfortunate things won't happen to us, they inevitably will, but with trust in living processes we can let go of a great deal of fear and worry about what could possibly arise.

Faith is a term I might have chosen in place of trust, but it is a word too easily confused with belief. Religious people sometimes refer to themselves as "people of faith", which if it were always true would be wonderful, but what they usually mean is that they are people of belief. Belief means deciding to accept a particular set of ideas or dogma as truth. That's fine for whoever chooses to believe in a religious system, but it is not the subject of this conversation. Faith and trust, however, are independent of belief since they are established from *felt experience*. Once someone has experienced trust within a two-way relationship, they can learn to trust other people and aspects of their lives. They can let go of the need to anticipate, rehearse, control and conceptualize every experience. Unexpected and painful things will happen during a lifetime, but trust means accepting what is rather than denying, or fighting against, reality. This places us in a far better position to deal with whatever arises, and it is something that horses understand perfectly.

Sandy, a woman in her 50s, had great difficulty trusting in either herself or anyone else. To perform even the simplest task, she would run through her head all the possible things that might happen, mostly of a negative nature. She is convinced that she will always screw things up somehow or that another person will do so for her. From our previous sessions it had emerged that she was brought up with a sister ten years older who constantly warned Sandy of what she was likely to do wrong. Combined with her conditioned sense of self that tells her that if she is going to do something it has to be perfect, this gave her good reasons not to start most things.

I invite Sandy to take a horse for a walk around the arena anywhere she likes, using obstacles to move around or not as she chooses. Her first comment is, "I don't trust myself to do it properly." We discuss what she means by "properly" and she comes to understand that there is no right, wrong or "proper" way of walking a horse, other than keeping safe. What she really meant, she concludes, is that she was afraid of doing something less than perfect. So, we set the goal as one of "feeling safe" rather than achieving, then we discuss what that might entail. When she feels ready, she walks off with her horse. After 20 yards or so, she and the horse stop and stay in the same place for several minutes. Having agreed that I wouldn't intervene unless she beckons me over, I stand and watch as the horse's head gradually lowers. I don't know what is going on, but from what I can see it is a peaceful and still situation. When she returns, she says that the horse had "asked" her to trust him to stand quietly and be still. She says that she felt she was breathing in time with him and that he trusted her. She says that being with him having no expectations of her and accepting her as is, was a profound experience that she expects will help her to begin on a process of trusting herself by setting small and realistic goals.

It's difficult, but certainly not impossible, to trust another being if we don't know their language or if one person dominates the conversation and fails to listen. In the next chapter we focus on the very important subject of learning horse language.

Footnote

1. Practical issues include explaining confidentiality and safety with horses, having a code of ethics and requiring clients to sign an indemnity agreement.

Chapter 15

Horse Language

This chapter and the two following are included here not for purposes of teaching horse language to our clients in a comprehensive way, but rather, to ensure that within the triangle of trust, the lines of communication between practitioner and horse are well established. Clearly, we need to take care that we only invite horses into this workspace whom we trust and who trust us, and for that to happen we need to have worked with our horses to the point where we are secure in communicating with them and (more especially) secure in listening. However, in this work it isn't necessary (or even desirable) to teach equine body language to clients apart from the essential signs of the relaxation horses exhibit once some sort of pressure is released. Therefore, most of this chapter applies to practitioner-knowledge rather than client-knowledge.

The principle of pressure and release is foundational in communication with horses. It is most readily seen to operate in a herd when young horses are disciplined by their mother and other herd members. A foal is familiar with pushing and bumping into his dam to encourage milk to flow from her teats, but a nursing mother has quite strict protocols and has no problem telling him, with a little bit of a shove, when she has had enough. By the time the colt is about 12 months old, the mare and the rest of the herd have taught him how to live politely in equine company. They do this by pushing him around until he naturally moves away from pressure. They use very specific points of the body to push on (cheek, neck, shoulder and hindquarters), then the subsequent response is naturally rewarded as the pressure releases.[1]

The technique of applying pressure and releasing it as soon as a response comes is called negative reinforcement, meaning that the horse experiences an unwanted disturbance for a short period, but as soon as he does what is asked of him the disturbance stops. The release is the most important part of the pressure-release pairing, and if it occurs immediately after his try it is very effective in letting him know that he did the right thing. Negative reinforcement must not be confused with negative punishment, which is to inflict pain or discomfort *after* undesirable behavior. As well as leaning towards cruelty, the horse doesn't understand this very well (neither do dogs), so he usually learns little other than to fear and distrust the person dishing out the punishment.[2] Although punishment is ineffective in building a solid relationship, sadly, we still see plenty of evidence of it being used. For instance, during the 2021 Olympics, in one equine event broadcast for the whole world to see, punishment was dished out in heartbreaking lashes to a horse perceived to have given less than a perfect performance.

Horses understand about positive reinforcement too, which is to give them something they like when they do something we want. Food is commonly used as the reward, but I don't advise it since a horse can turn that around and mug you once they know food is present. However, I have seen horse trainers highly skilled in trick-training use food effectively as positive conditioning, and there are ways to use it well.[3] Dr. Robert Miller in *Understanding the Ancient Secrets of the Horse's Mind* suggests that a food reward be used only intermittently (called partial reinforcement) which is more effective than giving a food reward after every desirable behavior.[4] Two forms of positive reinforcement we can always use effectively, though, are to give a rub or scratch on a horse's favorite itchy spots. Another reward they love, probably as much as food and personal space, is *doing nothing*. After I have asked a horse to back away from me for instance, I will stand and observe for as long as it takes until I see more than one sign of my horse going into a state of deep relaxation, including her head being held lower than her withers. Giving horses our time, both freely and with patience, is the best reward ever.

Using pressure release does not have to be seen as dramatic, or even obvious, to an onlooker. One of the most memorable examples I have witnessed of the use of subtle pressure release was from Elsa Sinclair. She has developed a collaborative training method with horses in partnership, that she calls Freedom Based Training. She spends many hours with her horses reading subtle body language while asking their permission to make physical contact through gradual approach and retreat. It would not do her work justice to try to describe it fully here, but it is well worth looking at her website.[5]

This is not a book of instruction in natural horsemanship. There are already many such excellent books, videos and podcasts, and there are many fine teachers accessible worldwide. The ideal manner of learning horsemanship in my view is to have regular lessons and/or to attend workshops from more than one teacher to get different perspectives. Here, I am simply outlining the basic principles (rather than techniques) of applying horse language that I consider applicable to equine assisted practices. Personally, I have moved away from practicing set procedures in groundwork (although that is probably a necessary stage to go through), and instead I like to ask one of three questions: What? How? How much?

WHAT: Say I want to ask my horse to step backwards, away from me. That's a "what", so the first step is to have a clear mental picture (not a verbal command) of my horse stepping back. Being able to visualize what we want is the first part of the "ask" and in a finely tuned relationship it is perfectly achievable for a horse to respond in due course to that mental image alone.

It might take a while to get to that point, but for a start, mentally visualizing what you want your horse to do ultimately leads to clear communication. We might want something as simple as asking for our horse's attention, for him to put his head down or move his feet. It is our conceptualization of something happening that gives the horse the first set of instructions. This is not magic, it's science: when we activate intention in our body-mind, a whole set of physiological changes takes place in and around our bodies that a horse is more than capable of detecting.

HOW: What tools shall I use to move my horse? I'm not talking about physical tools of ropes and whips and the like, but tools such as physical pressure, intention, focus, movement and energy. Let's think about how horses do this. Have you deliberately spent time observing horses grazing in paddocks (or looking at videos of horses in the wild)? Spending an hour every now and then sitting in a paddock with horses while watching them question and respond to each other is the very basis of understanding. An obvious thing to notice is that horses locate and move each other through vocalizations, but sound as a tool should not be top priority for us. (Horses respond to loud and unfamiliar noises, but they do so out of fear and that is a response to be avoided.) You will also notice their concern for space within the herd. How to ask for space can be either explicit or subtle. Dams bump their foals out of the way, and horses move each other by simply looking at the part of the body they want to move. This is a constant pattern of behavior, but they do it so subtly at times that it can take some doing to notice that anything has been communicated at all. Horses can move each other around simply by raising their heads one inch higher or by moving their ears back slightly. They can move another horse by taking one step with intention towards them or just by looking at them. At the more energetic end of the spectrum one horse may choose to charge another, necessitating a very quick move by the targeted horse who might otherwise be bitten. There's a wide range of tools that horses use with each other, which for the sake of conciseness can be considered in four categories that increase in intensity with each step:

1. intention and focus
2. movement
3. light touch
4. active energy

There is a fifth step, but not one we should take ourselves, where one horse gives another a serious warning or launches an actual attack. This is horse business only. In my view it is *never* necessary for a human to hurt a horse. I have heard horse trainers justify the use of excessive force by saying that whatever we do is nothing compared with one horse biting or kicking another. But we are not horses, so this is not our business and neither is it necessary. If nothing works for you through the previous four steps, stop, take a break, check your attitude and presence, and start again while making sure that your signals are clear. Once this works well with your horse you can return to the earlier tools and ultimately you will be able to ask him to move in response to intention alone.

HOW MUCH: This is to some extent embedded within the four "how" tools as they graduate from soft to more intense. However, each one of those tools can be used with varying intensity too. I find it useful to think of a sliding scale of pressure from zero to three, where zero is not applying any pressure at all as you stand relaxed with one foot cocked while directing your energy away from the horse. Then at scale one, use one tool in the lightest manner possible. At scales two and three you will gradually increase your energy levels and range of movement until you get a response. Then move back down in energy so that you can work your horse at one in the scale.

Where does the intensity stop? As mentioned earlier, I've seen horses pushed with such intensity that they raise their heads high, ears go back and eyes widen, while responding with all sorts of avoidance behaviors. There is nothing to be gained from such a response. Even if you do get what you are asking for, you have done so by breaking trust and instilling fear, which is the opposite of what we are aiming for: meaningful and ethical relationship. Besides, no animal (human included) learns well through fear. They might learn something, but it's unlikely to be what you want them to learn. The levels of intensity as I describe them here might differ from what others in natural horsemanship recommend, and that's fine; you will want to find principles and terminology that work for you.[6]

What I would warn against is learning a whole set of formal procedures to practice with your horse repeatedly as you try to perfect your groundwork techniques. I did this for years (knowing no better at the time), and when I did achieve a good working relationship with a horse, I reckon it was through bighearted horses giving me the benefit of the doubt. Fortunately, horses are very forgiving and they are capable of putting up with us mindlessly practicing techniques, but it's certainly not ideal. As a rule of thumb, I would suggest doing a particular routine (hindquarter yields for instance) no more than three times in succession. There's always tomorrow, and with horses the old saying of "less is more" certainly applies. I find it worth reminding myself that I am not teaching nor training my horse, rather, I am *teaching her that I know her language*. She won't respond in the way I expect her to until I have convinced her that I know enough of what she knows. This seems the complete reversal of some horsemanship approaches, and I mostly learned it by preparing horses for equine assisted work. Essentially, they taught me this important principle.

In natural horsemanship there are a number of methods and approaches. Some methods are very similar, while adopting different terminology and explanations. Others are confusingly diverse yet equally convincing. I believe that everyone needs to figure out what works best for them, and given that horses also differ we need to find out what works best for each individual horse. You will know what's best for you and your horses once you take the time to fully identify your values. The bottom line for me is that my horses stay emotionally below fear and anxiety. Eliciting a fear response does not help relationship building in any meaningful way. I become aware that I have failed in this respect as soon as my horse reacts with a high head or wide eyes.

As for my own emotional levels, I watch those just as carefully, knowing that horses read our emotions closely. You can be assertive when you need to, but it's counterproductive to get angry or frustrated with a horse. Assertive simply means showing where the goals and boundaries are, whereas getting angry with a horse is emotional abuse. If you do unwittingly feel angry (none of us is perfect, after all), walk away for a while. Make sure as you go through the levels of intensity that you stop before you get emotionally involved. Over time you will learn to decrease the pressure to find the softest way of asking. Once you have achieved softness with a horse you will look as though you are doing very little (hence the misleading term, "horse whispering"). It is worth repeating that you are not training your horse, you are showing her that you are learning her language. At times you will get the grammar wrong, but your horse will appreciate you for making the effort and will help you over time to refine your ability to "speak horse".

Inviting your horse

Enter your horse's paddock or barn with her halter clearly visible in your hand. Start to walk towards her in a curved line, stopping each time she looks at you as you look away. If she walks away, do the same in the opposite direction. Resist the urge to "stalk" her. You are allowing her to have a "no" experience if she wants. Start again and take the time it takes to get alongside her, then offer the back of your closed fist to sniff. Allow her to do this three times, taking the pressure off in between each greeting. Put a hand somewhere on her body and leave it there until she either moves away (in which case, start again) or she relaxes her ears, nose, mouth and neck. As soon as she relaxes, go to another part of her body. Introduce her to the rope by putting it on various parts of her body, removing it each time she relaxes. Put the halter on then take it off when she relaxes. Do this three times, then walk away.

This is an exercise for the horse in truly accepting you, but it is also a great exercise for you to inquire deeply of your own motives. How strong within you is the desire to "catch" your horse and get on with doing something? How prepared are you to let her take the time she needs? Is your relationship with her prepared to be boundless? Ask yourself: "Am I giving some of my time to this while thinking about the next thing, or am I accepting the timelessness of the process?" How patient am I? Am I patient within limits? That's just dishing out a little bit of my precious time. When I listen to somebody telling the story of who they are, am I prepared to give all the time and attention necessary for that person to be truly, deeply heard?

Footnotes

1. For a detailed and precise map of specific points on the horse's body that both humans and horses can utilize effectively, see Wilsie (2018) p. 42.
2. For clear-concept books on procedures and practices using pressure-release (negative reinforcement) from an ethical

basis see: Brannaman (1997), Tabernaberri (2007), Kutsch (2021), Miller (2007) and Wilsie (2017, 2018).

3. I highly recommend observing Dr. Nadine Lindblom of Equine Connection Academy working horses she has trained through positive reinforcement: https://www.nadinelindblom.com

4. Miller (2007) p. 57.

5. Elsa Sinclair's work can be viewed at: https://www.tamingwild.com

6. Using only three levels of intensity means that everything fits between minimum energy "1", maximum energy "3", with something in between. I believe that if there were a fourth level of intensity, it might be regarded as license to punish the horse and/or venting frustration.

Chapter 16

Listening to the Horse

There are occasions when it is wise to loosen up on pressure-release methods of communication (i.e. negative reinforcement) and learn to use trust much more when working with horses. Dr. Janet Jones in *Horse Brain, Human Brain* suggests that "negative reinforcement teaches a horse to obey and respond, but it doesn't build much trust between horse and handler [and] does not offer the added benefit of teaching the horse you are on his side."[1] Dr. Allan Hamilton goes a little further, adding that, "Negative reinforcement ... may prevent an animal from carrying out a certain behavior because he is afraid [and] the lesson does not accumulate in his personal repertoire. It is devoid of happiness or any personal sense of success and accomplishment."[2] Negative reinforcement should never elicit fear (but unfortunately it is often used that way). It works well when teaching horses how to respect boundaries, how to stand still when asked, how to move when asked, how to walk calmly on the lead, how to yield and so on. But in the establishment of a trusting relationship between practitioner and horse we can go beyond that. A relationship with horses built on trust should be capable of allowing into it, as a matter of respect, occasions when we can accept "no" in response to a request, just as we usually do for fellow humans.

But haven't we all been taught that we must never allow a horse to say no to us, that we shouldn't let them ever refuse a request? There's good reasoning behind this, just as there is in the belief that it's not a great idea for a toddler to refuse a parent's request and on every occasion make up her own mind about what she does and doesn't do. With both the horse and the toddler, orders and requests are most often given for reasons of safety and well-being (the well-being of the parent comes into the equation too, of course). To live safely within a community, both horse and small human must learn that not every choice they make is entirely self-determined. Unlike the horse, the toddler grows up and is eventually able to access his prefrontal cortex and, with luck, remember his childhood learning. The horse, though, is already grown up for the most part so if we don't allow her to ever say no, not only are we telling her she has no agency but we are also not respecting what she, as an adult animal, might know that is best for her. Imagine what it would be like to always have your opinions, beliefs, and ideas overridden by someone else. (Hopefully, you do simply have to imagine this.) Would you respect and trust that person? Would you feel validated? It stands to reason that we don't always want a horse to make the decisions. On the other hand, I can think of several occasions in which I have handed over decision-making to my horse with positive results.

- I'm going for a long trek with a small group of riders. We are in the country, but start out late, so before we are halfway to our destination it turns pitch black. I can't see a thing and neither can any of the other riders, so we have no choice but to let the horses guide us to the overnight hut through streams, up and down hills and through forest. I have no option but to trust my horse every step of the way. Fortunately, a couple of the horses know the way since they have been there before, or it might have been a different outcome. The sense of total trust I allow this horse in the pitch black of night is an entirely new experience.
- On a solo trek I am injured from a homemade spring-loaded latch hitting me in the face as I open a farm gate.

Being prior to cell phones there is nobody else around, so I face either a long walk home in my dazed and bloody state, or I can hop on my horse and ask him to take me home. This he does willingly as he makes all the decisions along the way, including crossing country roads and walking through streams.

- Riding in the back country I face long steep hills to traverse, and I figure that the best way to do this with my quarter horse mare (who I'm sure is part mountain goat) is to give her a loose rein and ask her to choose her own way. She does this far better than my previous attempts to find the best footing for her in steep terrain. I learn that trusting a horse at the right time is a beautiful experience.
- I am in the open country and ask my gelding to race up a hill. It was exciting and I wanted him to keep going once we reached the top, but he would not listen to my request to keep cantering, instead stopping suddenly. This was terrain I had not been in before, and little did I know that at the top of the hill there was a steep fall into a quarry. Nothing visual gave a hint of the massive drop. Oddly, my gelding knew, even though he had not been there before either. After that, I was much more respectful of his "no".

Riders could get into trouble if they handed over *all* decision-making to horses, but in a meaningful relationship I believe there must be the capacity for either partner to hand over some decision-making some of the time in acts of trust. There are times when there might be good reason to listen to a horse's no. Pain, for instance, would be a good reason, or your horse might just get out of bed the wrong way one morning. Listening to a horse's no assists in the development of a trusting relationship for the simple reason that she feels understood. This doesn't mean that no must forever remain no. It can be modified by asking again, maybe more slowly or with more patience, or no might simply be the horse saying that she needs to digest the request a little. Sarah Schlote, an advocate for respecting a horse's yes and no, makes the point that ethically, horses engaged in equine assisted practices should be able to have a say in their involvement, a stance I wholeheartedly agree with:

> *Even if equine-assisted practices are typically for human benefit, this does not mean that such programs cannot also seek to benefit the animals in some way. At the very minimum, the interaction will be neutral for the animals, and ideally both would gain from the interaction—the ethical concepts of "do no harm" and "do good" apply equally to the human client and the equines involved.*[3]

In an equine assisted setting, in my opinion, it is essential to respect a horse's no. Without their willingness to be involved in a client session, little of value is likely to take place, and ethically at Earthhorse Aotearoa we do not wish to coerce any horse to work with us. Megan Kirby of The Equine Psychotherapy Institute expresses the same view in her book *An Introduction to Equine Assisted Psychotherapy*: "It is important that practitioners can offer horses opportunities to choose to participate ... [but they] can choose to say no to practitioners if they do not want to participate in sessions with clients."[4] Endearingly, horses are just as likely to offer the opposite response, deliberately choosing to work with a specific client. Whenever this occurs, invariably the horse provides that person with a therapeutic session precisely relevant to their needs.

Sometimes it is appropriate to release the pressure when horses give a definite no, as this allows them an experience of attunement in which they feel accepted and understood in the relationship. This idea aligns with attachment theory's recognition of "the importance of providing safe haven conditions in relationship, which are foundational to the development of trust".[5] The tricky part of taking notice of a horse's no, is in determining when she is giving a definite no for a good reason and when requests (such as boundary setting) have yet to be clearly understood. Like many things with horses, it is down to feel and intuition in knowing how to listen to a horse's yes and no. Negative reinforcement can certainly be taken too far, and it can undermine trust, but we mustn't throw out the baby with the bathwater. I find that the most beneficial place to experiment with listening to yes and no is when going into the paddock to halter my horse. Allowing some element of no into the relationship at this point helps enormously to build trust with a horse. Sometimes she is simply asking me to go a little bit slower with the checking in and haltering process, or she wants me to take notice of something in the environment that she is interested in.

The concept of allowing a horse to say no might sound radical, even dangerous, but I have taken to heart and put into practice advice from the eco-psychologist Dr. Michael Cohen. He makes the seemingly unusual suggestion (for a Westerner) that as a basic and pervasive exercise for establishing a meaningful connection within natural surroundings, we need to *ask permission of the natural area* for us to be there. He says that if subsequently "the area still feels attractive, or becomes more attractive, you have gained its consent." Conversely, if a sense of attraction does not arise, he recommends moving on to another area.[6] Asking permission of nature is fundamental to Cohen's method of teaching reconnection with nature within the discipline of eco-psychology. Up until becoming familiar with principles of eco-psychology, it never occurred to me to ask permission of nature. Whenever I have taken a walk in a forest, sat beside a stream, or wandered down a beach, I have simply regarded it as my right to be there. Asking permission of nature might seem an unusual concept, but it is not. It is a fundamental principle for most indigenous cultures. Dr. Robin Wall Kimmerer in *Braiding Sweetgrass* reports that Native American tribes ask permission of a tree before cutting it:

> *Traditional harvesters recognize the individuality of each tree as a person, a nonhuman forest person. Trees are not taken but requested. Respectfully the cutter explains his purpose and the tree is asked permission for harvest. Sometimes the answer is no. It might be a cue in the surroundings ... that suggests a tree is not willing, or it might be the ineffable knowing that turns [the cutter] away. If consent is granted, a prayer is made, and tobacco is left as a reciprocating gift.*[7]

In my country, Aotearoa New Zealand, the indigenous Māori people also believe in asking permission and giving back to nature to keep it and themselves healthy and mutually supportive. This principle, called *kaitiakitanga*, means guardianship over the land and is based on the knowledge of a deep kinship between humans and the natural world. Humans are not thought of as in any way superior to nature, and in fact humans and nature are seen to be seamlessly connected. Māori understand that all of life is connected in an intricate web, and to understand the world humans need to recognize and respect interdependent relationships within the web of nature.[8]

Asking permission of nature and giving back once we have taken something are unfamiliar ways of being in Western culture, although ecological sciences have made inroads into discerning and valuing interconnectedness within the totality of nature. However, for so many centuries, rather than ask permission humans have been more likely to burst onto a natural scene with digging, cutting and chopping instruments to do whatever they think they need for their own gain. This is an indicator that humans consider themselves separate from nature, although paradoxically we operate in quite a different manner within human society. For instance, when people visit each other's houses they usually knock on the door or call out. Only those whose closeness and trust is a given, such as close family members, would consider walking in unannounced. From anyone else, barging into a house is an expression of power and authority. What is the difference when we walk into a forest or into a paddock with horses grazing in it? This is their home and we are but temporary visitors, but we assume absolute agency and superiority over our horses simply because they are animal-animals while we are human-animals. We might very well own or rent the land that the horses live on, but that means nothing to horses (and ownership of horses means nothing to them too, for that matter). Ownership of land and other beings is a humanly constructed concept to which no animal (or traditional human culture) has any way of relating.

How would we ask for permission from horses? From experimenting with what it means to ask permission of a horse before entering her home, I have found this effective: before arriving at the paddock I send a mental image to the horse with whom I wish to connect. The mental image could be one of walking calmly up to the horse and rubbing her on the shoulder or scratching her favorite itchy spot. This needs to be a picture-image, not a word-thought. I also put attention on my breathing to make sure I am fully at ease. When arriving at the paddock I stand outside the fence for a while and send a request to the horse for permission to enter. This is not a thought, but a feeling directed from the heart. When walking into the paddock I like to greet all the horses, not just the one I wish to halter. When I approach the horse I want, I walk in an arc towards her rather than in a direct line. If she turns away from my approach it doesn't necessarily mean that she doesn't like or respect me. She might be giving me space out of respect, or maybe she just can't be bothered with humans just now. Or it might be that I approached her in a less than ideal manner. Maybe I made a "bee line" towards her or somehow broadcast a sense of urgency.

I have learned the value of Sharon Wilsie's practice of approaching horses in an arc, giving them space and offering them the back of my hand to sniff three times. This advice is based on knowing that horses ask permission of each other to enter their space, and that space is a valuable commodity to a horse. They also don't much like direct lines, and neither does nature in general. This approach works, even if only to give the horse an opportunity to sort out whether she's willing to spend time with me just now. It feels respectful, and it gives the horse a chance to not engage if that's what she needs. Wilsie in her book *Horses in Translation* also suggests looking in the same direction as the horse, mirroring the direction of her gaze to impart empathy for her concerns.[9] This makes sense since we now know that when humans imitate each other's body language a rapport is established through the mirror neuron phenomenon.[10]

Sometimes the yes/no process takes no time at all and at other times it can take five to ten minutes. If my horse prefers not to sniff the back of my hand three times she is saying no, but that doesn't mean I will walk away and leave it at that. I might go and ground myself for a minute or so, then circle the paddock and try again. When this happens, I usually notice a sensation within my body of some sense of urgency from my mind running a story about the scarcity of time. Even feeling this to a small degree is enough for a sensitive horse to prefer not to come with us. They have an aversion to urgency emanating from humans, and even a whiff of hurriedness can alert some horses. Usually, if I get a no from a horse it is likely to be just once, after which she allows a further approach. Since applying this method, I rarely have had a horse entirely unwilling, but when it has happened I've respected that horse's point of view. Allowing a horse to say no builds trust, especially with one that has been traumatized:

One of our horses was so traumatized by her previous living situation that it was impossible to get anywhere near her for several months after joining us on the Earthhorse Aotearoa farm. At first I simply followed her on the track from a distance, approaching and retreating. Every time she looked at me, I looked away slightly (taking off the pressure) as I let out a sigh. When I eventually got close enough, I added the hand-sniffing routine, accepting no as an answer each time. Then one day there was a yes, which came more and more frequently from then on. Now, several years on, after greeting her in the paddock within the herd all I need do is offer her a sniff of my hand, look towards her hindquarters, then walk away as she follows me without a halter or rope. It was well worth putting in the foundational relationship building but I also thank our other horses for teaching her the ways of the herd. They provided an environment of trust and gave this beautiful mare a real equine family.

Respecting the horse's point of view is an ethical value that has come increasingly to the fore in the last twenty years or so. Several books recently published indicate exactly what the author's values are in their titles: Andrea Kutsch's *From the Horse's Point of View* and Carlos Tabernaberri's *Through the Eyes of the Horse* being classic examples.[11] Short quotes from these two books throw light on the theme I wish to bring to the fore. Kutsch writes:

To this day, I have always maintained that we need to practice seeing things from the horses' point of view. We need to learn to understand their natural behavior and to find and offer appropriate solutions that they can follow without fear. Because, without us, without our actions and ambitions, horses don't have any problems at all.[12]

Kutsch follows with the comment that this point fascinates her; it also fascinates me that horses have no problems (or none they can't deal with as nature intended) without human input, without our egos driving us to "use" horses to fulfil our own assumed needs. The subtitle of her book is *Horse Training's New Frontier*, which alludes to the huge steps forward that horsemanship has made recently. It really does seem as though we have reached a new level of interspecies communication, respectful horsemanship and mutual compassion. The ethic of seeing things from the horse's point of view as a *practice* (as Kutsch puts it) is a truly spiritual approach. When it is treated as a practice (i.e. as something to *put into practice* daily) it can't fail to lead to transformation of the human-horse relationship. Equally, it is a practice that is transferable to the human environment as we learn to see the points of view of other people. We can experience that it takes nothing away from us when we are compassionate. Rather, it transforms our relationship with horses through our own sense of I AM, as well as our relationship with other human beings. Tabernaberri expresses much the same ethos in his book:

If you want success with horses, get rid of your ego. People so often let egos get in the way of many things. When you work with horses, it's the horse that matters, and he doesn't need your resumé, or list of achievements, to decide whether you're good or bad at what you do ... Fighting horses happens when you fail to feel like horses do.

All you need to do before you handle your horse is put yourself in his hooves.[13]

Getting rid of ego is not an easy task and it's probably unrealistic since ego is a mental structure that we need in order to live within human society. We just don't want to be *controlled* by ego. Tabernaberri has perfect advice on how to put our ego to one side when we are with horses, namely, to put our mind *inside the mind of the horse*. This is nothing less than exercising compassion. We can also make a point of being alert enough that when we notice our ego arising we simply note it and catch the reactiveness before it expresses itself overtly. Even noticing our ego after reactiveness has emerged is a step in the right direction. Horses give us feedback in situations where frustration, irritation or anger do arise in us as they react with direct honesty. If we learn how to "read" them accurately they become our exacting teachers.

Footnotes

1. Jones (2020) p. 152.
2. Hamilton (2016) p. 131.
3. Sarah Schlote (2018) "Can Animals Consent" [online]. Available at: https://naturallifemanship.com/can-animals-consent (Accessed 1 April 2023).
4. Kirby (2016) p. 139.
5. Sarah Schlote (2020) "Connection Before Concepts: A Comparison of 3 Pressure-Release Methods" [online]. Available at: https://equusoma.com/connection-before-concepts (Accessed 1 April 2023).
6. Cohen (2007) p. 23.
7. Kimmerer (2013) p. 144.
8. Te Ahukaramū Charles Royal, "Understanding Kaitiakitanga", *Te Ara — The Encyclopedia of New Zealand*

[online]. Accessible at: http://www.TeAra.govt.nz/en/ kaitiakitanga-guardianship-and-conservation/page-1 (Accessed 1 April 2023).

9.   Wilsie (2018) pp. 27, 50.

10.   de Waal (2019) p. 95.

11.   Kutsch (2021) and Tabernaberri (2007).

12.   Kutsch (2021) p. 4.

13.   Tabernaberri (2007) p. 10.

Chapter 17

Reading the Horse

Allen Boone in his book *Kinship with all Life* gives a personal account of discovering how to communicate meaningfully with animals. He establishes communication with animals on three principles: firstly, having respect for an animal's intelligence while seeing them on an equal plane of existence; secondly, quietening one's mind so that thoughts don't get in the way of communicating; and thirdly, providing a listening mind without judgment of any kind.[1] For anyone involved in talk therapy this advice will be familiar since the three aspects of respect, being present and listening without judgment are exact requirements for any counselor, psychologist or psychotherapist. With an animal we don't need to do anything special to establish meaningful communication, we just need to *listen differently*. There is a new language to learn but the real substance of communicating with a being of another species is much the same as within our own species. We will have differing means of expression but essentially, humans and horses experience the same things: pleasure and pain, loss and gain, joy and sorrow.[2]

Animals speak to us in ways that evoke feelings and require intuition. Our job is to discern the subtle differences between our own thoughts and desires, and those that come to us seemingly independently from the animal's body language and presence. Most of us are familiar with this process already through experiencing nonverbal communication with the people we are very close to. As we work with horses and clients we must continuously read the states of both, not only for reasons of safety but because this is how we bring presence into equine assisted spaces. With some exceptions, reading another human's state of being is relatively easy, we do it all the time without even realizing, but it requires considerable observation and practice. Learning the language of horses is fascinating and rewarding, but to dwell on it further would divert from this book's purpose. Not only has the subject been dealt with effectively by many other authors and teachers of horsemanship, we are not asking our clients to "speak horse", but to "read horse", hence I am approaching the subject from that perspective.

If you are a current or aspiring practitioner in the equine assisted space, no doubt you will already have a good working knowledge of horse body language. This is essential because it is our job to continuously interpret what is going on for the horse and to know how she is responding both to the client and to her immediate environment. We need this knowledge to work safely, but it is also valuable to help our clients discover for themselves how to read a horse. This is an essential tool when thinking of the triangle of trust, specifically when showing the horse that we understand and respect her point of view. It is something that practitioners can master, but we don't always want to teach this to our clients directly. There are many situations where we need to take note of what we believe is going on for the horse, while allowing the client's perceptions and interpretations to drive the process. Most of the time clients should be allowed to find personal significance in a horse's reactions regardless of what you believe is going on for the horse.

However, there are some situations where it is useful for clients to read equine body language such as when developing empathy and seeing the world from the horse's perspective. In such an exercise we can question our clients about how the horse is standing: is she standing on three legs (one leg resting) or four; is her neck tight and her head held high; is she breathing slowly or fast; is she attentive to you/us or is she distracted by something else? These questions enable clients to assess how comfortable a horse is with whatever is playing out and to change their behavior with the horse while looking for further signs of acceptance and relaxation.

The ears of a horse are particularly expressive: if both are upright and facing forward, the horse is listening to what is happening ahead of her. If one ear is focused sideways towards the client the horse might be wondering what people around her are up to while simultaneously listening out for what her paddock mates are doing. Often both ears actively move around independently of each other as she scans her whole environment. If the ears point backwards, she is listening to what is going on behind her. If, however, the ears are genuinely pinned back, i.e. completely flat against the neck, I wouldn't be hanging around asking a client what that means! Ear pinning happens so rarely though, and we are more likely to see it with horses in a band or herd as one horse reprimands another. If such aggression is ever directed towards a human it's best to back off, but I have never witnessed such a direct confrontation between horse and human other than in films.[3] A question I like to ask clients is whether the horse's ears are "talking ears" or "listening ears", a distinction that I invite them to define for themselves, and that invariably leads to useful analogies.[4]

Assessing what is happening around the eyes of a horse yields further useful information. A relaxed horse will blink approximately every ten seconds, whereas a horse that doesn't blink is one that is worried, tense, uptight or even ready to "explode". If the eyes are so wide open that the upper eyelid is "tented" the horse is likely to be anxious or uncomfortable, whereas a very relaxed horse will have loose upper eyelids.

We can look also for where the head is in relation to the body. A raised head indicates that a horse is concerned about something, or that she is at the very least not relaxed. A neck in parallel with the back is a more relaxed horse but one with her head lower than the top line is very much at ease. Close to the ground is a vulnerable position for a horse's head because it is the ideal place for a predator to grab hold of the nose or throat, so a horse that lowers her head around people is showing trust. It is a sign to look out for as we ask our clients: "I notice your horse has lowered her head. What do you think she is saying to you? What has she picked up from you as you've been talking?"

The mouth and nostrils give us vital signs of relaxation too. Are the lips held tightly; is the lower lip drooping; is she licking and chewing (coming off adrenalin); are the nostrils flared or moving freely? These are all signs of her varying levels of alertness, concern, trust and relaxation. Finally, is she making a sound? Is she calling out to the herd with head high and ears forward? Or is she doing that endearing low-pitched nickering? Is she silent? Ask clients what these things mean to them rather than supplying the answers yourself, and allow the conversation to move to parallel situations in their own lives.

An exercise I find useful is to ask someone to assess the mental state of the horse within a scale of one to ten (relaxed to tense). This can provide a mirror in a learning or therapy space as the client assigns feelings to the horse. They might be assessing the horse accurately or they might be projecting their own feelings, but either way it offers valuable information for discussion. We need to remember too that horses effectively pick up and reflect the physical-mental states of people around them. Sometimes a person doesn't fully recognize how they are feeling until a horse reflects their mood back to them. If your client assesses the horse as anything above five, ask him to help the horse relax down to one or zero by gradually letting go of tension, then explore the number of ways in which the client can also let go. The numerous opportunities for somatic awareness clients is what it's all about.

Kate, a woman in her late fifties who suffers from anxiety stemming from an earlier life-threatening event, comes for several counseling sessions. The trauma happened two years previously but no matter what self-awareness or relaxing practices she follows she can't stop thinking about the event and is bothered by frequent flashbacks. Kate spends a fair amount of energy "holding herself together" both mentally and physically. Her breathing is shallow, she can't stand or sit completely still and she talks incessantly while darting from one subject to another.

We go together into the round pen in which a gelding stands free. Kate enters, stands near the rail and observes him. This horse had been standing relaxed with a lowered head but now he lifts his head high and walks around slightly agitated. Kate wants to pat him, but he keeps away by an arm's length all the while looking over the rail as though he really wished he were on the outside. She is sad that the horse doesn't want to come to her or let her approach him. We stand still and I ask Kate to assess her level of stress on a scale of one to ten (one being completely at ease physically and mentally, and ten being highly concerned, tense, worried, anxious). She puts herself at seven on the scale so I ask her to point out all the things the horse is doing that reflects that level back to her. There is a lot going on with the horse that she notices. Then we do some grounding through a slow body-scan. After a while Kate sees that the gelding is less agitated. We practice "box breathing" as a technique to lower stress (four counts in, hold for four, four counts out, hold for four, and repeat) all the while observing the horse's head gradually lower and his eyes relax through blinking. Kate reassesses her tension as a five on the scale and I invite her to do whatever she feels she needs to release down to four, then three. She acknowledges some areas of tension in her body and by accepting them and moving around, she lets go more tension. She notices the gelding licking and chewing and moving his nostrils freely, then the gelding walks up to her and places his nose on her arm. Finally, she declares she is at one on the scale as the gelding indulges in a big yawn and rolled-back eyes. She has just had a most effective biofeedback experience.

Returning to Allen Boone's advice referred to at the beginning of this chapter, if we wish to communicate meaningfully with a horse, we need to regard him as our equal being on this Earth; we need to take care not to let our own inner business get in the way; and we need to read the horse without making any judgments of right or wrong. A great place to start this process with a client is to invite them to observe horses interacting with each other in a group of two or more.

Footnotes

1. Boone (1954) pp. 73–80.
2. This is a partial quote from a phrase attributed to the Buddha: "Praise and blame, gain and loss, pleasure and sorrow come and go like the wind. To be happy, rest like a giant tree in the midst of them all."
3. A very dramatic but real instance of a horse attacking a human occurs in the documentary *Buck* on the life and work of Buck Brannaman. This human-attacking horse was a stallion who had been mentally damaged through misguided handling.
4. For "maps" on horse ear gestures and other observable behaviors, see Kutsch (2021) pp. 84–118.

Chapter 18

Herd Dynamics

Through getting to know the dynamics within a herd of horses we see a microcosmic image of the various leadership types and qualities evident within human society. Observing herd dynamics is valuable since we see what it is like to live within an internally regulated and generally peaceful social hierarchy. While horse society is not free from conflict by any means, it is contained within an environment of energy conservation and group preservation so that disagreements are short-lived and effective.

It is relatively easy for us to assess the dynamics of a herd or band: who is the lead mare, who is second in charge, who is at the bottom of the hierarchy and so on, while also seeing how those dynamics are subject to change. For instance, there is often a "lead mare in training" who learns by observation, sometimes by being physically close to the lead mare and by temporarily taking over the leadership from time to time. Just as in human society, there is an inevitable and necessary jostling for position. The leadership dynamic is relatively fluid because no horse is in her prime forever, or lives forever for that matter, so training a second in command is vital. While not everything about herd behavior is peaceful, it is fair according to equine societal rules, and horses generally acquiesce and recover quickly when reprimanded by another.

At all times in a band or herd, each horse has a role to play. There is usually a sentinel for instance: one horse who is looking around to make sure there are no cougars or lions creeping around in the long grass. Even though in this country (Aotearoa New Zealand) we don't have big cat predators, horses don't know that and they instinctively keep their environment under surveillance. Again, this is a fluid role within the herd, as horses take up the sentinel responsibility for a few minutes (or seconds) and then pass it on to another.

Equine herd hierarchies are quite strictly enforced. One of our geldings, a one-time high performing dressage competitor, was weaned too early and was brought up on his own, so despite being humanely handled he missed out on learning how to operate within horse society. Our horses continually move together as a herd within a wide-ranging "track system", which is the closest we get to a natural herd environment while keeping horses domestically. It falls short of what a wild herd would experience but it's more natural than keeping them in separate paddocks in ones or twos.[1] But our poor ex-dressage gelding doesn't always know where he fits within the highly mobile herd. He is at the bottom of the pecking order, he doesn't have a friend to practice mutual grooming with, and he keeps his distance from the others by an extra horse length. This has nothing to do with his size since he is the biggest horse in the herd; he just never fully learned the rules of horse society. But he makes unwise moves at times such as attempting to move up in the hierarchy, creating a nasty dynamic for a while during which he might receive a few bites on his hindquarters. He eventually sees the wisdom of returning to the old order for a quieter and safer existence. I know human beings who make impulsive and inappropriate moves like that too! Remarkably, it is not always the leaders of the herd who put the "bottom" horse in his place, it is the "second-to-bottom" horse who does that. Neither do the lower-in-hierarchy horses involve themselves in what is happening higher up. Everyone knows their place relatively speaking and they don't involve themselves in business further away from them. There is, in other words, no micromanagement going on within the horse herds that I have experienced (but undoubtedly there will be exceptions). If there ever is a leader who involves herself in everybody else's business, she doesn't remain as leader for long. The head mare's job is to nurture, maintain peace, and provide safety.

This leads to another characteristic of horses: they are very forgiving. The gelding I've just mentioned who goes through phases of receiving bites on his flank and hindquarters holds no grudges against the one who pushes him around. When one horse pushes on another for whatever reason, once the issue is resolved (someone gets out of the way) they both immediately go back to grazing. This, once observed, is a useful concept for people to take away as a strategy for coping with conflict in their own lives — not the biting part but moving away and letting go!

I used to assume that horses grazing together were doing nothing other than eating grass, but I was mistaken. I now see that they constantly look after each other through present-moment awareness while communicating through subtle body language. Now I enjoy helping other people discover for themselves the intelligence of herd communication. In our workshops at Earthhorse Aotearoa we invite people to observe the herd and comment on what they see, down to the slightest gesture. Sometimes it is the simplest of actions that draws attention. Participants have commented, for instance, that each horse in the herd faces a slightly different direction while standing in a paddock and that it is not a random process. The way the horses position themselves in relation to each other enables them to survey the whole area, scanning the landscape with their ears while grazing and browsing. Another useful observation is noticing that each horse takes up their own space, pretty much equidistant from each other.

Linda Kohanov in *The Five Roles of a Master Herder* would say that horses each manifest one of five possible leadership roles of Dominant, Leader, Nurturer, Sentinel and Predator as categories she derived from researching the practices of nomadic herding cultures.[2] In our work at Earthhorse Aotearoa we utilize this information by observing horses that are free to move around each other together, especially at feed time. People are asked to describe the role each horse plays within three general areas of leadership, dominance and subservience. In this context I find it beneficial not to suggest specific categories or roles but to let people come up with their own ideas and terminology. This is a creative process in which each person's observation about individual horses is always "correct". It might not be the interpretation that a seasoned horseperson might intuit, but since humans are adept at projecting personal traits onto a horse (or other people), how they view themselves is the truth of their experience.

As a group of clients peacefully observe the herd, unfamiliar loud machinery starts up in the neighboring farm. All the horses look up at once, heads high and ears forward, with bodies taut and ready for action. They instantly form a straight line facing the direction of the noise, much like an army contingent at inspection, but before making a move they wait for the head mare to let them know whether it is a fight, flight or freeze situation. We see them all with one ear on her. After about ten seconds she turns her back to the noise and lowers the angle of her head, saying in effect, "Don't bother about that, it won't hurt us." One by one the others turn their backs also and return to grazing. Again, without fuss or effort each horse takes up a unique direction while maintaining a respectful space from each other. This recovery happens despite the machinery noise carrying on with the same intensity. But there is a discernible change in the group now, as one horse at a time acts as a sentinel, raising his or her head to look around for a few seconds, moving their ears around like the sensitive antennae that they are.

How does a simple observation like this teach people about their lives within human society? Even though human groupings are larger, more complex, and more variable than a horse herd, the structured nature of equine society shows what could work for us too. What we saw in this exercise was horses naturally keeping within their own bubble at a safe distance from each other. On average, that bubble was one to two horse lengths. Any time a horse found herself too close to another, she took a few steps away. A horse stepping away from another might indicate submission, but the tone of body language in such a scenario could just as easily indicate willing cooperation. But if a horse finds it necessary to ask another to move too abruptly, too often or too much, she might receive a threatening kick or nip. If several threatening kicks into the air or displays of dental prowess don't send the protagonist away, then an actual contact kick or bite might come next but that is rare in an established herd. Boundaries played out this way are normal for horses as they affirm and renegotiate their place in the hierarchy, modelling for us how we could be. An observation many people make is just how quickly the horses forgive each other: "Those two horses are mutual grooming, but they had a spat only a minute ago." It is not that horses don't have disagreements or the need to reprimand each other, it is that they don't let it affect their relationship within the herd. They don't dwell on disharmony since, for one thing, they lack the neocortex capacity to ruminate, and for another, it would be a waste of valuable energy. Humans certainly do have the capacity and the psychological drive to blame, resent and sulk, hence the job of becoming a peaceful negotiator in human society takes considerable skill and awareness.

One lesson seen from horses working out their hierarchies is noting how consistent they are. They mean what they say and don't muck about being excessively polite, but at the same time are reluctant to get involved in conflict in the first place. They would rather walk away or make a little threat such as a pretend kick. (Horses know that there is no advantage in having seriously injured members within their herd, so they rarely kick to injure.) Another lesson is seeing how quickly they get over themselves, for instance how well they defuse their anger. Humans typically make negotiations unnecessarily difficult and complicated, while horses won't agonize over hurt feelings and neither will they hold on to resentment. They don't walk around seething all day, saying to their mates, "Guess what he did to me," and the horse receiving a reprimand doesn't sulk for a week either although they might learn to be wary. Even though they have immense strength and fighting capability, except for stallion fights in the wild, horses tend to avoid serious scrapes. When they are in power struggles they recover pretty much immediately. They know that it is in their best interests to be calm, peaceful, and available to deal with whatever greater external threat might come along next. Horses accept what just happened and get over themselves, while putting the well-being of the herd first. Human beings have a long way to go to learn (or relearn) how to be like that!

Leadership in action

In an individual herd-observation exercise I ask a client to describe the roles of each horse and ask which one they identify with in terms of their own personality. Then we go into a deeper description of that horse's characteristics. Did he show his place within the herd in a calm or agitated manner? Did he seem confident or nervous in his role? How much energy and movement did he use? Was he respectful of the other horses? Did he hold any resentment? The next stage is to ask the client what they regard as ideal leadership characteristics, being careful not to invite shame or embarrassment as they identify differences between the actual and the ideal.

There is one massive difference between horse and human group dynamics: putting stallion fights to one side, horses don't go to war against each other. The greatest threat to horses isn't other horses but other species. For humans, however, the greatest threat imaginable comes from fellow humans. We not only have the capacity to kill each other and have done so on a huge scale throughout history, we also represent huge threats to each other's egos whether we are talking about individuals or whole nations. Horses, though, are hardwired to put the herd before individuals and as a result are masters at conflict resolution and communal living. When we observe equine group dynamics, not only is fluidity ever-present but so is cooperation. Horses offer a perfect model of consensual leadership free from ego.

Leadership does not unfold in a straight line or sit within neat categories. I often observe the lead mare in her role and I see that most of what she does is in the interest of keeping the herd safe. I see her leading the herd with subtle but clear body language from the front of the group or by directing them from behind. I see her reprimanding a young horse, I see her protecting the horses at the bottom of the hierarchy and I see just how effectively she raises the alarm when needed, turning it off again for immediate calmness. Sometimes she must be forceful, but this is not from egotistical motivation. Although it might not always be immediately obvious, the reason she does anything at all is for the safety and well-being of the whole herd.

We human beings are different socially because of our higher order thinking capacities and egos and because, in

Western cultures at least, we have cultivated and elevated the concept of individuality. If we need an example of how to live harmoniously in a group, horses show us how to lead with care, compassion, and give and take. Observing herd dynamics is especially rewarding for emotionally damaged children when they see horses being kind to each other and releasing their tensions quickly. The concept of going back to grazing has become a helpful theme for more than one child with serious anger issues. And on a one-to-one basis horses teach us in very practical ways how to set boundaries with each other so that issues of tension and situations of conflict need not get in the way of harmonious living.

Footnotes

1. The "track system" imitates the horse's natural environment whereby they have access to a continuous track with varying surfaces for their hooves with the water trough at one end of the track and hay at the other, within a mixture of hilly and flat terrain. This keeps them moving and seeking, which is much healthier physically and mentally than keeping horses in little square paddocks. In our track system, at any one time they have open access from the track to one of seven paddocks to which they help themselves in a pattern of rotation. See Jackson (2014).
2. Kohanov (2016).

Chapter 19

Horse Boundaries, Human Boundaries

Horses maintain very clear boundaries with each other, serving the same purpose for them as they do for humans: they keep everyone safe within a herd while achieving or maintaining delineated hierarchies. They rarely significantly hurt another herd member because they all know their place within the herd, albeit with some fluidity. A micro-movement from an ear or a pointed look is, evolutionarily speaking, preferable to a full-on assault. If a horse hurts another it is generally because he didn't take notice of several prior warnings or he broke an established herd rule. When a human is hurt by a horse it is usually either accidental or the result of someone failing to accurately read the horse's warning signs.

Almost everything we need to know about horses establishing and maintaining boundaries with each other can be learned through observation, which is a great foundation generally for equine assisted work. On an individual basis, though, there are so many ways to learn directly from the horse. A client who learns to establish their own boundaries from a horse will realize it is a concept transferable to human society. But this is not where I would start. I recommend starting not with the human's boundaries, but with the horse's personal boundaries. Why? It is an ethical issue. To not start with the horse's point of view is disrespectful. If we don't make the effort to find out how he negotiates his boundaries with us, we are disregarding one of his most essential concerns and we are objectifying him. This is also a safety issue: why would you start working with a horse before knowing how his sensitivities are playing out?

I invite my client Zak into the round pen to be with a gelding who is standing there freely. I ask him to stand with his back on the fence and observe this horse to "read him". Zak notes that the horse raised his head a little when he entered. For a reading out of ten for how relaxed the horse is, Zak suggests six (ten being the most relaxed). I ask him to look around the muzzle and describe what is going on with the horse's mouth and nostrils. He notices the gelding's mouth firmly shut and still so he revised his assessment down to four. We do some breathing exercises and I remind him not to direct his energy directly towards the horse. After a few minutes the horse relaxes to an eight. We practice relaxing breathing exercises and imitate the soft nickering sound that a horse makes when releasing tension. This works a treat as the horse imitates Zak and relaxes to a ten.

Now I ask Zak to take steps towards the horse's near shoulder and to stop the moment he sees the gelding show any sign of tension. Zak takes two steps as the horse raises his head and turns his ears on him. Zak stops. I ask him to stay there while audibly exhaling. When he sees his horse's eyelids relax and muzzle twitch he steps in again. This time the gelding doesn't make any change so Zak stays beside his shoulder. After a while I suggest that we have not yet met the edge of this horse's bubble (the delineation of his boundary). He has not asked Zak to move away so I suggest he put his hand on the horse's withers who turns slightly to look at Zak and returns to his forward-facing relaxed demeanor. I ask Zak where the edge of the horse's bubble is and he says, "Right now it is on the surface of his skin." Zak says he feels that the horse has invited him into his personal space which he regards as a great honor.

It is important to remind clients to always have their eyes on the horse's head during this exercise so that they can continuously read micro-movements to assess levels of tension and relaxation. Most people look at their own hand when they place it on a horse, so they need reminding to assess their horse's state of tension/relaxation by looking towards the horse's head.

I ask Zak to step backwards towards the horse's hindquarters, stopping beside his girth while reading the horse's reaction. The gelding's ears go back a little because he is listening to Zak. This is a good example of a horse prioritizing his sense of hearing as he is highly aware of Zak being there even though he is not looking at him directly. Zak stands there until the horse relaxes to a 10, then he steps away to reward the horse's deeper relaxed state and to give him space.

This exercise is not about training the horse to allow touch and movement around and over his body. It is not an exercise in desensitization. It is about finding where a horse's bubble is and giving him the space he asks for. It is about approaching the subject of respecting boundaries from the horse's point of view, and it is about listening to his yes and his no. Zak's horse was very relaxed that day but we can't assume that any horse will have his bubble sitting at the same place each day. All horses are different and any horse can vary from one day to another, just like people. The following week we do the same exercise with a mare.

Zak steps into the round pen and the mare steps away. Is she giving a message that she doesn't want to engage with Zak, or is she "giving space"? I ask the question, but neither Zak nor I know the answer just yet. Zak reads the mare as six out of ten (equally balanced on four legs, ears moving around, but eyes wide, and her mouth in a fixed position), so he relaxes his own breathing. He mirrors the mare's movements, looking where she is looking, sharing her concerns. After some time, the mare relaxes to a nine, giving some nice sighing and yawning responses. Zak takes a step towards the horse's shoulder, but at two meters away her head swings around and gives what Zak calls "a pointy face". He stops right there and shows with his own body language that he is demanding nothing from the mare, who relaxes back to eight. Zak works all around the mare in this manner and discovers that the horse's bubble is about two meters wide all around her body. If Zak tries to move in any closer, our mare shows that she is challenged.

That's interesting, because a couple of weeks earlier we had an observation session with the herd, and Zak saw that this mare kept all horses away from her by a horse length. That is, except for one gelding with whom she enjoys mutual grooming and another mare with whom she sometimes stands nose to nose. This showed us how to continue working. Zak decided that we should approach "knuckle to nose" only (greeting with the back of a closed hand to emulate a horse nose).

Zak offers the mare the back of his hand to sniff. Then he releases the pressure by looking away and exhaling. For the second greeting, the mare sniffs Zak's hand, but at the third greeting she turns her head away. Zak gives the mare space and walks away. We observe other horses for a while then return to the mare. Each time Zak offers his hand, she only allows a greeting ritual once or twice. After three or four more repetitions of the ritual, our mare gives three knuckle-to-nose greetings and Zak follows by rubbing the mare's forehead, which she clearly enjoys. Now Zak can rub the mare's neck and shoulders and return to stroke her nose while she remains still and relaxed. Zak moves away and sits on a mounting box, then the mare quietly walks up to Zak and asks to stand with him. Zak had just experienced how patience and compassion (walking in another person's shoes) can profoundly change a relationship and he was able to take this new understanding into his home life.

What just happened? We had a dignified mare indicate that she highly values her own space. My client respected the mare's wish, and after further demonstrations of no, she willingly stepped towards Zak and they stood together in a beautiful exhibition of trust. This horse very specifically demanded respect for her need for space, and once she trusted that she would get it consistently, willingly invited Zak into her bubble. Once they shared space together Zak was able to touch this mare all over, scratching her itchy spots and having a cuddle.

This exercise combines very nicely with observation of a group of horses in an arena to figure out their social rules. Who is allowed to stand next to one horse but not another? Who is actively pushed away and who is drawn to another? And so on. The communication tools horses use with each other are subtle but clear, and once we start to see them, our own observational abilities become increasingly reliable.[1]

Humans as relational beings also need to establish clear boundaries with each other. Detail differs from culture to culture, but it is universal for humans to observe unwritten rules about how close to stand next to someone, whether to look directly into another's eyes, whether to ask personal questions, whether or not to touch (how, where and when), and how much emotion to show. However, in modern Western society, for all manner of reasons, many are unable to uphold boundaries effectively with others. We give way to others because we want to be liked, we don't want to offend, we don't feel confident (meaning we feel inferior) and as an ingrained habit from childhood we prioritize another person's boundaries over our own.

Those of us brought up in Western society tend to call our bounded zones of being "personal space", but this is never a fixed delineation. For instance, I might stand quite close to my best friend but not my employer; I might allow myself to be emotive with my partner but not with acquaintances; I will generally hug people I know but rarely do so with strangers; and I will speak quite personally to close friends but not to the person I buy my bread from.

Out of insecurity or diffidence, some people are either not clear about their boundaries or are inconsistent whereas horses are quick to work out their boundaries with each other. When horses are with humans they are likely to test us out to see where we fit within their hierarchy. Will we let a horse push on us? Do we accept it when he shoves his big nose in our face, or do we think it's cute? Do we move out of his way all the time? We generally need to teach any horse we meet that we don't want to be pushed over, trampled on, chewed on or have our heads knocked off. Just as horses teach each other where their boundaries are, humans must also show horses where our boundaries begin and end. If we don't, chances are some horses will assume we are lower than them in the herd hierarchy and might experiment with pushing us around. Having a horse fool around in your space is not cute, it's dangerous, and he is testing how much he can be in command of your space. Some people have difficulty setting boundaries with horses though because they want the horse to love them and they equate pushing a horse back a step or two with rejecting them. When this situation arises it can lead to valuable talk because if someone is weak or inconsistent in boundary setting with horses it's pretty much guaranteed they have similar issues with at least one significant person in their lives. However, once a client realizes that by accessing and engaging her own energy she can gently but firmly move a massive animal away from her, the exercise becomes a metaphor for boundary-setting at work, at home and with friends.

A valuable aspect of boundary-setting is when a client asks a horse to step towards them. Many a horse will take one step too many, so people feel the need to take a step backwards to get out of the way. But when we step backwards from a horse crowding us it signals submission. Once people recognize what they are doing and what it means to the horse, I invite them to repeat the exercise while using energy or movement (or both) to stop the horse at an arm's length. Again, most people have difficulty with this initially because they feel they are rejecting the horse's "affection" and it takes a while to learn that's not the case. A client experiencing for themselves how they can arrest the movement of an animal many times their weight and size is very empowering.

Sam loves to watch the herd members jostling for space and authority during a free-for-all feeding session that we call the "bucket dance". He astutely observes their pushing, shoving, allowing, watching and boundary negotiations, all of which leads to animated discussions of how Sam sets his own boundaries. He observes that horses sometimes push each other around but that they don't hurt each other or get into fights. What do horses do to avoid hurting each other? They show their displeasure through body language then walk away, forget about it and go back to grazing. Sam is very impressed with the horses' strategies for getting along with each other and the following week he brings along his diary entry describing all the ways he has noticed himself choosing to give way to other people out of kindness and when he decides to stand his own ground to set healthy boundaries.

When working with boundaries, the physical space between client and horse becomes a metaphor for other kinds of boundaries such as emotional space, touch and verbal boundaries, bringing into consciousness a wealth of personal discoveries. Emotional space is also very important to horses as they will often tell another to move away even though there is no danger of having their grazing usurped. Clients learn when doing this work with horses that physical space equates to emotional space. There is always an emotional component to maintaining boundaries. Someone who fears that asking a horse to stand a little bit away will hurt the horse's feelings can recognize similar situations in their human environment as they equate preserving emotional and physical space with rejection.

The next step might be to invite a client to mentally identify a person who does not respect their space and to name the horse as that person, then see what arises as they work together on an exercise. Boundary work is one of the most valuable learning situations with horses. Not only is it essential to have boundaries well established with the horses from both safety and respect perspectives, but boundaries are also the foundation for working with anger, as we discuss later on. As Dr. Gabor Maté demonstrates so effectively in his patient case studies, boundary violation is the foundation of early trauma and is the trigger for anger expression as an adult[2] so if we can help someone with their boundaries it can have very positive and immediate repercussions.

Footnotes
1. To see how an experienced observer of horse language can decode the subtle behaviors of wild horses, watch

onnection with Horses

Sharon Wilsie's commentary on the Konik horses of the Netherlands at: https://www.youtube.com/watch?v=v4_DW9o9OGY (Accessed 1 April 2023). See also, Wilsie (2017).

2. "Anger in its natural, healthy form is a boundary defense, a dynamic activated when we perceive a threat to our lives or our physical or emotional integrity." Maté (2022) p. 378.

196

Chapter 20

Intention, Visualization and Focus

How we think, what our intentions are, what we say to ourselves (about ourselves, others and experiences), and what we visualize, impacts how we feel, how we behave and how we build relationships. We have a responsibility to ourselves, to horses and to other people to know our own intentions and motivations. This also happens to be, in my experience, the first requirement for working in the equine assisted space. How effectively we recognize our own ego in action and how practiced we are at lessening its influence on our behavior and attitudes not only determines the quality of our relationship with horses but it also determines how effective we will be when working with people. Noticing our thoughts and motives is the first requirement for loosening ego's grip, and the second is to accept those thoughts without judgment. Accepting whatever arises without making any kind of judgment invites supportive and creative spaciousness.

Our thoughts are silently transmitted to others—horse and human—more readily than we care to admit. But most of us build a protective shield around ourselves by projecting outwardly how we wish to be known although it is possible to see (or at least feel) the incongruity of a person expressing something contrary to what they genuinely experience. An example of incongruity in the human world is a salesperson trying to sell you an item such as a house or a car, while acting over-the-top-friendly, positive and familiar. I will not purchase from someone pretending to be my friend simply to make a sale, especially one who thinks they know exactly what I want. We can't sell lies to our horses either: they are acutely aware of incongruity. Knowing that horses are sensitive to our whole being, including both conscious and unconscious states, should give us a few clues about how to communicate with them. Horses become uncomfortable with artificiality, and through their reactions teach us firstly, that our thoughts are powerful predictors of our behavior (we become what we repetitively think), and secondly, that through our behavior, body language, energy levels and feelings we communicate our innermost states of being without trying. What a good number of people on the planet are realizing (which seems like a new thing but is as old as humanity itself) is that intention is transmittable:

> While training in an equine bodywork modality the instructor asks me to walk the horse I am with, over to a different paddock. This horse is jittery and walks with a high head. I am told to form a mental image of the horse walking relaxed with his head down as we go. I think, "Fine chance that will happen," but I do it anyway and it works. From now on I know I will continue to explore how human intentions, thoughts, visualizations and focus communicate to horses.

I see real and honest communication happening all the time while working with people in the presence of horses, and it is the horse's exacting response that draws out a person's true state. I might for example suggest that a client walk a horse around the arena while she works on something specific, then I might notice her stop as the horse shows reluctance to go forward. Almost invariably when I inquire about what was going on I get a reply along the lines that the client was doubting her ability to keep the horse walking, or that a negative thought popped into her head just before the horse stopped. Horses are not able to read human thought as such because they don't have verbal language, but they certainly detect the physiological markers that accompany doubtful and negative thinking.

For my own work before inviting someone onto the farm I ensure that I am honest with our horses about my own state of mind. If I sell my horse a false story, pretending to be perfectly fine when I'm not, it puts the seed of incongruity into a working arena in which someone else is about to step. It is worth checking in with yourself before stepping into your horse's stall, paddock or arena. For just 30 seconds, you might check in with your breathing, feel your booted feet firmly on the ground and scan your body for points of tension. This is time well spent because it keeps you and others safe. If you are in a less than perfect frame of mind, which can happen of course, then all you need do is admit it to yourself and bring it to the horse. We only need to be honest and congruent, not perfect.

We have a mare who is very sensitive and exacting. She is a beautiful riding horse but in the last three years has been increasingly reluctant to let me halter her when she's in the paddock. I know she would be compliant if I had some carrots in my pocket, but I consider that to be a form of deception so I need to do something else. I have tried all the relaxing techniques I know. I've meditated in the paddock with her, approached in nonthreatening ways and been careful not to direct energy from the center of my body (hara) directly towards her. It is especially unsettling to my ego when I see that she doesn't have the same problem with other people so I figure it must be something to do with my mental position. It dawns on me that although I am being emotionally congruent I am being conceptually incongruent. I am careful to match what I feel with what I am expressing but my mare is demanding something else; she wants me to be consistent in my thoughts too. Thoughts have emotional content, so that's not surprising really.

I review my relationship with her and remember that for a variety of practical reasons I have been trying to decide whether to keep riding her, and it occurs to me that subconsciously I have been asking her to tell me what to do! I have been unable to decide through weighing up the pros and cons using mental processes alone and have been torturing myself with indecision. No doubt I have been torturing her as well.

One day as I walk into the paddock I spontaneously give up the struggle of trying to decide, genuinely settling into not bothering either way. It feels as though the question has resolved, as though a decision has made itself without any effort from me. Now I walk into the paddock and my mare walks up to me, leans down to put her head in the halter, and happily walks beside me on a loose line.

I have had so many experiences of horses picking up on mental positions and emotions that these things no longer surprise me (although it is still wonderful when it happens). This has led me to purposely work on intention and visualization with people who want to work with the horses. The moment someone loses their focus while walking a horse on line for instance it is immediately obvious. That is the moment when the horse is likely to stop or head in the "wrong" direction. It is something you might be aware of too if you are a rider, when just thinking "trot" or "canter" can be enough for a horse to respond accordingly. You see this in the best dressage riders where it looks as though the rider is physically doing nothing while the horse performs precisely and beautifully. Although the horse is responding to very subtle physical cues from the rider, mental imagery undoubtedly plays its part in a top performance as it does for any athlete.

Accessing the life force

This is another practice for accessing your sixth sense, or as Tolle calls it, the inner body. Practice this on your own first until you get used to it, then take it to your horse. Allow yourself to relax totally, then without moving ask yourself how it is that you know your body is alive. Can you sense the aliveness in your hands, in your feet, in your chest? This is a favorite exercise of Tolle and is a deceptively simple but highly rewarding practice.[1] Once you can do this alone, try the same thing while standing next to a horse. Then do it on behalf of the horse. Can you feel the aliveness coming from him? Can you feel his energy field? Can you feel your energy fields intermingling? If you have any doubts about feeling energy fields do this simple experiment: hold your hand two or three inches away from the skin of your horse and wait. Before long, your horse's twitch muscle (which runs under the skin of his whole torso) will go crazy under where your hand is hovering as he picks up on your energy.

Some intention practices with horses

The following exercises are not about horsemanship but are to guide yourself initially, and then your clients, to recognize that they have the capacity to affect another being through intent, energy and imagery. The aim of this work is not to achieve something, not to get a result but to discover an inner capacity that might not previously have been realized or trusted. It is the discussion that you initiate with your client that constitutes the real work, and what shape that takes will vary according to your training in the specific discipline in which you work.

1. Try this on your own before inviting anyone else to do so: stand next to your horse at one end of an arena or small paddock and imagine her walking to the far side. Access

a visual image of being there, of feeling what it is like to walk with her and of seeing the two of you walking there together. When the time feels right, walk to the fence yourself and mentally invite your horse to follow. "Inviting" is different from "willing", which implies an element of authority and force, whereas an invitation feels warm and interesting. This might not work the first time you try it but don't give up. If you feel spacious and calm and keep practicing, over time (days, weeks or months) you will have her following you everywhere. The important thing to remember is not to turn back to look at her or to call out.

2. Again, practice this yourself if you have several horses together in a herd (i.e. two or more). Stand at the side of a fence and invite one of them to come to you. Do not call your horse, simply have a mental image of her approaching. Give it five minutes, and if she doesn't come, then call by name. If that still doesn't work, when walk to your horse and halter her by inviting her to put her head in the halter as you hold it under her nose. It is vital that you don't give up in frustration and "catch" your horse. There are three steps here: mental invitation from a distance, calling, and approaching. If you do all three in a calm state with no sense of urgency, eventually (even if it takes a year) your horse will come to you from mental imagery alone.

3. Ask a client (making sure you are also practiced at this) to walk a horse on a lead line while alternating the pace from medium, to slow and fast, in any order. Don't tell them how to do it, but simply suggest that they ask for the change of pace mentally rather than verbally or through physical means. Naturally, they will impart their intention unconsciously through changes in their own posture and

energy but that doesn't matter since intention will be the main driver.

4. If you have a horse that you have been working at liberty, invite a client to move him around while making changes of direction, possibly going over and around obstacles. It is likely that they will "loose" the horse from time to time but reassure them that's normal and not a failure. Question your client about what she or he recognizes internally that encourages the horse to respond to them. This is not a technique (although it can easily become one) so assure them that getting any response at all from the horse is all that's required. Even no response can lead to fruitful talk with your client. The aim is to recognize the kind and level of energy that works or doesn't work with a horse. If there is no response at all, reassure them that it's not failure either but is an opportunity to explore different energy levels and imagery.

One issue likely to arise in this work is the alignment of a client's body language with her intention. When we set things up so that attention is focused on mental processes it's very common for a client to forget that her body posture, movement and state of tension/relaxation send strong messages to a horse that could be a lie to her intention and imagery. When this seems to be the situation to you as practitioner, explore your client's somatic awareness, allowing her to explore possible solutions and different somatic states of being. All we need to do is ask a question such as, "I wonder what you could do with your body that matches your intention?" This is a powerful invitation that in my experience so often brings a client into a deeper somatic awareness. Remember though that a client's personal discovery is far more valuable than being shown what to do. This is about inviting awareness of the body-mind, not about teaching horsemanship. It's a fine distinction to make and is worth bearing in mind as a practitioner.

The next two chapters are about expanding the way we look at the world by opening up to a wider vision (literally and metaphorically) and by opening up space in the mind through meditation and mindfulness.

Footnote

1.   Tolle (2005) p. 52.

Chapter 21

Expanding into Spaciousness

English-speaking people, and possibly others too, use the concept of seeing for so many descriptors: "I *see* what you mean ... I can't *see* myself clear on that ... *see* if you can find a way ... let's *see* how it goes..." Vision as a metaphor for knowing is thoroughly embedded in the English language, which is something one soon realizes when talking with a sightless person. In this chapter I equate seeing (both as vision and metaphor) with awareness and attention, and argue that horses can teach us how to move beyond our limited habitual ways of breaking down experiences into small, manageable packages. Modern humans are so adept at concentrating on individual detail, often very small detail, that we can do so to the exclusion of the wider picture. As useful as it can be to focus on small details (and science does this in the extreme), it often happens at the expense and understanding of the wholeness of a situation.

This chapter focuses on recognizing that we have agency over the way we view our environments in a physical (and hence, metaphorical) sense that can expand our personal realities. The British psychoanalyst and educator Dr. Marion Milner in *A Life of One's Own*[1] searched through her own personal diaries of several decades for clues into the nature of happiness. Although her book was published almost a century ago in 1934, her insights from self-observation remain relevant and profound. She noticed that she had two quite different ways of perceiving visually: through what she called *narrow attention*, and through *wide attention*. Narrow attention, she characterized as selecting what serves our immediate interests while ignoring the rest. Milner recognized that narrow attention "saw everything in relation to something else, as a means to some end, [ensuring that] contentment was always in the future." Wide attention she characterized as a kind of perceiving that "wants nothing" but is available to take in the totality without seeking to attend to detail within a narrow focus. She describes how by chance she herself discovered the knack of holding wide attention, realizing that experiential delight arose from there. She discovered that many experiences have meaning only when considered as a whole and that she could take in the whole picture rather than focusing on small details when viewing paintings in an art exhibition, something which I have since verified for myself:

Gradually my mind settled down to complete absorption, oblivious to all but the harmonies of shape and colour which once again took on a life of their own and continued to grow out of the paint the longer I looked.[2]

While applying wide vision to art she felt she truly appreciated it and was fully emotionally engaged, whereas up to then she had viewed art through narrow attention in a futile attempt at understanding the work, which at best felt like a pretense.

Wide attention can be experienced through more senses than vision. As a lifelong musician I have only recently learned to listen to music without feeling compelled to identify the performers, genre, composer, structure, harmonies and other individual features that for so long I had regarded as necessary to consider. For most of my life I could not sit through a concert without my mind making educated responses to detail (which were never satisfying on an affective level), whereas now I am able to recall the wonder of the wholeness of sound that I experienced as a child. Returning to an analytical perspective always remains as an option to dip in and out of. What we really need is a balance between the two. To make the gear change to wide attention, listening becomes a form of meditation on the phenomenon of the full soundscape. To mentally put detail to one side while listening to music as a totality of experience involves the heart and soul in a fulfilling experience.

As hunter-gatherers of old, humans had to be good at focusing attention on single objects while at the same time being fully aware of their peripheral surroundings in case they inadvertently became some predator's lunch. Modern humans have inherited the ability to pointedly focus attention on a single task, idea or object, becoming so good at it that we are so much less adept at wider focus. For some people wider focus is largely a foreign experience since in modern life it is rarely called upon. We actively avoid using a wide vision in our urban environments, partly because there is no need to look any further than the next intersection, the computer in front of us or the things we do with our hands. Single-pointed focus is demanded in most employment situations as we have become single-minded specialists in both work and play. In prehistoric times as predators but also incidentally as prey we would naturally have shifted from wide vision to single-pointed focus as required.[3] These days we don't often employ wide vision in the physical sense unless we are on the ocean or walking in natural open spaces, but when we do it can come with an incredible sense of renewal for mind, body and soul.

In Western cultures, specialists who are highly skilled at doing one thing are usually more highly valued than generalists yet the latter calls on significant skills and organizational ability. I recall my university working years where managerial efforts to encourage interdisciplinary collaboration were, more often than not, met with lukewarm responses. It is rare (but not without possibility) for academics, steeped as they are in their own specialist areas, to see beyond their own domain and through cross-disciplinary cooperation come to deeper understandings and wider applications.

There is a famous psychological study that you have probably already come across, where experimental subjects were tasked with watching a video of a basketball game in which one team wore white shirts and the other black shirts. The task was to count the number of times the players in the white team had possession of the ball. In the middle of the game, a "gorilla" walks into the middle of the play, pounds his chest then leaves. More than half the observers failed to notice the gorilla, even when prompted afterwards. This dramatically illustrated how close attention (narrow focus) prevents humans from seeing important surrounding detail.[4] If our hunter-gatherer ancestors were equally bad at noticing detail around them I doubt that any of us would be here today.

Working with horses on the theme of taking a wider view (literally and metaphorically) shows us that we can train ourselves to see the bigger picture and consciously shift between that and single-pointed focus. It is clear when observing horses that they are expert at shifting from narrow focus to a wider view and that they switch from one to the other with ease. They also seem capable of fixing their attention on one single thing while maintaining wider awareness at the same time. They might be fully absorbed in a detail like a single blade of grass while simultaneously remaining hyperaware of their wider surroundings in case a hungry cougar comes for a visit. With eyes situated on the sides of their heads their survival capacity is enhanced through a wide range of vision. As grazers and browsers living in herds (even if only a "herd" of two in a domestic situation), they constantly survey their environment for mutual protection. They do this while calmly aware, utilizing their capacity for wide vision. By observing how they negotiate within their environment they model how we too can seamlessly shift focus from wide vision to single-pointed focus, and back.

While doing focus work with people I have become increasingly aware that problems are solved and dilemmas resolved much more readily and satisfactorily in wide vision awareness than in single-pointed thinking. In fact it was a client who initially showed me how horses teach us this valuable life-skill.

While working with a young woman, Lara, whose emotional issues prevent her from focusing on single tasks and following them through to completion, we talk for a while then I invite her to work with a horse. We focus on several tasks such as weaving between cones and going over and around obstacles but several difficulties arise because the horse isn't picking up on Lara's focus very well and shows frustration figuring out what she wants. Lara wonders whether providing leadership to a horse might translate to looking ahead to where she is going instead of directly in front of the horse's feet. She saw for herself that her focus was too short. The horse responds, showing her how much better leading works when Lara focuses ahead. However, there is still a certain lack of conviction from the horse and this leads us to a discussion of how horses encourage each other to move. Having observed the herd in several previous sessions she picks "energy" as a motivating force and decides to be conscious of her own energy as she asks the horse to walk with purpose and vitality. This works well for her so as a further experiment she chooses to be aware of expanding her range of energy as she leads the gelding around in an exploration of expansiveness. This wakes him up (a laid-back horse who uses no more energy than necessary) as he responds with increasing enthusiasm.

Now a metaphor emerges that relates directly to Lara's feelings of inertia when it comes to her work and home life. She walks her horse around again to explore sensations of expansion as she looks both forward and upward, noticing the canopy of 200-year-old trees forming a perfect dome shape surrounding the working space. Having never noticed this before she realizes that she has just experienced the wider vision of horses. This gives us many images and analogies to work with in subsequent sessions, especially to do with focus, commitment to what she is doing in the moment and extending her life force into any space she occupies while returning to single-pointed focus as needed.

Serendipitously, as I began to work with clients on wider focus I came across Dr. Paul Holman's book *Living Space* where he thoroughly explores concepts and practices of spatial awareness. This book is well worth exploring in itself but one concept I have found especially useful in this context is remembering that we live in three dimensions while occupying a central point within life's unity. Holman points out that "consciousness is the central fact of significance and worth, and that we are always standing at the centre, both physically and existentially." He goes further to explain that a vital aspect of discovering spaciousness is to "STAY AT THE CENTRE" (his caps) as we manage the directions of up and down, left and right, back and forward.[5] He offers a number of exercises to help us realize where we stand within the three dimensions (and six directions) and points out that the one direction we are most unaware of is the one behind us. He is quite right of course and I am reminded of this often when my Labrador dog, who loves to wander freely around the farm when it is least convenient to the humans working on it, has perfected the art of sneaking up behind me and rushing past when I open the gate to our enclosed living space. When

I consider the ability of the horse to see within virtually 360 degrees I realize how limited I am in knowing my environment fully. We can't develop eyes in the backs of our heads but we can use our other senses like hearing and general awareness to develop a knowledge of what is happening behind us. And there is plenty of anecdotal evidence that we can feel another person staring at the back of our heads, or someone silently following us. If this is the case it is neither the sixth nor the seventh sense (as defined in Chapter 4), but something else altogether that is beyond the purview of this book.

An exercise I practice myself and give to people who feel directionless or stuck is to emulate the horse's wide vision (although for humans we are talking about 180° rather than 360°) then return to single-pointed focus. This can take several different forms with one being to initially work through a grounding exercise so that a person is aware of where they are situated, then to offer a guided meditation to expand their awareness down through their feet and up through the top of their head. Your imagination can come up with various ways of suggesting this but one that Holman suggests that I have found effective is "breathing" through either the top of the head or through the feet. It is a beautiful way to experience health emanating from the breath and travelling through the body. For spatial awareness left and right, ahead and behind, I find that listening to sound works well. The suggestion that we become aware of the specific direction of sounds as though we are experiencing a 3D sonic map around us is hugely revealing of where we feel we are situated within our immediate environment. This can be accompanied by reminders during the meditation that the person, meanwhile, remains at the center of experience.[6]

I might choose to follow spatial awareness meditation with an invitation to walk a horse on line as the client takes a position next to the horse's head while maintaining a soft forward and upward visual focus. While maintaining that position without getting ahead of or behind the horse the task is to be aware of the horse's head through peripheral vision. It is difficult for most people to resist the urge to glance at a horse's head, or to fixate on what's directly in front of their feet, so it's not something that can be accomplished in one session. This works best if I also walk in parallel on the other side of the client so that their peripheral vision is in balance on both sides. In preparation for such an exercise I might employ Holman's suggestion of holding two outstretched hands in front of one's eyes then slowly move both outstretched arms to the side while tracking them without turning the head or moving the eyes. It is also good to ask the client to walk between two horses in this exercise but I would reserve that for people who are very confident and for horses who are totally trustworthy and familiar with being led as a pair.

Why would we want to develop awareness of our peripheral vision? Because it can lead to totally fresh experiences of the world. Scientist Dr. Iain McGilchrist in his book *The Master and his Emissary* points out that it is the right hemisphere of the brain alone that deals with the peripheral field of vision and that also tends to be the hemisphere that deals with new experience.[7] This means that by consciously applying wider vision exercises the right hemisphere of the brain counteracts, or at least balances, the logical, analytical left hemisphere that deals with detail.

Since practicing wider vision I have enjoyed frequent experiences of spontaneous spaciousness. I have always had an eye for detail and would typically look closely at a leaf or bark on a tree for instance but since consciously activating wider vision I can take in whole patterns rather than detail; the whole canvas rather than the brush strokes. The detail is not sacrificed though, since it becomes part of the lively pattern along with all other details with no single piece taking priority of attention over another. There's nothing wrong with concentrating on a detail such as a single leaf, but to mentally stand back and take in leaves moving together in a coherent pattern on a tree and then to see trees forming a single coherent pattern together brings an experience of vibrancy in which all inner commentary ceases.

Both Holman and Milner highly value spacious awareness, promising that it has the capacity to lead to new visions and experiences of reality, as do I. Horses experience spaciousness as their default: simply by being themselves they add a depth of experience that we wouldn't normally have. If we let them, horses can bring to the relationship either what is missing in us or that which is dormant. Through such experience there can be a sense of completing each other through relationship. Dr. Janet Jones in her book *Horse Brain, Human Brain* applies her neuroscience knowledge of the human and equine brain to riding and training horses, and suggests that "horse training is partly a process of teaching your mount to depend on you for prefrontal decisions." Although we are not considering riding in this instance, it is a lovely way to say that we complete horses in some sense.[8] And conversely we could say that they complete us! This applies regardless of what we are doing with a horse, whether we are riding, working with them on the ground or observing. Another way of expressing this is to consider that when we are with a horse we are in relationship within a common environment.

Allow yourself to be led by your imagination and intuition while exploring spatial awareness with yourself and your clients. By remembering to do this in small ways every day your awareness of vibrant patterning in the environment (both natural and human-made) will increase as the right hemisphere of the brain gets more use. One way (but not the only way) to find the space for such exploration is to lead yourself and clients into meditation in the presence of horses. This is the subject of the next chapter.

Footnotes

1. Milner (1934/2011).
2. Milner (1934/2011) p. 80.
3. Numerous books and websites categorize horses as prey animals, and humans as predators, but the predator-prey binary, in my opinion, is too black and white a concept. Humans are put together physically to be good hunters and we are predominantly predators, but not entirely, since we too can be hunted.
4. Chris Chabris and Dan Simons conducted the original "Invisible Gorilla Experiment" in 1999 that has since been published in their 2010 book, *The Invisible Gorilla: How Our Intuitions Deceive Us*.
5. Holman (2018) pp. 205–6.
6. Holman (2018) p. 57.
7. McGilchrist (2009) p. 40.
8. Jones (2020) p. 183.

Chapter 22

Meditation and Mindfulness

Meditation is both conceptually simple and accessible to everyone. The difficulties are remembering to do it, not regarding it as something to achieve, and realizing that the purpose of it is to increase awareness of inner processes so that our lives are not controlled by unconscious thought patterns. Simply observing how repetitive and pervasive our thinking patterns are, and how much space they take up in our being, is in itself transformative as it leads us out of unhelpful mind traps and into awareness of *what is*. We can see our random thoughts and acknowledge them while choosing not to run away into a story, in other words by disidentifying with them.

Whichever formal meditation technique you use, whether it's awareness of the breath, gazing at the flame of a candle or reciting a mantra (silently or aloud), the effect can be much the same. We usually need some sort of meditation object, and that object can be anything, including a horse. As we concentrate on the meditation object, we become aware of intruding thoughts which we can regard as merely passing clouds. Thoughts are not something to get rid of entirely no matter how random or pointless they seem, although some meditation teachers take the absence of thought as the primary objective. Moments without thought when they do arise, are peaceful and spacious but they are unlikely to recur through trying because effort brings with it the effect of creating more thought while encouraging self-judgment. Trying for a particular state of mind is an example of single-pointedness and is, in the end, counterproductive if what we are wishing for is spaciousness. However, if thought is simply accepted as a natural mental phenomenon with no judgment of whether it is good or bad, right or wrong, the mind can be brought back gently to the meditation object whenever we notice it has wandered.

You might choose to practice meditation formally for 10 to 20 minutes every day, and/or you might choose to use micro-practices. One micro-practice I like is using whatever "down time" comes my way such as when I'm stuck in a supermarket queue. The meditation objects can be all the things I see around me such as the groceries in my shopping trolley and the people walking and standing nearby. Or I might concentrate on inner body awareness. Eckhart Tolle drew my attention to this practice through his podcasts[1] and I find it such a healthy exercise since it takes me away from frustratingly watching the clock and wishing myself forward in time into a better moment. What's more, with present-moment practice, by the time I wheel my groceries to the car I feel calm and at peace rather than unsettled and bothered. Sadly, humans can spend their whole lives wishing they were in a better moment than the one currently experienced and I must admit that at least half of my life followed that pattern.

In a traffic jam or supermarket queue, once you have noticed yourself slipping into a mind frame of frustration, another healthy option is to put your attention onto somatic awareness. You will most likely notice at least one of a churning stomach, tense shoulders, jiggling legs, shallow breathing, clenched hands and tapping fingers. Simply noticing these things helps us to release them, and the more we practice in this manner the more attuned we become somatically. We become attuned to our bodies as reliable teachers. This is important because if I notice that I have tense shoulders for instance I can ask myself whether I am worried or upset about something, and if the answer is yes I can recognize the origin of the thought and let it go before it becomes a problem.

Horses are great allies in the meditation process. They help us in two ways: firstly, we can invite a horse to be the point of focus as we meditate on one or more aspect of him through our primary senses. This can be a visual feature such as his beautiful soft brown eye, the nutty smell around his neck or the texture of his velvet-smooth coat. In this way the horse as the focus of meditation becomes the mantra. I will explain later how this can be extended to working with clients. Another way to meditate with a horse is to practice more traditional meditations while in their presence. What do horses have to add to this process? For a start they are very grounded beings and if we quieten our minds they sense this. They are *of* nature just as we are, and despite 6000 years of domesticated life with humans they have not lost touch with their innate states of being. Simply through their presence they lead us to a place where we renew our interconnectedness with nature.

At the Earthhorse Aotearoa farm there is a huge native tree (Totora) estimated to be 250 years old in an area where the horses often choose to shelter. This has a large protruding root perfectly shaped for reclining upon. It is my favorite "do nothing" place and often I sit there and meditate as the herd wanders around. At times one horse will choose to stand close by, head down, eyes half closed as though in meditation with me.

While meditating under the tree for about ten minutes I get the idea that I ought to open my eyes. I see seven horses standing in front of me in a semicircle with their heads down as if asleep. In a profound moment of feeling totally at peace I know I belong intrinsically to nature. More than that, I *am* nature and there is no separation between me and a horse or a tree. I want to keep that special moment going but I see immediately by the horse's slightly more awake reactions

217

that trying to hold on to an experience causes it to dissipate. Nonetheless, something has shifted within, and eventually I move. The horses respond by gently wandering down the hill to their water trough.

Mindfulness, a practice derived from Buddhism but also practiced in most world religions by other names such as contemplation, is meditation on the move. I like to call it "meditation on the hoof". In essence it is conscious perception of the present moment, of the here and now, as experienced through the primary senses without interference from unnecessary mental commentary. Mindfulness is a practice in which you remind yourself of where you are and how events are unfolding in the present. Being mindful doesn't mean that you will automatically do everything slowly and in a dreamy state. That's not it at all; that's pretend mindfulness. You can do whatever you do at any pace you like so long as you aren't directing your thought energy into the future, into getting to some other place, or into worrying about something unrelated.

There's a famous story of a Zen master who was asked by one of his students, "What is Zen?" His reply was, "Chopping wood, carrying water," meaning that enlightenment or being fully awake in a spiritual sense is the result of being aware moment to moment of whatever you are doing without complaint and without desire to be somewhere else. It also means that while chopping wood there is no need to worry about carrying water, and when carrying water there is no need to worry about chopping wood.

Everyday mindfulness becomes easier as we use it and it makes our days feel pleasantly longer and more interesting. We notice things we would otherwise ignore and we learn to enjoy things that we might have dismissed as mere stepping stones to something apparently more meaningful. Once it becomes habitual, mindfulness leads us to delight in the simplest of things. Chopping wood and carrying water *is* meaningful. Everything we do and experience is meaningful.

How can we develop mindfulness? Working with horses helps enormously for the simple reason that we need to be fully aware of what is happening for reasons of safety. If there is need for awareness it is most definitely when we are with horses together with clients. Mindfulness is the key to being aware around horses: we need our mind on the job rather than somewhere else. Megan Kirby of the Equine Psychotherapy Institute (Australia) teaches that a practitioner's awareness is the most important aspect of safety in the equine assisted and learning space.[2] That assumes that the practitioner knows how to be mindful and aware, and of course this takes some practice. If you are a practitioner maybe you have noticed how calm and spacious you feel after you have worked with another person and a horse. That's what working with mindful awareness does for you but we can practice present-moment awareness (or mindfulness) anywhere and at any time. To bring myself into a mindful space, I find it useful to ask these questions: "What am I feeling in my body? What is in my entire field of awareness right now? What thoughts can I let go of?" Stopping to ask yourself such questions for a few seconds at various times of the day is a micro-meditation that takes you out of thought preoccupation.

Practicing meditating with horses

Whatever form of meditation you practice, do it sometimes with your horse/s in the paddock, arena or sitting in the barn. Work with the breath, a mantra or sensory awareness as you sit in silence with your horse/s. Leave your eyes open to keep safe and don't be surprised if your horses join you and appear to go to sleep. If you only have one minute to spare for this, then use that one minute. There are no rules, just honest intentions.

Mindfulness is essentially taking notice of what goes on around us, what we are doing, feeling and thinking without turning it into a story in which we lose ourselves. We can learn to be aware of our thoughts as objects in the mind instead of getting involved in them. Take note of how most thoughts appear in your mind of their own volition and see that most of them have nothing much to offer and are irrelevant to what is happening right now. Unless we are actively trying to solve a problem that the mind can deal with effectively, most thoughts are repetitive, circular and generally useless. Without those repetitive and capturing internal conversations we would be at peace. If thought stops entirely for a while it doesn't mean that we have suddenly become mindless or stupid. The opposite is true. Intellectual discoveries and creativity emerge much more effectively from spaciousness in which thoughts, when they arise, are simply treated as background noise. No doubt you will have noticed that if you are intensely interested in a book or something on your smartphone, you cease to hear what is being said around you, or if you have the radio on you fail to notice it. The brain is not capable of processing two streams of sound at once, so it switches back and forth from one to another depending on what the conscious mind decides is important enough to pay attention to. The same applies to thoughts. If we are concentrating on something we are doing, thoughts take a back seat. They are still there in the background and we can pay them attention if we choose to, but if we "give them no mind" they are simply like a radio with the volume turned down.

Can you recall moments when something happened that was so astounding that you stopped in your tracks and all thought ceased? If you remind yourself of those moments you might remember feeling intensely alive. Such moments of aliveness will continue to happen the more we take note of them. We can't banish useless repetitive thoughts (they will continue to be a distraction), but the more we consciously notice them while choosing not to identify with them, the less sway they hold over us. If we notice that we have been idly thinking about a specific subject for the last few minutes, if the thoughts are not useful, noticing them as objects passing through your mind is sufficient for change to begin. If you simply notice the thought, it loses its power over your mind. However, what we must be careful of in mindfulness practice is not being too "single minded" or single-pointed about it. If we make any kind of *effort* to be mindful, we are simply adding more stress. Rather, it needs to have a sense of letting go, of letting be, of *just this*.

During formal meditation in which we watch our breath, recite a mantra, or look at an object we become very aware of thoughts demanding our conscious attention. We notice how irritating and demanding of attention some of them can be. This is not failure, it's normal. Noticing them, labelling them and returning to the meditation object is the "doing" of meditation that exercises a group of mental "muscles" that help us become better at noticing, acknowledging and moving on. This noticing is something we can practice at any time, not just during formal meditation. In fact it is possible to regard one's whole day as a meditation practice.

A gentle way into meditation is to observe your breathing while either counting your breath or reciting a mantra such as "be still". This is not some sort of magical process but is simply the *noticing* that enables us to step out of repetitively demanding thought. During meditation you quickly discover that your mind chatters away more or less continuously and that you forget to notice your mantra, counting, breath or whatever your meditation object is. Discovering our busy monkey-mind can be irritating, but that's not the point. It helps us realize that *we are not our thoughts*, we are the *observer* of our thoughts.[3] The practice is to continually return our awareness to the meditation object without self-criticism. Eventually we get better at it or rather, I should say, we become accustomed to the process as our minds become quieter and we find ourselves carrying the ability into daily life to be still and at peace.

If you wish to practice meditation formally, the ideal is to find experts to teach you how to do it even though in essence it is quite simple. The reason I recommend finding a meditation teacher is because it's just too easy to complicate meditation through perfectionism and self-criticism. Without a teacher, after a few weeks of trying you may end up concluding that meditation doesn't work or that you are not any good at it, whereas truly anyone can do it. It is also a powerful practice to meditate within a group. If I had done this when I'd started meditating in the 1970s I would have avoided many pitfalls. It is just too easy to lose track of the point of it and to let it fall into being an activity of "achieving a good meditation", which besides being counterproductive is the exact opposite of what meditation really is. The space you are moving into contains no "shoulds" or judgments of any kind. I would also recommend finding yoga, qigong or tai chi classes that suit you since they beautifully combine meditation with breath and movement.[4] Then there is mindfulness with horses:

Linda, a woman in her mid-fifties, comes to work with our horses because she feels as though she has been "dead inside for at least a decade". She isn't sure whether people have souls but she figures that if they do, hers has long since moved to another country. Being a devoted career woman she has given her life to her work and now feels as though life is empty and pointless and she can't focus her mind on any one thing. She wants to find some meaning and is keen to learn to meditate but finds she can't keep her mind on her breath or a mantra. At the same time her inner voice tells her it is all a bit pointless and probably doesn't work anyway. To start with I suggest a mindfulness meditation where the emphasis is on developing awareness of all sensations, more than on a single phenomenon like the breath. I suggest to her that horses are in this sort of mindful state most of the time and that we can see this when we watch them grazing. So as a learning exercise we spend twenty minutes in silence watching the herd graze and I ask her to describe what she sees: "They are all eating grass, pushing it around and picking out bits. The brown one makes a snorting noise, but the other horses ignore it. Then he eats again. The light-colored horse shakes his whole body then goes back to eating. Another one swishes his tail and his friend moves to another spot to graze. They are all moving their ears about while eating and it looks like they see and hear everything around them. One horse brings his head up, curious about a sound that the others ignore. I see the breeze blowing in their manes and I feel it on my skin as well. One horse scratches an itch then puts his nose back on the grass. Another comes to sniff my hand, then walks away and joins the others. Time passed quickly and I feel incredibly calm and peaceful. It's not boring looking at horses. It reminds me of the mindfulness lesson I had earlier. It almost looks as though the horses are meditating and 'relax and eat' is their mantra. When they are distracted they don't become obsessed like I am by my thoughts."

This turned out to be a useful mindfulness practice for Linda as she put a major part of her awareness on the horses, giving her a break from her self-focused incessant thoughts. She came up with two ideas she could take from the observation exercise: one was noticing that she was perfectly capable of keeping her attention acutely on what she sensed in her environment, and the other was that she noticed how quickly horses let go of whatever grabs their attention if there is no need for reaction. I introduced her to the phrase "go back to grazing" and she was pleased to take away that concept to remind herself to let go of negative and obsessive thinking. She also volunteered that it seemed to her that horses are "soulful" and that if they have an inner space called "soul" then there's no reason why she can't have a soul-space, even if only as a comforting metaphor.

As suggested earlier it is impossible for humans to access actual and full reality. Beings can only ever experience relative and partial reality: relative to the sensory capabilities of each species, relative to their cultures, relative to their personal histories and biases, and relative to the brain architecture of the species. It is fair to say that there is not one single reality but many realities all depending upon varying conditions. There is ant reality, cat reality, horse reality and human reality, and given that there is neuro-physical variation among individual humans it's fair to say there is also individual reality. So if we don't access some sort of universal reality we might wonder whether it is possible to access the universal soul, or even one's individual soul. The best spiritual prophets, sages and advisors tell us that we don't access the soul by thinking about it or by accumulating knowledge. It can only be accessed as lived experience. But to say we "access" our soul is not quite right either. We *are* souls, so to own that truth all we need is to clear away that which obscures the soul. The task is to still the mind and allow space between thoughts through meditation and mindfulness practices, thus allowing a parting of the heavy curtains of ego. Horses, whose egos are negligible compared with humans, literally don't have the capacity to obscure their minds with conditioned thinking as we do. A well-adjusted horse (i.e. not mentally damaged through maltreatment) shows us how it looks to react honestly within his environment without ulterior motives, emotional baggage and neuroses. Horses have the capacity to show us how it is to live from the foundation of the soul. Look at horses in the pasture and you will see that they are masters of stillness. They have no problem at all standing in the warm sun or the cool shade doing nothing for hours on end. They live from the soul and reside in stillness. They have no need for entertainment or mental diversion. If you want to know how to live from the soul, ask the horse to teach you how to be still. This sort of experiencing can't be put into words, rather, we learn and grow through observing from an open mind.

There are many ways to meditate with horses. The simplest but very powerful way is to sit in the vicinity of one or more horses while practicing a traditional meditation such as following the breath. This is a more powerful practice than meditating in your own home, because the horses participate too. They bring their energy into the process and meditate with you because for them it is their natural state of being.

Walking meditation can also be practiced with a horse. This can be done in two ways (although with imagination you will find other ways too). First, is to walk your horse on a lead line in a paddock or arena, going wherever he wants to go, accepting whatever pace he wants to set, short of actually stopping. The practice for you is acceptance, being in the moment and letting go of goal setting. Another practice is to walk with your horse on line while matching steps (left with fore-left, right with fore-right). Start at a reasonable pace then gradually slow down through intention of communicating energetically rather than through putting any kind of restraint on the halter. During the walk be aware of your own physical processes as each foot moves and takes the weight, then as each foot leaves the ground.

Breathing exercises with horses can take several forms too, but the one I like the most is to lean next to the horse's torso in such a way that I feel his breath, matching my breathing to his.

Then there is sharing space while doing nothing for five minutes. This is possibly the most rewarding practice of all. Be aware of everything in your and your horse's sense environment: all sounds, sights, smells and skin sensations. He will experience them differently from you because our sense organs and his have differing sensitivities, but you are sharing the same environment nonetheless. Notice how you are thinking about what is happening between you. Do you think you are with your horse or that he is with you? Are you observing him or is he observing you? Are you the subject looking at the object or is it the other way around? Can you sense that you share beingness, that you share the essence of life?

Practicing expansion

You are already part of the universe, but you might believe that your being stops at the outer surface of your skin. On one level you know that can't possibly be true since when we hear and see things from a distance through our primary senses it is as though we are at the origin of the sight or sound. Take the experience to another level and be aware of everything currently happening on the surface of your skin as you stand with your horse. Can you feel the weight of your clothes and the gentle breeze on bare skin? Are you aware of the ambient temperature? Then extend your awareness to six inches out from the skin encapsulating your body. Imagine it being transparent and infinitely flexible and then extend your awareness out further to 12 inches. Extend your awareness to include your horse, the barn, and the trees or whatever is around you. Extend further to the natural boundaries of the land, then look up to the sky and extend as far as you can see. Finally, feel into what you can't see. Stay there for a while, then come back ... gradually.[5]

Footnotes

1. Eckhart Tolle's podcasts are available at: https://eckharttolle.com (Accessed 1 April 2023).

2. Meg Kirby, https://www.equinepsychotherapy.net.au (Accessed 1 April 2023).

3. There is more to us than thoughts and the observer, but to separate and identify the two is a good start for awakening practice. Other parts of ourselves include the inner critic and the ego but none of these parts are really separate and autonomous entities. Running beneath it all is the True Self, the Soul, the Atman, or Universal Spaciousness, call it what you will, which we can feel from time to time during meditation and during moments of awe.

4. For another inroad into somatic-based meditation I recommend the book by Dr. Tamara Russell (2015) *Mindfulness in Motion*.

5. This is a practice I adapted from Ram Dass podcasts: https://www.ramdass.org/

Chapter 23

Balancing Yin and Yang

The principle of yin and yang that is central to ancient Chinese Taoist philosophy teaches that all things in life are in balance and that opposites sit together within a continuum of mutuality. Yin is feminine, dark, receptive and negative; yang is positive, bright, active and masculine. The interaction of these two characterizations is both the expression and underlying principle of the totality of life. Every human being has the capacity for both yin and yang, feminine and masculine, positive and negative, dark and bright, receptive and active, and the more these seemingly opposing energies and characteristics are accepted as mutually supportive the more balanced our lives are.

Through observing nature we see the interconnectedness of all things and how everything we do, say and think depends on everything around us. Nothing can possibly exist alone because everything affects everything else. Even thoughts (because they are energy) can and do change the world. They either add to the burden of the world or they ease it. We can take this further and see that we are more than dependent on our environment: we are beings with an environment. We are nothing at all without an environment within which to live and breathe. We are inseparably part of the *totality* of being.

I stand next to my horse, sensing that it is not his skin and mine that define where we begin and end; it is the physical space between us that intermingles our assumed boundaries as individual beings. I have a felt sense that we share that space equally as though it is merely a soft cloud of convenience between us. The cloud belongs to me, and it belongs to the horse. It defines the beginning and the ending of our two form identities but there is no place within the cloud that is uniquely mine and no place that is uniquely of the horse. For a moment I know that we are together as one.

Both yin and yang are essential for life, relationships and healthy living. The most successful (i.e. well-functioning) human beings, incorporate both yin and yang (whether they name them as such or not) and experience them within a continuum rather than as opposite energies. In a binary system such as gender, we might consciously identify with one end of the binary or the other (although there is choice to manifest at any point within the binary) but regardless of where we are in that system we recognize and respect those at the other extreme.

In the horse world the mare and the stallion beautifully embody yin and yang but they are adept at modifying their yin-yang characteristics when needed for the sake of the herd. Yin and yang principles are readily observable in action in a herd of horses. A prominent example comes from the lead mare who sometimes drives the herd from the back and at other times leads from the front, taking the herd to water, feed and safety. Other horses in a group will also take yin and yang roles as they express their desire to dominate an area of pasture and as they see various needs arising in the herd. Typically, there will be at least one horse in a group of grazers acting as a sentinel (taking either a yin or a yang role depending on the situation), roles that are also swapped freely within the group. People express both yin and yang qualities when dealing with horses: taking on a yin characteristic we ask a horse to come to us in a draw, then taking on a yang characteristic we drive him away. The joy comes when we can move between yin and yang (draw and drive), flowing freely between the two in a dance with our horse.

There are two main ways I like to explore yin and yang concepts with horses. One is to invite clients to observe horses in a group as they graze or eat from piles of hay as I ask them to write down all the expressions of yin and yang that they observe. People can be amazed to see that any single horse expresses both qualities, moving seamlessly from one to another. For humans who like to categorize themselves as this or that it can be quite a freeing experience. Horses don't need to assign themselves strict categories to find out who they are.

Another way I like to explore yin and yang is to invite clients to work at liberty in a round pen. A horse able to walk calmly with someone positioned beside his head or neck is likely to handle the lead rope being taken off and work at liberty in a round pen. In equine assisted practices the aim of liberty work is not to have the horse obey a human's commands, nor to encourage him to walk with or follow the client. If that happens naturally, all well and good, but it doesn't need to be the aim. Working horses at liberty as an aspect of horsemanship is stimulating but for equine assisted work we are looking at a different concept. For one thing there is nothing to be achieved while working at liberty in the equine assisted space. The advantage of liberty is that horse and human are on an equal footing without the rope between them (so they are in a sense naked), and a client's emotions and feelings will intensify as a result. The practitioner's job is to track and help deepen emotions and insights through inquiry with the client.

The two exercises below are helpful in practicing being relaxed in the balancing of both polarities.

Exercise 1

Allow your client to discover how she can move a horse from one space to another. Avoid showing her how to do it since it is empowering for people to discover this principle for themselves, but if it doesn't work the first time there would be plenty of room for questioning how she feels about the task. Lead your client towards finding her own solutions.

Practitioner to client: Without either using your voice or touching the horse, move him from the arena into the round pen. Find a way to do this with kindness and without arousing fear or using force. All you will have by way of equipment is an unattached lead rope to wave gently towards the horse as you feel you need to. See if you can "ask" your horse rather than "tell" him what you want. Be aware of what difference it makes where you stand in relation to your horse. Be aware of how much energy you need to project towards the horse. Be aware of your intention, focus and body language.

Exercise 2

This exercise at liberty (no rope or halter) is a well-known horsemanship practice whereby a horse is trained to stay out on the circle until the person invites him in. We use it in the learning context with clients as a way for them to experience their own yin and yang qualities and assess whether they feel them in balance. The horses are not asked to do any more than from one to three complete circles. The horses we invite into this exercise are familiar with the task so there is no sense of the client training the horse. The beauty of the exercise is that the client discovers how accurately and instantly the horse reads their energy levels.

Practitioner to client: I invite you to go into the round pen and ask for connection with your horse. Before going into the round pen, observe the horse and send your intention to him by way of a greeting. Take your time with this. Once you are in the round pen, with a soft focus and a relaxed body position keep your attention on the horse and be aware of your breathing. Before you start, wait until you can breathe slow and relaxed and wait until your horse is in a similar state. Using the lead rope for movement, gently send your horse away from you so that he moves in a circle, then after one complete circle relax your energy, turn your back on him and walk back to the center of the circle. He will most likely follow you. Keep turning away, look at the ground and relax. Once he comes up to you give him a rub or a scratch and relax with him.

Reflection

- How did you express yin and yang with your horse?
- How did the draw and the drive feel different?
- Were you equally comfortable with both?
- Were both equally effective?
- How do you use yin and yang in your everyday life?
- Do you think you are predominantly yin or predominantly yang?
- How can you experiment with accessing the less-used side of yourself?

There is no right or wrong with these exercises in terms of getting the horse to perform, rather, a client's awareness of their own yin and yang qualities gives them a playful tool for exploring personal qualities. They can explore their willingness to communicate through give and take, through leading and following, through changing energy levels, through conscious intention, and through kindness and compassion.

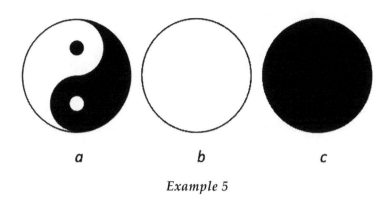

a　　　　　*b*　　　　　*c*

Example 5

Example 5(a): Shows the yin-yang symbol. It is a beautifully balanced design with a wealth of embedded meaning. Yin and yang are nestled together as two identical elegant shapes in reverse and retrograde positions relative to each other. Yin (black) delineates yang (white) and yang delineates yin. Yin has a little bit of yang in her by way of a small white dot and yang has a little bit of yin in him by way of a small black dot. Neither is exclusively yin or exclusively yang and they both need each other to make a complete whole.

Example 5(b): All of yin is removed. Yang has no shape without yin. The black circle circumference is there for convenience to distinguish yang from the white background, but without this arbitrary boundary, yang doesn't exist. Yang as white on white (like with like) is invisible and formless.

Example 5(c): All of yang is removed. Yin has no shape without yang. If the solid black sphere was on black paper yin would not exist. Yin as black on black (like with like) is invisible and formless.

In the full yin-yang symbol everything is in balance: black mirrors, supports and delineates white and *vice versa*. There is no beginning or end to any part of the symbol. It is interactive, inclusive and mutually supportive.

Accepting and exploring your own yin and yang qualities can only occur within an attitude of acceptance and of realizing that these aspects of ourselves are not in competition with each other but are complementary. Although it is useful to think of ourselves as containing many parts, the pathway to wholeness and spaciousness requires us to accept them all.

Chapter 24

Accepting the Good with the Bad

We live in a binary world of day and night, left and right, up and down, hot and cold, but in the West we tend to polarize by identifying with one end of a binary over another without realizing it is impossible to experience one end of a binary without taking account of the other. For instance, light and dark are intimately connected since without one there cannot be the other; music would not exist if it weren't for the silences between notes; we wouldn't understand pleasure were it not for pain; and the positive end of a magnet would not exist if there were not also a negative end. Opposites don't sit in ruthless competition with each other, they support each other and we experience them differently according to how we identify with them.

We naturally want good things to happen in our lives but without the experience of bad we wouldn't know what good is. Furthermore, good and bad are stories we tell ourselves. We might interpret something that happens as bad at one time but afterwards see that it has led to something useful or good. Recognizing this helps us reassess our personal stories. Sometimes we also tell ourselves something is wrong because we need to feel sorry for ourselves or we want to criticize others for their actions. Then there are times when something good that we have been striving towards finally manifests (such as a new relationship or new job) only to discover months or years later that it is not making us happy. If we think about all the bad and good things in our lives we might see that they are fluid concepts that change with time. Here is a Taoist lesson of the relative nature of good and bad. It is a 2000-year-old story of the good (and bad) fortune that follows a farmer's loss of his horse.

> *Once upon a time there was a Chinese farmer whose horse ran away. That evening, all of his neighbors came around to commiserate. They said, "We are so sorry to hear your horse has run away. This is most unfortunate." The farmer said, "Maybe." The next day the horse came back bringing seven wild horses with it, and in the evening everybody came back and said, "Oh, isn't that lucky. What a great turn of events. You now have eight horses!" The farmer again said, "Maybe."*
>
> *The following day his son tried to break one of the horses, and while riding it, he was thrown and broke his leg. The neighbors then said, "Oh dear, that's too bad," and the farmer responded, "Maybe." The next day the conscription officers came around to conscript people into the army, and they rejected his son because he had a broken leg. Again all the neighbors came around and said, "Isn't that great!" Again, he said, "Maybe."*
>
> *The whole process of nature is an integrated process of immense complexity, and it's really impossible to tell whether anything that happens in it is good or bad—because you never know what will be the consequence of the misfortune; or, you never know what will be the consequences of good fortune.*[1]

Right and wrong is another polar pairing that gets humankind into a lot of trouble. All arguments, whether of a personal nature or between one nation and another, come from the assumption that both parties assume they are right. If we are honest, we see ourselves doing this all the time as we assume that our opinions are more than opinions. We think they are defined as the truth by our own experience, understanding and values. But we forget that our experiences and understandings are always limited, and that our values, while they suit us, might not suit others. We forget that our point of view and that of others can often coexist and that we can agree to be different. When we put things into definite categories it not only makes us judgmental and defensive of our mental positions it also divides our mind into separate and conflicting parts. Polarization is a form of insanity from living with conflict in our individual psyches, and this habit of living through conflict has not only infected human society it has also resulted in many an international conflict.

> One evening an old Cherokee told his grandson about a battle that goes on inside people. He said, "My son, the battle is between two wolves inside us all. One is Evil. It is anger, envy, jealousy, sorrow, regret, greed, arrogance, self-pity, guilt, resentment, inferiority, lies, false pride, superiority, and ego. The other is good. It is joy, peace, love, hope, serenity, humility, kindness, benevolence, empathy, generosity, truth, compassion, and faith." The grandson thought about it for a minute and then asked his grandfather: "Which wolf wins?" The old Cherokee simply replied, "The one you feed."[2]

When we consider good and bad we so often carry into that space assumptions that we should always end up with the good, the best and the perfect. We judge other people from the perspective of this assumption, as we do horses. Not being able to accept the imperfections of individual horses has led to many a horse being rejected as not good enough and sold on. We probably all know people with the funds to buy an expensive well-bred horse for competition only to discover that he or she has an unfortunate habit or fault. Instead of working on that habit or fault the poor horse is so often passed on. It must be the horse's fault if they are not performing to the highest standards, right? But sometimes a competitor will give an unlikely horse a chance. Charisma, a horse ridden by the New Zealand equestrian Mark Todd in the 1980s was not initially regarded as a competition prospect. He was only fifteen hands high and tended to be overweight, hence his nickname "Podge", but under Mark Todd's tutorage and sportsmanship Charisma went on to win gold at the 1984 and 1988 Olympics. We far too easily give up on horses, as well as on other people and ourselves, with little idea of the potential we are missing out on.

Do horses have concepts of right and wrong, good and bad? They have preferences of course and will avoid certain things but since they are not driven by word-based thought they don't think narratively or in binaries. They avoid pain and discomfort but in all other respects (and often for pain too) they are masters of acceptance. Horses accept what *is* because it is vital to their survival. They can't afford to spend their energy on past, future or denial. Animals do suffer of course but they don't get involved in a commentary about fairness and causes. Horses have evolved to know it serves them better to reserve their energy for the real possibility of immediate flight or fight. If they hadn't evolved this way they would have died out long ago. And whatever does happen they accept as having happened. (Which doesn't mean they forget. They simply don't dwell on what has happened.)

Acceptance is the way out of polarized thinking such as good *versus* bad, or right *versus* wrong. Acceptance does not mean that you necessarily like what has happened or that the current situation is comfortable. What it does mean is accepting the inevitability of a situation and that includes accepting our emotional response. What has happened, has happened and can't unhappen even if we are able to mitigate the circumstances somewhat. A practice that epitomizes the principle of acceptance of what is, is the first step of Alcoholics Anonymous that requires an admission from the person seeking release from their drinking problem that they accept they are "powerless over alcohol". Without that single admission the recovering alcoholic would before long entertain ideas that they have their drinking habit under control or that they could safely step into moderation (even if they have tried and failed with that strategy numerous times). Embracing something seemingly negative like the AA first step with its paradoxical acceptance of being powerless over something is a necessary step towards enjoying the fullness of a sober life.[3] Admitting to being powerless over aspects of our lives is liberating and empowering.

Let's return to the yin-yang symbol to see if we can take acceptance into the duality of good and bad by seeing how one needs the other. Remember what happened when we removed either yin or yang from the traditional diagram? (Example 5) The other polarity simply disappeared because it needed its contrasting opposite to exist. If I swap out the concepts of yin and yang for good and bad and go back to what I wrote about this exercise earlier, this is how it reads now: Good and bad are nestled together as two elegant identical shapes in reverse and retrograde positions with each other. Good delineates bad, and bad delineates good. Good has a little bit of bad inside, and bad has a little bit of good inside and they need each other to make a complete whole. When all of bad is removed, good becomes formless, shapeless and invisible. Good within an environment of good is invisible, so the concept of good becomes meaningless and ceases to exist. When all of good is removed, bad becomes formless, shapeless and invisible. Bad within an environment of bad is invisible, so the concept of bad becomes meaningless and ceases to exist. Good and bad need each other.

What does this mean for us living on this planet? It means that we can accept the possibility of experiencing opposites as structurally supportive necessities within the totality of being. We might be rich now but one day we might be poor. If we are young now and live long enough, one day we will be old. If we are fit and well now, one day we could be weak and sick. It is far better to accept that difficulties inevitably arise through our lifetimes than to pretend that such things only happen to other people. To think otherwise is a pervasive and unhelpful lie.

Sophie comes to us at Earthhorse Aotearoa because she lost her father to cancer a year ago and is having a hard time processing the grief. She says she has been sad almost all the time since he died and that her life feels as though it has stalled. We discussed how she feels, then we approach the horses in the arena. The mare who so often elects to work with grief comes forward and allows herself to be haltered. After a grounding exercise in which Sophie identifies her physical response to grief as tightness in the heart area, I suggest that she name the mare Grief and stand with her for a while. I stand back to give her an opportunity to express her sadness and feel comforted as the mare nuzzles into her. She comments that her father had been her best friend and that now she feels all alone so I suggest she take the mare for a walk and ask of her what Grief needs from her now. She comes back after a few minutes and says that Grief needs her to let the emotion happen, to sink into it fully without grasping it or pushing it away. She does that literally as she puts her face into the mare's mane and sobs. After a while Sophie lifts her head and says she has an image of herself wearing grief like a garment. I ask her how she could reenact that with the horse and she says she wants to put a saddle blanket on the mare. We do that, then Sophie walks the mare around the arena leading her between two large cones at which point Sophie stops and says that the cones feel like a doorway into a new place of acceptance. At this point she takes off the saddle blanket and drops it to the ground. She is overcome with emotion as she expresses her need to accept that her father is no longer here and that she doesn't need to carry grief as a burden. We extend the talk to acceptance of all the nurturing, friendship and love she had received from her father, accepting and being thankful for those wonderful times. Finally she accepts that it is OK to feel her sadness but that it doesn't need to define her and restrict her life.

What do horses do when bad things happen to them? They react as they need to out of self-preservation, then accept what is. They know they can't indulge in regret or blame and of course their minds wouldn't even conceptualize in this way. Leading someone to an understanding that they too can accept what is, without regret and blame and without labelling experiences into exclusively bad and good, is one of the greatest gifts you can pass on. The remaining chapters consider some models of how acceptance and non-dual thinking can be explored in the psycho-spiritual realm. If you do not work in the therapy space I hope nonetheless that you will appreciate how such models described can help you to exercise your imagination within your own discipline and understandings.

Footnotes

1. This is a Chinese parable from 2000 years ago as retold by Alan Watts [online]. Accessible at: https://bremeracosta. medium.com/parable-of-the-chinese-farmer-f012db83694d (Accessed 14 July 2023).
2. This story is of Cherokee origin although its source is impossible to verify [online]. Available at: https://medium. com/@EdwigeRobinson/the-wolf-you-feed-7095a0cd7586 (Accessed 31 January 2022).
3. See also Acceptance and Commitment Therapy (ACT).

Chapter 25

Projection and Metaphor

Projection is a naturally occurring phenomenon that we use as an effective tool for personal insight. Human beings can be surprisingly unaware of which emotions truly belong to them and which belong to others as they habitually project their motives and emotions onto other people through an unwillingness to own motives and emotions. When we project unconsciously onto others it leads to significant misunderstandings as we try to hand our uncomfortable mental positions to another person. A typical projection is accusing (or even thinking) that someone is angry with us when in fact it is we who are angry. The ego has difficulty seeing this because it loves to blame other people and situations for its own emotional discomfort and insecurity.

When a client projects onto a horse it brings unconscious meaning-making processes to a place where they can be recognized and questioned. By way of a simple example a client might say that her horse looks sad or unhappy, while you might have a different assessment of your horse. In the equine assisted space you wouldn't deny what the client says since that would make her "wrong" but you might ask questions about why she thinks the horse feels sad, then encourage her to unfold her own story of sadness. Through such a natural process we invite clients to recognize and explore their projections (without calling them that) and enable them to observe, as if an outsider, how they seek personal meaning through story-making.

Projection can arise if a horse steps away from a client when she is expecting close contact. She might offer an interpretation of the horse not liking her, whereas you might see that he simply wants to hang out with a horse friend across the fence.

It would be disempowering and undermining to point this out to a client, and would achieve little of therapeutic or personal learning value, but an inquiry focusing on how it feels not to be liked; under what conditions someone feels disliked or rejected; what they do to feel liked, inevitably leads to personal insight.

People so readily take an animal's behavior personally (as we do with the behavior of other humans). I had a situation early on in this work of a client who in every session, regardless of which horse she worked with, commented that the horses kept pinning their ears back at her. On each occasion she said the horse was angry at her. Several times I explained that rather than "pinning their ears" the horses were simply moving their ears around freely as they listened to everything going on in their environment, which included my client. But I realized that by slipping into horse-instructor mode in that way I was missing a therapy opportunity. Since the comment returned in subsequent sessions, I turned the conversation to, "Does this horse remind you of anyone? Who else in your life do you feel is pinning his or her ears back at you?" and subsequent followup questions. I should have done this in the first place for it led to revealing talk about ongoing anger incidents with a particular family member. Unsurprisingly this client's practice of projecting her emotions onto others played a crucial part in the ongoing conflict with the family member. Projection is a gift in this work when clients are led to recognize the process for themselves. The beauty of doing this with the participation of a horse is that projection is not an abstract idea. It is both visible and relatable.

Like projection, metaphor arises naturally. Humans so readily fall into metaphorical thinking which, to paraphrase George Lakoff and Mark Johnson from *Metaphors We Live By*, is pervasive in language, thought and action in human society. How we think and act is fundamentally metaphorical in nature.[1]

Stories arise naturally in work with horses and we need to be on the lookout for them so that we can provide the space for a client's personal themes to unfold. This might mean that a session develops in a direction different to what we had in mind, so we need to be flexible enough to allow the client's imagination to actively direct the work. Unpicking stories (or dreams) is always personal to a client and they must be allowed to make their own connections to narratives in their daily lives.

So much in our world of experience is understood through metaphor. It's possibly the most usual way humans make sense of experience, and in areas such as religion, philosophy and even science, metaphor is central to how we explain, understand and process our lived experiences. The concept of trust readily invites both analogy and metaphor. How can we even define the word trust without creating stories to say what it is like? Dictionary definitions generally put it as a belief in fidelity and reliability, but the words trust, belief, fidelity and reliability are abstract concepts that themselves beg for metaphor and analogy to flesh out meaning. In a real sense all words are metaphors since by definition they are symbols for something.

As well as arising as a natural phenomenon, metaphor can be consciously applied in the equine assisted space. It is a simple but effective exercise to invite clients to name their horse as the thing/person that currently concerns them, just as we did for Sophie. Through discussion while a troubling emotion or behavior emerges as a theme for the client, we may suggest naming his horse after the emotion/behavior while taking the horse for a walk to see what arises. Something always does arise because humans can't help being story makers and seekers of meaning. It is so natural for us to understand our world through story that, in my experience, setting up a metaphorical experiment with a client has never been met with incredulity. Most people jump into it readily and are equally quick to extrapolate meaning from whatever arises with a horse. This process works whether we deliberately choose a metaphor from concepts arising from discussion or whether one arises naturally from clients' projections:

Jason walks our gentle thoroughbred around the arena during a private session. He walks ahead, pulling the horse with the lead rope while looking behind to see if he is coming. On this occasion the horse isn't following very willingly at all. I inquire from Jason why he thinks his horse isn't walking willingly with him and he wonders whether looking at the horse directly in the eye might not be helping. He says, "Maybe it's making the horse nervous?" (Which it was.) I ask Jason to experiment with finding a more trusting way of walking his horse and he finds that walking beside the horse's head while focusing ahead is much more effective.

This experience becomes a powerful metaphor for how Jason leads his life. In discussion he sees that (metaphorically speaking) he has a habit of looking behind to know how he is doing. He also "drags" others around at work to some extent rather than walking beside his colleagues. In so many aspects of his daily life he investigates his habitual behavior and identifies ways in which he can try other strategies. He also knows that he habitually seeks approval and direction from others. We all do this of course but for Jason it was largely unconscious until he worked with a horse. In his experience over several weeks of discovering for himself how he can walk with his horse in trust, he brought behavioral patterns forward into consciousness thus freeing himself from their habitual nature.

Allowing the imagination to run free in the interest of allowing personally meaningful stories and projections to emerge is essential in this work. In this respect, whatever people project onto a horse, whatever meaning they derive and whatever story they weave from what the horse is doing is not only directly relevant, it's also true. The truth of the stories comes from the client's unconscious mind, so we never want to confuse that with a contrary interpretation of what we think the horse is actually experiencing. It is challenging at times to remember that this is not a process of learning horsemanship skills. I have more than a few times inadvertently blurted out what I considered to be the real motivation for a horse's behavior, only to remember that the client's story is always right. It is true and rich material for therapeutic and learning processes. In this respect, unpicking the meaning within a story is rather like dream work in depth psychology.

Alistair a soldier returning home from action with severe PTSD[2] came for a series of sessions with the horses. From a grounding exercise he identified a place in his neck and back where he held considerable discomfort. In response to my questioning he described the discomfort as a solid black triangle with sharp corners. He recognized this as his held-on-to hurt and anger. I suggested he walk a horse around the arena with awareness of this discomfort and "ask" the horse what to do with it. He returned to say that the discomfort in his neck and back grew into an enormous black cloud that followed him and the horse as they walked together. We worked on this metaphor over several weeks and among other exercises asked the horse to carry the black cloud. At first Alistair was reluctant to give such a burden to a horse but eventually he felt a willingness from the mare to take it on. After walking around the arena with her several times Alistair returned with an expression of lightness and joy, and explained that with the mare taking on his heavy black

cloud he "saw color for the first time". He didn't mean
that he had never been able to distinguish between colors
previously but that this was the first time as an adult that he
was fully conscious of color as a phenomenon. This sense of
joy remained with him.

Footnotes
1. Lakoff & Johnson (1980) p. 3.
2. PTSD is what this client presented with after having been
   diagnosed by other health professionals. As counselors we
   do not diagnose clients but we do work with whatever the
   client presents.

Chapter 26

Fear and Anxiety

As is true for all emotions, fear serves a vital purpose for humans as it does for all other animals: it helps us survive as individuals and as a species; it tells us to jump out of the way of danger; it tells us not to trust a threatening person or animal. It keeps us safe. However, we humans have a habit of both fearing things that are not real threats and of clinging on to fear needlessly. We fear things that are not actually an immediate threat, i.e. we fear some possibility in the future that might never happen. We get attached to fear and use it for almost anything: fear of loss, fear of change, fear of rejection, fear of love, fear of success and fear of shame. The list is endless. We think that if we worry sufficiently about things and hold on to our concerns that we will keep ourselves safe from pain. But it doesn't work that way since in the very act of holding on to fear we deplete our energy for what is needed in the present moment. Very few human fears relate to what is happening in the present moment but when they do there is usually an immediate corrective action we can take (like jumping out of the way of an oncoming car) after which the fear dissolves. Problems arise when fear fails to meet up with an anticipated threat and subsequently doesn't get an opportunity to be resolved. This is where fear can turn into anxiety.

At times I am approached by potential clients who admit they are afraid of horses and wonder whether they should do this work. Of course it's fine for them to opt out through lack of confidence but it occurs to me that if they have got to the stage of making an appointment and showing up, their attraction to working with horses can overcome their fear if we take things slowly enough. With some questioning I make sure that being around horses isn't likely to trigger a phobic reaction, then I point out that firstly, fear is a very good place to start in this work because it keeps them safe, and secondly, that they don't have to do anything that makes them feel uncomfortable. They can step back or opt out at any time. We can even start by observing horses from behind a fence, which can usefully occupy a few sessions until they are relaxed enough to make physical contact.

Observing and talking about fear while observing a group of horses is a valuable exercise in itself. When observing a group of horses I might ask a fearful client to look for the slightest sign of fear (or *heightened alertness* is probably a better term) in the horse. It is bound to arise at our farm because one of the roads beside our arena is a reasonably busy highway. At any stage there could be a car pulling a trailer with a flappy tarpaulin covering, or a motorbike with a noisy exhaust system or someone in the farm next door shooting. We even have helicopters overhead occasionally. Something is bound to happen that will attract a horse's attention. When that happens, I ask my client to describe what he sees unfolding:

> Client: That dark horse over there heard a gunshot and raised his head suddenly.
> Me: How long did he keep his head up for?
> Client: About two seconds.
> Me: Did the other horses do the same thing?
> Client: One of them did, that one with the stripe on its back.
> Me: What did she do?
> Client: She looked up too.
> Me: For how long?
> Client: Maybe two seconds.
> Me: Then what did the horses do?
> Client: They relaxed again.

The discussion might then center on why the horses were quickly able to assess that there was no immediate danger. They decided instantly that they didn't need to run away to safety, and one of the key factors was that the mare figured there was no problem so she gave the herd a signal to relax. We might then discuss what signals of safety people can rely on in their human environment by identifying personal "islands of safety" in the presence of fear. Who are the people you feel safe with? Where are the spaces where you feel safe? What can you say to a trusted person to tell them you don't feel safe?

Matthew is an intelligent and highly energetic eight-year-old but he is frightened and emotionally volatile. In his first session he is introduced to three miniature horses but his fear overwhelms him so that he needs a fence or gate between himself and the little horses. Fear is ever-present in his life and it becomes clear over several sessions that he has very few personal resources for dealing with his worries. I ask him to identify where he feels fear in his body and he says it lives mostly in his stomach. I encourage him to accept this feeling as something which is trying to keep him safe and I reinforce his need to step away when he becomes anxious. I invite him to interact with "his" miniature horse but often in a session he refuses to go near any horse. When that happens I work with his horse instead as Matthew watches. I ask him to tell me how the horse is feeling and what he might be thinking.

By the sixth session Matthew has learned to lead his horse around gently, to push the horse away when he does not respect personal space, to groom respectfully, to pick up and clean out the horse's hooves safely and to hug his horse safely around the neck when saying goodbye. By the tenth session he runs around with his miniature horse and kicks a ball around, both enjoying the fun. As Matthew overcomes his fear of horses his caregivers report that he is less afraid at home and is much more compassionate with his siblings.

Once a young person (or anyone for that matter) learns to conquer one significant fear the skill is transferable provided the process is discussed fully and he understands how his strategies worked. Working with a horse that is fearful (or spooky) can offer us opportunities (within the bounds of safety) with positive effects for both client and horse. We have a young mare who takes some time getting used to new things in her environment, so at times I introduce her to something new.

I worked with a young couple who had considerable issues accompanied by a raft of fears. For one session we focused on our young mare from the point of view of her fear. She was in the arena on her own, with the rest of the herd nearby. I introduced a large hoofball at the far end of the arena. Immediately her head rose up and she looked interested but fearful. My two clients gently rolled the ball back and forth between them while we observed the mare. When she was frightened she turned away to face her friends but as soon as she turned back to look in the direction of the ball my clients stopped moving the ball and let her relax. We kept this going for a while and varied the pace, direction and distance of the ball from the mare. Because we were rewarding the horse with stillness (taking off the pressure) whenever she faced the ball and stood still we called this "facing the fear", which gave us a richness of opportunity at each resting point for discussion about the couple's fears. At the same time this was an exercise in seeing the world from the horse's point of view and offering her our reassurance.

From fear it is relatively easy for anxiety to emerge. Although mammals and humans share the same emotional pallet, anxiety is an almost uniquely human emotion arising from held fears and accumulated negative thoughts. Anxiety is a product of the prefrontal cortex's unique functioning capacity working overtime on imagined future scenarios. Fear of hypothetical situations can be exaggerated through story formations, evoking further emotional reactions and avoidance behaviors. A fear of "what might happen" becomes what feels like a certainty that something awful *will* happen. When someone fears that something awful but unfounded will happen right now, we are edging into the realm of phobia.[1]

A harmful aspect of anxiety is that it persists in the body-mind within a feedback loop: the body does not know the difference between the *thought* of something terrible happening and the thing *actually* happening. We react in the same way as heightened levels of cortisol and adrenalin produce sweating, increased heart rate, and increased blood pressure and tension. Such bodily reactions can evoke further fear that maintains or builds on the original level of fear. When fear of future scenarios becomes chronic (constantly present) we call it anxiety.

Horses obviously experience fear but they rarely become anxious unless they have been "tortured" in some way. Their brains are not as predisposed to anxiety as ours are because they don't have the prefrontal cortex capacity for complex story-making scenarios, nor do they have the words for such stories. Instead, their nervous systems and brains have evolved to solve problems through escaping from them in lightning-fast reactivity as one of the fastest movers in the animal kingdom. They don't need executive functioning to figure out all the possible "what ifs" when they can simply escape perceived danger.[2] Sometimes the danger might be imaginary (as we know from spooky horses) when they react before thinking. But this behavior makes a lot of sense since there is no survival advantage to prey animals in hanging around to figure out how dangerous or otherwise an unexpected stimulus might be to them. Besides escaping (flight) the other options for horses in fear are fight and freeze.

We humans also have the fight-flight-freeze reactions to fear but we can learn to exercise choice over our reactions to a much larger extent. We can also learn from horses how to access our mammalian ability to be somatically aware and fully conscious of our surroundings so that fear doesn't arise. We can learn from horses (and nature in general) how to live consciously in the present, trusting that we will react appropriately to danger when needed instead of torturing ourselves with imaginings of what might happen.

Anxiety is held-on-to and amplified fear as a result of identification with an imagined negative future. When a horse is anxious we can observe several important signals (shallow breathing, high head, wide eyes, fixed stare, tight mouth and ears facing what's happening). Inviting a client into a discussion of how anxiety manifests in horses might be followed with questioning along the lines of:

- Do you react in a similar way when you're anxious?
- What usually happens in your body when you are anxious?
- Is the horse reacting to something physically present or to something in his mind?
- Can you identify what is happening in your body right now?
- Can you sit with what is happening in your body right now?

Exercise: Once clients identify their own somatic discomfort, invite them to take that discomfort to a horse for their reaction and "comment".

Acceptance is recognizing that anxiety (thinking of it as an entity) is trying to look after us. When we feel anxious we can choose to accept it in this moment, and we can even thank it for trying to keep us safe. Anxiety is not always rational (although it usually has rational origins), but even if you no longer know why anxiety is telling you it is dangerous to do something otherwise ordinary, we can thank it anyway. Acceptance is allowing yourself to feel into where the anxious feelings are somatically, and to let them be there while letting go of resistance and containment. It does not mean you *like* what you're feeling, it's simply recognizing that anxiety exists in this moment and that you are choosing not to fight against it. Accepting emotional states is the first step to them losing their sway over us. In addition, identifying a safe zone in the body is valuable. Ask your client to find a place in their body without tension present where they can go to mentally when anxious.

- Ask your client to recall or observe a horse's shifting emotional states and ask her how the horse deals with it.
- How long did it take for the horse to recover?
- Did the horse seem to accept what happened or is he still thinking about it?

Exercise: Invite your client to name their horse "Anxiety" and take him for a walk, asking what it is that Anxiety wants or expects.

Alertness is the conscious state of observing the inner body and the outer environment with the purpose of noticing the play, or patterns, between them. Everything is alive to our senses but we are rarely conscious of the patterns of experience until we see something stand out against a still background. All animals look for change from a safety perspective but they also enjoy the novelty of noticing something new or unexpected. Invite your client to observe a group of horses eating grass or hay, taking note of every movement and change she sees.

- What signs of alertness do you see in the horses?
- Are all the horses equally alert at the same time?
- What do you feel like when you are alert?
- How can you be alert right now without added anxiety?
- What would help anxiety to change into alertness?
- As a herd, how do horses help each other to be alert?
- Does anyone help you or look out for you?

Exercise: What can you invite a horse to do with you that demonstrates alertness without evoking anxiety?

Awareness is being fully present in our current environment without holding on to stories about what has happened or what might happen next. Ask your client:

- Is there anything wrong with what is happening in this moment?
- If so, is it a thought that you can let go of?
- Does your emotion lessen when you let go of the thoughts?
- Can your awareness be soft as you let go of a need to control what is happening right now?
- Look at the horse. What is he seeing, hearing, feeling?
- Where is the horse's attention?
- What does he do when his attention changes?

Exercise: Take your horse for a walk and imagine that you are experiencing his world through his senses. Allow yourself to experience his awareness and yours working together supportively.

Jack arrives anxious about something unfolding at work with a colleague. We talk about it, discussing which aspects of the situation he might be able to change or deal with as he itemizes the things over which he has no control. Jack accepts his anxiety as being a real thing, acknowledging that it signals a situation that could be a threat to his employment. I invite Jack to stand with one of our mares in the round pen and silently talk to her about his situation. When he comes out of the round pen he describes how tense the horse seems to be, which he interprets as the horse picking up tension from him. We talk about whether it is possible to accept his anxiety bit by bit rather than try to eliminate or avoid it. He sees that anxiety is showing him that something needs his attention and he comes up with some possible steps to take to allow anxiety to move down in energy to a state of alertness.

Jack goes back into the round pen to the mare and thinks about several of the steps he had proposed. I notice that he appears to be more at ease physically and that the horse is also more relaxed. Jack takes that as a sign that his ideas are worth testing at work in the week coming. We discuss alertness as a state in which he can be aware of future scenarios without identifying with them, in other words being enough of an observer of his thoughts that he doesn't need to run with the whole story in his head.

Over several weeks as he becomes used to being alert in this way he sees the possibility of taking a further step down in energy into a space of still awareness. Here he can let go of his worries and look at his historical problems at work objectively without evoking fear. He retells stories to the horses of his workplace situations and invites them to help him see alternative interpretations. The process of stepping down from anxiety into still awareness allows him to let go of the idea of the inevitability of something bad happening.

With the mare he practices a wide-vision exercise and returns with a big smile. He says that being consciously aware of the physical space he is in, while inviting soft vision, takes his mind out of a worrying, highly focused space. He walks the mare around next while reciting a mantra he has come up with: "There is nothing wrong right now." He decides to actively use that mantra during the next week, and on his return he reports that when he said that to himself his mind would sometimes return with the thought, "It's fine right now, but what about later this afternoon, or tomorrow." When he heard his mind coming up with reasons why he needed to hold on to anxiety it made him laugh. He said that he was able to switch to the memory of the mare's calm and unworried state and imagined feeling calm like her. He was able to avoid falling into a pattern of anxiety, therefore working through the problem at work.

Equine assisted therapy can go further than working with analogy and metaphor, towards exploring aspects of a client's story to find an honest perception of themselves as if from an outside perspective.

Footnotes
1. Dealing with phobia is a complex and specialized area that I would always refer to specialist therapists.
2. Where horses can develop anxiety is where they are fully restrained such as in crossties in a horse trailer. If they realize they have no means of escape, unless trust has been built beforehand, they can become sweaty and emotional.

Chapter 27

The Personal Story

We all carry around a personal narrative of who we think we are. We have an internal story of what kind of person we are, what we are good at, what we are lousy at, what sort of company we like to keep, how clever we are (or not), how we think we look, and so on. We have interpretations of how our personal histories have shaped us, what influences (good or bad) our parents had on us, how pleasant or otherwise our childhood was, what hardships we have endured and which opportunities have come our way (or not). These stories of who we are not only define us but, in addition, give us reasons for why certain things have happened. They help us make sense of our lives but they also work against us in that they are not the whole truth. Personal stories are based on values that were given to us from our family during childhood and they encapsulate the norms of society so that we can usefully fit in with our culture. They serve the purpose of helping us integrate with society but the stories that carry the values and beliefs we hold might not be what we would choose as an adult to base our lives upon.

There usually comes a time when it is both necessary and healthy to examine and challenge our personal stories, or they can trap us. A great number of our narratives are to do with the collections of problems and traumas which every human being experiences in unique combinations; through resistance to change we become defined by our problems and trauma. The more problem-saturated our stories become and the more we retell them to ourselves and others around us, the more solid and unchangeable they feel. As if we are tracing with a pencil over and over the outline of a figure, they appear solid and form such a part of our identity that we come to believe we *are* our problems. They seem to make us what we are, for which reason we resist letting them go. That is, until something disrupts our worldview and we are forced to look at ourselves.

What very few of us see in our problem-saturated stories is that our interpretation of what has happened in our lives so far is not *our* interpretation at all. We receive our model of judging ourselves through conditioning from our families and all sorts of outside influences, and we end up claiming those judgments as our own. Until we question our conditioned beliefs, values and ideas, the distorted story of who we are will be kept alive. Sadly, our conditioning rarely serves us well into adulthood. At some stage in life most people are forced to question received values and identity. This is healthy as we enquire into which beliefs and values we choose to claim as our own. However, it's one thing to know which parts of the story we wish to move on from and quite another to build a fresh identity. The good news is that the simple act of recognizing conditioned thoughts, values and habits (so long as we do so without judgment) has the effect of weakening their influence. The first step towards psychological wholeness and freedom from the conditioned mind is to notice conditioned thoughts and accept them for what they are. They can never be entirely banished because they are the foundation of our ego development and therefore a necessary process of learning to be human. However, they can be subjected to the illumination of awareness.

How we project our self-image to the so-called outside world is very important to us. Most of us have set ideas about who we are, how others view us, how successful or otherwise we appear and how our personality is viewed by others. We can call this our *form identity* as distinct from *soul identity*.[1] We claim a form identity as our own and believe it is who we are. It includes personal values such as how trustworthy, kind, hardworking, clever or talented we are perceived to be. But we have so many attributes to live up to (or we think we do), and we fail in so many of them that our form identity can be anything but a source of comfort. For example, my father came from a working-class family of twelve in which good behavior and hard work was cause for family identity and pride. My mother was middle class, a social climber, and a perfectionist, and everything she did was beautiful and seemingly perfect. Hence, I received a mixture of values ranging from diligence, hard work, perseverance, endurance, pride and perfectionism. These are not bad things in themselves unless they become exacting taskmasters and measures of personal value, which they did for many years. Recognizing these received values was the beginning of them loosening their grip.

Most of us are aware of a voice in the head telling us who we are, making judgments, comparing ourselves with others, constantly criticizing or praising. This voice is often referred to as the "inner critic" or "inner judge". The problem is that we don't always recognize our self-criticism as conditioned thought. We too readily believe it to be self-generated and true. But our personal stories are self-limiting. We tell ourselves all through our lives that we are no good at certain things or that we are failures at this or that. These are judgments that might be based on as little as what one teacher or parent said to us when we were children that from then on became fixed identities and self-fulfilling prophesies as we lived up (or down) to them.

Jay Earley and Bonnie Weiss in their book *Freedom from your Inner Critic* identify seven types of critic naming them as: perfectionist, inner controller, taskmaster, underminer, attacker, guilt tripper and molder, each with their attributed behaviors and characteristics. These categories are illuminating, though not exhaustive, and for the purposes of equine assisted counseling I find it more engaging for the client (especially children) if they come up with their own name and description for their self-critical thinking.[2]

We generate emotional responses to our inner critic, and until we see that the source of anger, fear, shame or whatever comes from our version of conditioning we can't find much distance from our emotions. Anger, for instance, is an inbuilt human response to experiencing the uncomfortable gap between an ideal of what we think should happen, and reality as what really happens. It is not anger itself that we need to control, it is our mental interpretation of it, i.e. the story of what happens around the anger that we need to recognize so that it doesn't control us. It's less a matter of controlling anger, and more a matter of finding personal agency through inner observation. We can do this inner work at any stage in our lives, but if we can help young people with their anger, we give them valuable lifelong skills. In my work with young people I have seen too many examples of negative self-images established early in life and when these are mixed with a lack of meaningful human attachment the results can be tragic.

Chloe had lived in over twenty foster homes by the time I met her as a nine-year-old. I quickly discovered that she was expert at preempting being moved on to yet another foster home by exhibiting behaviors her foster parents or caregivers wouldn't tolerate. She learned not to make meaningful attachments with another person to avoid the hurt of further rejection. This kept her in a painful position of detachment and separateness. However, she readily made strong attachments with the horses, especially to one of the miniatures because animals (unlike humans) had never let her down.

Chloe loves being with her favorite small horse but she doesn't open up emotionally until one day she says,

"Sometimes I think I am a bad person." I encourage her to externalize the feeling of being bad by "naming" it and discussing what it "wants" from her. She takes the lead by calling it her "bad friend" who entices her to do "naughty" things. This way she doesn't have to take full responsibility for the badness she feels inside. Then we role-play with the horses to explore her bad friend's "personality". We name the horse as her bad friend and ask him to complete various tasks such as weaving among cones, then we explore the meaning she makes of the horse's behavior. Over a period of weeks this enables her to see how her self-critical thinking sabotages her life. She loves writing and drawing so we make up little booklets about her journey with the horses that she takes home, to which she adds more stories. Responding to my questioning and the role-playing with horses, Chloe increasingly experiences her problems as residing outside of herself, hence gaining some emotional distance. Eventually she volunteers the thought that her "bad friend" horse can't help being bad. He does naughty things because he thinks nobody loves him. That's a great insight for a young person. She says that she will love her horse so that he can be her good friend. Soon after, the fostering agency move her to another home in a distant city, so I don't know how she fared. My cherished hope is that this experience with the horses has seeded an awareness of self-value, that she can feel her trauma to be "outside" herself, that it is not her fault and that she continues to be supported in her healing.

Unfortunately, the probability is that since she has missed out on secure attachment in her early years, Chloe will most likely always carry a sense of not being good enough to be loved fully. Hopefully the influence of that fundamental belief on her life will diminish the more she learns about her conditioned thought patterns.

I remember back in the 1970s and 80s that "positive thinking" was a popular self-therapy, and my friends and I sought to improve ourselves by inwardly reciting affirmations to counterbalance self-limiting beliefs. This seemed perfectly achievable while actively reading the self-help books telling us how to improve our lives, but I don't know of anyone who changed themselves fundamentally through such means. It certainly didn't work for me at the time. Self-affirmation can work in conjunction with other strategies but on its own it requires a divided mind: one part that believes that a negative attribute exists within and another that counteracts it through affirming the opposite. The most that such a strategy can achieve is an internal argument with yourself, effectively turning you into two entities. Try as we may, we can't fool ourselves because whichever side seems to win the argument, we are aware of the other side waiting in the wings with counterarguments.

What does work is noticing our conditioned thought patterns as they arise, i.e. so long as we don't attach judgment to them. But how do we know what comes from conditioning and what is relatively real or relatively true? It is helpful to undertake a course of psychotherapy to discover such connections, but we can also do a certain amount of work by asking a three-part question of habitual thought: *is it true; is it helpful; is it kind?* If we respond to any part of that question with a no, we can safely disregard the judgment and move on. It is not necessary (indeed, it's inadvisable) to get into dialogue with oneself to attempt to untangle the historical threads of self-critical thought. In response to the thought "I am ugly", there is no real answer since judging ugliness is relative to everyone else on the planet, and to whose standards are we comparing ourselves? We go around in circles with such an internal enquiry because there is a massive variety of culturally defined views on human bodily aesthetics. Who knows what beauty is? The protruding surgically altered lips of today may well be seen as an ugly aberration by the next generation (if not already). I might not be able to determine whether the thought "I am ugly" is factually true, but I can certainly see that it is neither kind nor helpful.

The stories of who we are evolve throughout our lifetimes as we accept the changes that naturally occur. However, form identity is very resistant to change since it is an aspect of the ego and wants to maintain itself. But resisting change is as unhealthy and painful as a child growing out of his shoes. Even if I am comfortable inside the story of who I am, that story is unlikely to sustain me into my middle years and old age. For instance, if the most defining characteristic with which I identify is being physically fit, strong and athletic, my emotional attachment to such an identity must surely take a hit as I grow into old age. The inevitability of aging brings valuable lessons since we can either resist it within an environment of fear and rigidity, or we can let go into the natural process of change and experience what it must teach us.

As we involve horses in the narrative processes of our clients, they bring the whole process alive. Horses so readily participate in clients' story-making processes, and equally, people readily share their storylines with horses. Once someone is ready to tell an aspect of their story that they feel stuck in they can invite a horse to listen to the narrative. Sometimes people are not ready to talk to us about their stuckness but are willing to share it with a horse. Observing what happens in that conversation between horse and client opens the enquiry.

Bridget comes to Earthhorse Aotearoa for a demonstration session and to interview us for an article she is writing for a magazine. She is excited to experience some aspect of the work as we do a grounding meditation from which she identifies tension in her neck. I encourage her to describe the pain in detail, then suggest she take a horse for a walk around the arena to see what arises. She returns to say that the thought "she's a pain in the neck" keeps coming to her and realizes that represents someone in her life who upsets her constantly. I suggest she walk her horse again while thinking of the mare as this person. When we talk she says that the mare is not annoying her, and that if she had been, it would not have been in any way deliberate. Bridget sees that the mare is being herself, just as the annoying person is also simply being herself. She volunteers that how they are, really has nothing to do with her. It is not her responsibility to own another person's behavior. Nor does she need to react. We confirm this awareness by taking the mare for a walk again, allowing the horse (as the "annoying person") to be just as she is. As Bridget externalizes the problem instead of taking it personally, she comes up with a fresh perspective, saying, "I can let [person X] be how she needs to be without an emotional response from me."

Horses bring insight into story-making and story-identifying processes because they reflect (or mirror) a person's true emotional state and, much like the Rorschach test, allow people to project their own meaning and emotion onto a pattern, in this case a horse. A client wanting to free themselves from negative or painful aspects of their history might retell it wrapped up in old interpretations, but when allowing horses to become part of the narrative, entirely new interpretations are likely to emerge. It is difficult to lie, elaborate, embellish, exaggerate or elicit sympathy when telling one's personal story to a horse. As part of a person's form identity, a story is often held on to tenaciously because it is comforting in its familiarity but I have witnessed clients let go of dysfunctional identities when session after session they see their own dysfunctional stories reflected back to them by a horse. The horse doesn't know they are participating in the identification of stories of course, they are simply interacting honestly and directly to a client's current emotional and somatic state. At times the stories that emerge are heartbreaking.

> Sam, the ten-year-old boy we introduced earlier, notices during herd observation that one horse seems to be protecting another. It appears to him that this mare "has the back" of her friend. I ask Sam, "Who has your back?" He names his supportive adoptive family and one friend at school. I ask if there is one horse that he feels has his back and he names one of the miniatures. I ask him what he could do to show that he has the mini's back and he replies that he would like to lay a long stick across his back for reassurance and walk around with him, which he does with ease. We get into a fruitful conversation about trusting people and at the end I ask Sam why he especially likes this horse. He replies that it is because this mini wasn't wanted and was going to be sent away to the pet food company before we adopted him (which is true). Sam then says, "That's why I love him, because I was three years old when I was given away." By loving the mini he is nurturing the younger child in himself who has been so profoundly hurt. In the following weeks we explore ways of understanding, caring for, and nurturing his horse within this framework of understanding.

Footnotes

1. Eckhart Tolle in his writings and podcasts refers to two different personal identities: *form identity* and *essence*

identity. In line with the theme of this book, I use the term *soul identity* instead of *essence identity* but the meaning is the same.

2.   Earley & Weiss (2013) p. 22.

Chapter 28

Externalizing and Scaling

No matter how problematic a client's narrative it loses much of its power when viewed objectively, i.e. when seen as a phenomenon occurring *outside* the person. The therapists' job according to narrative therapy, is to establish with clients that they are not the problem, *the problem is the problem*. Through questioning and subtle changes in language we help people situate the problem external to themselves.[1] For instance people tend to talk about "my anxiety" or "my depression" as though there is no space between the self and the problem as they fully identify themselves with the problem. (This is also a major issue in the diagnosis of medical conditions, but that's another story.) If you as practitioner simply introduce the definite article "the" while reflecting back to your client, the perspective of *being* the problem changes. Hence "your anxiety" becomes "the anxiety", positioning the problem external to the person and making it so much easier to evaluate and examine without being emotionally overwhelmed.

In the externalization process we encourage a client to think of their problem as a "thing" or an "entity". Depression, for instance, might be described as "the gorilla sitting on my shoulders". For a child "my anger" might become the "shadow monster that visits me." Further questioning brings such entities into focus through enquiring about what color, what shape, what size, what texture and whatever other characteristics the client recognizes within the problem. For children, asking them to draw or write stories about the entity that visits them is a useful externalizing tool too. In equine assisted work by inviting the horse to take on the role of the external entity the horse externalizes the problem through analogy and metaphor. According to Michael White and David Epston in *Narrative Means to Therapeutic Ends* this encourages clients to disidentify with their problem so that something they might consider an inherently fixed part of their identity can become less fixed and less restricting.[2]

"Interviewing the problem" is a conversation we have with clients to help with objectifying and personifying the problem. First we remind clients that anger is not their anger, it is human anger in response to events around and within them. Then we can take the externalization process further by referring to it as something outside of the person that visits them, and together we can interview the problem to identify its many features. For children this can become a playful process. For instance we could ask questions like this for interviewing what a child identifies as a "shadow monster":

- What does shadow monster think it is doing (its purpose)?
- What are shadow monster's hopes and dreams for you (aspirations)?
- How does shadow monster get you to notice it is there (motivation)?
- What does shadow monster do that makes you feel bad (actions)?
- Do other people or places help shadow monster to upset you (situations)?
- Do you do what shadow monster wants (give in to it)?
- Can you remember times when you have been able to make the shadow monster go away (resist it)?

By externalizing a problem, clients learn to separate from the dominant story shaping their lives and relationships. They learn that "neither the person nor the relationship between persons is the problem. Rather, the problem becomes the problem, and then the person's *relationship* [my italics] with the problem becomes the problem."[3] Alongside externalizing and personifying the problem through talk, exploring a client's relationship with the problem while in the company of a horse is a great tool. This can be achieved by as simple a process as naming the horse as the problem, then working towards naming the horse as the solution. Externalizing the problem establishes a creative space between the person and the problem, enabling the relationship with the named problem to be fully explored.

Jacob, the twelve-year-old who called his recurrent anger and frustration the "shadow monster", takes one of our geldings for a walk around the arena. He decides to ask the shadow monster what its motivation is, what it wants of him. I watch as they silently walk around the arena three times looking as though nothing much is going on between them. However, when he comes back to talk about their communication he says that the horse (as shadow monster) wants to be "respected and loved". We talk about what those words mean to him, then Jacob decides to take the gelding for another walk while being open to ideas around respect and love. He reports back that he got the sense from the horse that he (the horse) had been badly treated and taken away from his mother when a young foal and that's what makes him angry even when he forgets he's been a foal. This story about the horse mirrored Jacob's experience of living with violence and neglect in his early years, which I already knew about from his social worker's case notes but we had not discussed previously. This was deliberate on my part because I do not bring up a subject from a third party, preferring to allow whatever arises to come directly from the client. When it comes to trauma though it is not only the thing that has happened, the wound created, that continues the suffering but also the ideas and interpretations wrapped around the story that keep the wound active. In Jacob's case, it emerged through more "walking the walk" with horses, that an influential adult had told him when he was around six years old that he would never recover from his traumatic early childhood experiences and that his life was probably "ruined". From that astounding memory we continued to work with horses personifying situations where he has acted as a person whose life has not been ruined, when he has known himself to be strong and responsible.[4]

A valuable exercise in interrogating the problem and externalizing is to ask a client to scale the problem as a means of seeing how it manifests, while identifying its characteristics.[5] Example 6, in a scale of one to ten (low to high), shows how this worked for Sean, a client in his forties who was wrestling with out-of-control anger. The process I use if a client is responsive to the idea is to question problems within categories such as actions, feelings, sensations, triggers and solutions. The questioning doesn't have to be in any order, in fact it's best to allow the conversation to evolve organically with a client until a full picture finally emerges. It is likely to take several sessions to get to the full picture but there's no issue with the details of the picture arriving piecemeal so long as we write things down on the grid as we go:

Actions: Ask your client to rate on a scale of one to ten (low to high) where their problem was the last time they experienced it, then to describe what happened. Ask them what a one would look like on the scale, then what a ten would look like. They may not be able to find words for their actions on all ten points on the scale, but gradually over several sessions it is generally possible to fill in most gaps.

Feelings: This is often the most natural way in for clients to talk about the problem. "What feelings and emotions go with each point on the scale?" These are very personal, and clients usually come up with feeling-words easily and fully over several sessions.

Sensations: Identifying sensations in the body that relate to each point on the scale is crucial to this process since it enables somatic signals to be recognized the next time the client gets to certain points on the scale. Clients are often unaware of physical warning signs until they have had a few discussions along these lines, so recognizing somatic signs as they arise opens a valuable space between the sensation and the problem.

Triggers: It may not be possible to find triggers for every degree of the scale of an emotional state (such as anger in this example) but there will always be key triggers that the client is aware of. Identifying them is an essential part of this process as it empowers the client to see what is happening as it arises.

Solutions: Discuss how the client has in the past positively dealt with the problem. There have usually been some moments where, for instance, full-blown rage has not resulted because the person has done something to arrest it. Identifying where existing strategies have worked previously is valuable information to build upon.

Scaling exercises are based on a client's actual experience, and it is essential to keep it that way so that solutions and realizations come from the person's remembered experience. This empowers them through the process while helping them see different perspectives through questioning. If the scaling exercise takes place over several sessions I use a whiteboard or a large piece of paper that can be added to from one week to another. A full picture of the problem gradually emerges by asking questions such as:

- How does your body feel and act when your anger is at level three?
- What are some of the possible things to do when you are at level two?
- What happens before the anger gets to level six and overtakes you?
- What are the warning signs you might observe at each level?
- What triggers can you identify that take you to a four?
- Do you have thought patterns that add to the problem?
- Is there one place on the scale where you feel totally taken over by anger?

SCALING ANGER

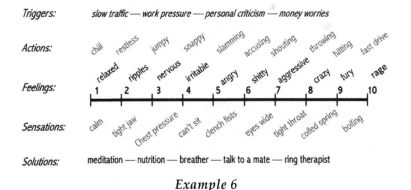

Example 6

What emerged from the scaling exercise with Sean (Example 6) was a new awareness that if he got to level three, unless he recognized anger arising at that stage, he could reach level ten in a nanosecond. If he ever got to five on the scale it was, in his words, "all over". He realized that as soon as he noticed himself feeling jumpy and nervous, he would need to activate his solutions of listening to a podcast or taking a breather. One method he discovered for himself at home was to take a breather outside, to lie face down on the grass and breathe in the smell of grass and soil. A lover of nature and wilderness, this usually centered him and brought him back into equilibrium.

With the help of the horses we worked on his anger by creating scenarios and allowing projection and metaphor to arise naturally. He added another calming solution: breathing in the scent of a horse's neck. If at home he couldn't go outside to breathe in the scent of the earth, it was enough for him to remember taking in the scent of a horse while relaxing his breathing to calm him down.

As an adult with considerable self-awareness, he had recognized the historical causes of his anger, but that self-knowledge had not helped him to either control or avoid his dangerous outbursts. It wasn't until he had fully explored his somatic experience of rising anger and was able to recognize both triggers and solutions, that he transformed habitual patterns of his behavior.

While working in this way over several months, conversations we had about his birth family turned to a description of his mother's life. It emerged that his aunt (mother's sister two years older) had accidentally caused the death of their younger brother. This tragedy became pivotal for both his mother and aunt, overshadowing their entire lives. Since generational trauma is passed on to new family members, Sean realized that he too had been carrying a burden of unresolved guilt, shame and fear for which he had not even known the cause.[6] Over time, Sean approached his mother with the aim of fleshing out the detail of this generational trauma as we engaged the horses in metaphors of forgiving, letting go and compassion for lives past and lives lost. With understanding, patience and personal insight, Sean grew towards wholeness and peace.

It is important when working with a client's anger issues to reassure them that anger isn't in itself "wrong", but that it serves a purpose and is biologically ingrained. Anger is "human anger". It is not uniquely generated by the individual, but while the neural systems that generate anger are inborn, we do have the choice of modulating our responses or amplifying anger through thoughts of revenge and retribution.[7] The place where clients can exercise agency is in the small gap between anger and its modulating thoughts. I remember the joy of surprise that a client expressed to me on discovering that he could sense the microsecond before anger arousal as an opportunity to choose between an angry reaction or accepting the emotion without a felt need to respond physically. Options included walking away, taking "time out" and calmly expressing his disappointment to a family member. These were scenarios we fruitfully worked on together with the horses taking metaphorical roles.

The other valuable understanding around anger (or any emotion) is that other people and things don't *cause* our anger, rather emotions result from triggers generating already established emotional circuits. It is rarely appropriate to explain this process to clients, but it's useful to help them realize that while they are triggered by outside stimuli the choice of response remains with them. As the influential neuroscientist Dr. Jaak Panksepp outlines in his book *Affective Neuroscience*, the option of choice as exercised through emotional education or willpower is unique to humans. He says that "animals, because of their limited ability to conceptualize the nature of emotions and intentions, do not appear to have such options."[8] The other choice that humans have is to choose a different story or to rewrite their current story to align with who they wish to be and how they wish to experience their life.

Footnotes

1. Alice Morgan (2000) p. 17. See also White & Epston (1990) chapter 2.
2. White and Epston (1990) p. 38.
3. White and Epston (1990) p. 40.
4. In Narrative Therapy, events that are situated outside the definition of "the problem" are called "unique outcomes" and are identified to modify a rigid personal story.
5. The technique of scaling is central to Solutions Focused Therapy.
6. For a fascinating account of the influence of generational trauma on a person's life, see Mark Wolynn (2017).
7. Panksepp (1999) p. 190.
8. Panksepp (1999) p. 190.

Chapter 29

Rewriting the Story

Through processes of externalizing, interviewing the problem and scaling, people find their old patterns loosening their hold, allowing a creative space within their personal story. While doing this work it is essential as Alice Morgan points out in *What is Narrative Therapy?* that both client and practitioner recognize that "problems only survive and thrive when they are supported and backed up by particular ideas, beliefs and principles."[1] She is not referring to religious beliefs but personal beliefs such as what kind of person we think we are. Personal beliefs need to be examined so that dysfunctional ones can cease to be part of our personal identity. So often beliefs and principles that come from the wider culture and family are not questioned but are accepted as true. When people start to see those old belief patterns clearly it gives them the opportunity to question whether specific beliefs are worth holding on to, or whether they need changing.

An experience of a client deconstructing and rewriting their story comes from a young man Stu who was rejected by his whole family. He was brought up in a morally strict community that regarded homosexuality as a personal choice that can, and should, be rejected. When he came out as gay to his family the response was immediately one of expulsion. By throwing him out with no further contact allowed with family, the parents' belief was that he would see the error of his ways and return reformed. This sensitive young man is devastated, particularly by not being able to spend time with his mother with whom he is very close.

He doesn't know whether he should return to the fold as a celibate or whether he should build a life outside of family and find a partner. I can't tell him what to do but what I can do is listen with compassion and ask questions to help him see his situation with some clarity. I ask Stu questions such as, "What are the fundamental beliefs of your family?" Stu comes back with love, charity and moral values. I ask whether he personally holds the same values. He replies that he believes in love and charity, but that morality is a confusing concept because it was on so-called moral grounds that his family rejected him.

As we begin the work he discovers that he has a strong inner critic with messages such as, "You are not strong enough to resist temptation," and, "You are not good enough for your family." One horse that Stu pairs with is very helpful in externalizing these voices. This horse has a great sense of humor (in a horsey sort of way) and whenever Stu takes on the seriousness of his self-criticism the gelding does something to make Stu laugh and in turn he laughs at the crazy things his inner critic tells him.

Gradually, as he expresses what is truly meaningful to him the values that Stu holds dear are disentangled from those given to him by his family. He rediscovers examples of how he has been kind, loving and moral according to his personally held belief system and he gradually tells his horse a new story of who he is becoming. He names his horse after his qualities and explores his interpretation of the horse's reactions. At the final stage of our work together Stu feels joy as the horses model acceptance while he tells them the story of who he is becoming. Over several weeks Stu has externalized the problem, examined his values, remembered exceptions to the story shaped by his conditioning and is beginning to rewrite his personal story.

As clients build a revised story of who they are, telling or demonstrating this to a horse takes various forms. It might be verbal, or the client might choose to use props in the arena to demonstrate an emerging story. The horse never fails to give his perspective (the interpretation of which ultimately comes from the client's unconscious mind) to consolidate goals, values and personal beliefs that better serve the present situation and goals. Through such a process clients come to realize that they no longer need to sing from the old hymnbook that they've inherited. They don't need to be stuck in a conditioned story not of their own choice, while patterns that no longer serve a useful purpose are replaced by values and beliefs of conscious choice.

Something to be wary of in helping clients rewrite their personal stories is to ensure that they emerge from *actual experience* rather than from the conceptual mind. We can all come up with ideas of how to be better and nicer people, but if they emerge conceptually more than experientially they may merely become new goals and standards that they fail to live up to. New Year's resolutions mostly fail for this very reason.

We humans are so good at holding onto negative personal stories that it becomes an essential part of our identity. Since people generally seek a therapist because they see they have a problem to be solved or emotional patterns to be released, their minds are naturally dominated by problems. As White and Epston the pioneers of narrative therapy say, their story is "problem saturated". Once work begins in externalizing the problem so that it is not so emotionally dominant, attachment to the problematic identity loosens. During this process we can also help clients to find "unique outcomes" as instances that contradict the problematic pattern: they find examples of where the problem has not had a dominating effect in their lives and relationships.[2] Such unique outcomes serve to demonstrate that there are exceptions to the problem's power in the client's life;

that there have been times when they have been authentically themselves without the problem's interference. Those moments provide confidence and become the building blocks of a new identity from which a new story can naturally unfold and lead to wholeness and a sense of soul-to-soul connection.

Footnotes
1. Morgan (2000) p. 45.
2. White & Epston (1990) p. 56.

Chapter 30

Wholeness and Spirituality

I suggested earlier that the spiritual dimension within is that which never changes, which is the underlying knowingness, and is essentially *whatever goes beyond thought*. But why would we want to go beyond thought? Aren't our intellectual powers the very qualities that set us apart from the rest of animal life? Haven't we developed a powerful brain out of an evolutionary need to guide us in everything? The cognitive function of our brain is certainly powerful and useful but we don't need to look at many examples of the history of human life on Earth to see that we have relied on the power of our logical and deductive capacities without it necessarily leading to a good place collectively. Humans have historically valued thought to the exclusion of other abilities regardless of the accumulated negative consequences.

Back when we were hunter-gatherers our prefrontal cortex's executive functioning was put to good use for planning and executing hunting expeditions, for making weatherproof shelters and for navigating large geographic areas. Creatures evolve in response to challenges in the environment, so higher-level thinking in humans must have given us the competitive edge in the struggle for survival. It worked, but it had the unfortunate consequence thousands of years later of us humans becoming so identified with our mental capacities that we have come to believe that we are our thoughts. By the time of the "Enlightenment" or "Age of Reason" of the seventeenth and eighteenth centuries, the belief that thought, logic and ideas are the engine room of human life had become thoroughly entrenched, convincing us to devalue intuitive ways of knowing.

We were warned of this possibility long ago. In Jewish scriptures of over three thousand years ago reliance on thought or cognitive knowledge was seen as dangerous, as exemplified in the story of Adam and Eve. This story is remembered chiefly for Eve and Adam eating the "forbidden" fruit, but really the problem was that they both ate from "the tree of the knowledge of good and evil".[1] Jewish culture understood that if humans regarded thought as the source of all wisdom (the tree of knowledge) and split experience into categories of good and bad, it was an act of disobedience to God, or as I would want to put it, it ignored the underlying principles of nature. The long-term results of ignoring the principles of nature are clear to see in modern human existence. Ignore the health of the body, including good nutrition and exercise and what do we get? Allow the human mind to come up with any discovery at all without considering possible applications for conflict or degradation and what do we get? Discover how to use the planet's resources to the degree that our greedy appetites dictate and what do we get? Allow our conditioned minds to rule our lives and what do we get? We get insanity all round of course.

If spirituality is a deep knowing within, that never changes but is the very basis of our being such as the air we breathe, it cannot be explained adequately through mental concepts or measured scientifically (at least not yet). Sceptics might take the position that not being able to measure spirituality is evidence that it doesn't exist, however, we still know only a small portion of life and human experience through the scientific method. Most of life on planet Earth has yet to be explained or measured by scientific instruments, yet that is no reason to ignore all phenomena outside of what currently can be objectively measured and analyzed. Spirituality is experienced beyond cognitive activity and can't be either confirmed or refuted by thought. If our inquiry into the spiritual dimension were to be entirely intellectually situated, we would never know the spiritual dimension because we would be looking in the wrong place. Or perhaps a better way of putting it is that we would be looking in the wrong way with preconceived ideas, judgments and desires. If you (as subject) looked into the eyes of a horse (as object) with preconceived ideas of what you might find, all you'd experience would be a visual image of the eyes of what you conceptualize as being a horse. You might admire him as a beautiful looking animal and imagine soulful connection and oneness with him, but that would not be the real thing. To truly experience something on a spiritual level we need to put our ego (our conditioned concepts of what should be) to one side and look with absolute innocence, or as Buddhism puts it, with an empty mind. If human experience is entirely filtered through mental concepts, how would we experience the aliveness of a tree, the sensation of being on a vast ocean, or the immensity of the sky, all of which are so far beyond our true comprehension?

Mark has been working with me and the horses for about six months. He suffers from a pervasive anxiety about the state of the world and is worried about what his responsibility might be within such obvious global dysfunction. He talks of pandemics (Covid-19, and viruses yet to emerge), climate disasters of the present and future, and worldwide ecological degradation. Every time he reads something on these subjects through the media, his suffering increases. He has taken the problems of the world into himself and feels guilty about pretty much everything he consumes and uses. At the same time, his exacting father has instilled in his mind that he should be a perfectly moral human being and Mark feels as though he is anything but perfect.

We have made some progress in letting go of these pervasive ideas but it is very much a case of two steps forward and one step backwards as he undermines himself from one week to the next, regardless of insights from the previous session. We work on accepting that which is (that which he can't change), but he picks up the load again during the week and puts it back on his shoulders.

He is a very intelligent young man and sensitive to many aspects of nature. He has dogs whom he adores and he loves being with our horses. He tells me how he cries when driving past a paddock of calves taken from their dairy-cow mothers. He weeps when he reads social media reports about cruelty to dogs and other animals, and he delights and laughs when seeing our horses running into a new paddock of fresh grass. He is politically active and talks intelligently about social justice. He is a sensitive and lovely person but the world is "making him miserable".

Mark and I work on the assumed idea of something or someone "making" us feel a certain way and he understands that he is choosing how to respond to situations personally. We practice meditation and mindfulness with the horses, and he is gradually becoming aware of his conditioned thinking.

At the six month point in our work together we discuss how he has already identified and worked with several issues such as his inner critic (conditioned thinking) and that he has understood conceptually that he takes on responsibility for things beyond his sphere of influence. I suggest it is now time to experiment with having no agenda so he goes into the paddock with all seven horses to spend time alone with them while "doing nothing" and having no expectations. He does this for three consecutive sessions. In the first two sessions he comments on experiences of heightened senses and bonding with the horses. In the third session I stand outside the fence watching as he walks up to each horse and greets them. Then he takes extra time with one horse. This young gelding looks very relaxed in his company and after five minutes or so lies down on the grass to sleep. Mark sits down in a safe place next to the horse's head and stays there for a while.

When Mark comes back out for a chat he says that he has never before felt so peaceful and that he used that time to meditate with his eyes open, bringing his mind back to the horse every time his monkey-mind took over. He says that he felt some moments of pure spaciousness where thinking was absent and that he was surprised to observe that he was fully functioning and conscious while at the same time experiencing a deep sense of "knowing". He reports that all he had to do was to let go of his worries about the world, to relinquish his need to fix and control and to accept things as they are right now. He says that the lying down horse was showing him how to surrender and accept what is, and what he experienced just then was the smell of damp grass and warm horse and a deep knowing that there was no need for anything more. Mark had just experienced the formless dimension.

The spiritual dimension is formless, meaning we can't touch it, examine it or hold on to it. Because we can't do those things, meaning that it cannot be detected scientifically, it can become cause for dismissal and denial but the only way to know the spiritual dimension is to experience it. The spiritual dimension is all too easily denied or missed because it can't be sought through the intellect, although its absence can be all too easily felt as a sense of emptiness, disconnection and meaninglessness. Because the spirit or soul is always there within us, and always has been (although it can be obscured by ego), we don't have to do anything complicated to experience it other than to still the mind and be aware of the spaciousness of the present moment. This can be enabled by consciously observing one thing at a time in our immediate environment without making a mental commentary about it. This can be anything. For Mark it was a horse and the sensation of sitting on grass on a warm summer morning in a state of spaciousness. As thought recedes into the background, you will at times come to a sense of nothingness or emptiness felt deep within your being. This is the state that Buddha called the "no-self", meaning that we are no longer captured by a stream of thought with which we identify personally. The spaciousness that is then free to arise is that which poets, musicians and mystics are driven to express through imagery. If it wasn't for humans being aware of this formless dimension, there would be no need at all for either art or mysticism.

One experience of awareness is the deepening sensation we call *awe*. A sunrise can instill awe in us. So can a piece of music, the song of a bird and the smile of a child. Such experiences capture our attention so perfectly that, for a few seconds, all thought stops, and we feel at one with where we are at that moment. You could say we *transcend* thought in such moments, and I would place a bet on every human having had these kinds of experiences more than once. Awareness (or becoming fully conscious) is not a mind-blowing experience but is something we all have, even if in small doses. I would go so far as to say that every one of us experiences moments of pure awareness every day but we might not recognize them as such, therefore they do not become more frequent. With practice, though, if we recognize these moments of stillness without trying to grasp them we will know them as our spiritual home to which we can return.

Another way into this dimension is to put our attention on our inner body to consciously experience it. (I discuss this below as "accessing the life force within".) This is a beautiful practice because the body is always there, so we can have access to this awareness at any time. Nobody around need even know that we are accessing our inner body awareness, although it's possible that they will sense a certain calmness around us when we do.

Can we also find the spiritual dimension in a church, synagogue, mosque, temple and ashram, etc.? Yes, it is perfectly possible given that accessing the timeless dimension is the primary goal of most religions. Religion has its place and deserves respect as the multifaceted expression of the human yearning to know the divine. But unfortunately the human desire for divine experience has fallen under the compulsion to wrap it up in thought and form structures. All too easily it is buried under dogma, as religion gets tied up in ideas, ritual and moralistic regulation. But against all odds, the truth remains in its essence inside every religion. A few highly evolved spiritual people (such as the Christian, Hebraic and Islamic mystics)[2] have successfully negotiated their way through dogmatic obstacles to arrive at the essence of spiritual experience but it's a difficult pathway. Personally, I have explored the pathway of formal religion several times, each time arriving at a point where I find the human-made conceptual obstacles too distracting. However, I do continue to study the words of Jesus of Nazareth, Lao Tzu, the Buddha and the mystics with great reverence.

The pathway to the divine is experienced within ourselves. Because spirituality cannot be fully conceived by the mind, Jesus constantly used metaphor and analogy to describe it. To point to divinity he used the metaphor of the "kingdom of heaven", repeatedly saying that it is within each one of us. He also said that we can access this dimension at any time. We don't have to go somewhere special to find it and we don't have to perform rituals. Our own divinity or depth of being has always been there in each one of us but has become so hidden by dysfunctional thought that it appears to be inaccessible.

We can take it for granted that humanity is suffering from separation sickness (separation from nature and the divine within), and that we have lost much of the emotional and intuitive skills that our animal ancestors relied upon. If we could get in touch with, make friends with, and truly reintegrate our animal nature with our intellect then maybe we would become the beings we were meant to be. Animals have not replaced their rooted connection to life with conceptual thought, so they don't suffer psychologically in the same way as humans. However, through connecting with animals and nature in general and horses in particular, and through developing a state of presence we open to the possibility of utilizing the aspects of our body-mind that have been neglected in favor of conceptualized realities. Once we learn to reserve conceptual thought for practical purposes, for the rest of the time psychological pain gradually recedes.

How do we lead ourselves and our clients into being aware of the spiritual dimension? In my experience it happens surreptitiously in that if people are open to what horses have to offer they can't help but respond to the soul of the horse with their own soul, whether named as such or not. As practitioners we use whatever therapeutic or learning practices we are skilled in to lead clients to a place beyond conditioned thought where they can experience a shared stillness between themselves and a powerful large animal. Once people access some freedom from their conditioned selves they begin to find the space necessary to identify with the unconditioned part of themselves, which we might choose to call the true self or the soul.

The underlying theme of this book is that through the presence of horses we can lead people to spiritual wholeness while working within any equine assisted practice. Given that you are still reading this, undoubtedly you will have been doing some of this work already and will be no stranger to many of these concepts from your own life experience. Whatever spiritual awareness I experience has not come from myself. I have applied the spiritual practices from the teachings of much wiser people and have put them into practice before adopting them in my equine assisted counseling work. It is essential that we work on ourselves and access our own divinity before attempting to lead anyone else. The good news is that we don't have to be the Buddha, or Christ or the prophet Mohammad before we do this work. Making a start is all that is required; horses will do the rest.

Footnotes

1. Genesis, chapters 2 & 3, Revised International Version of the Bible.

2. For instance, Saint John of the Cross, Saint Teresa of Ávila, Julian of Norwich, Francis of Assisi, Meister Eckhart, Bonaventure, Abu Bakr, Rumi, Martin Buber and Aryeh Kaplan.

Chapter 31

Transcending the Personal Story

It becomes clearer and clearer that we do not live in a divided world. The harsh divisions of spirit and nature, mind and body, subject and object, controller and controlled, are seen more and more to be awkward conventions of language. These are misleading and clumsy terms for describing a world in which all events seem to be mutually interdependent — an immense complexity of subtly balanced relationships which, like an endless knot, has no loose end from which it can become untangled and put in supposed order.

Alan Watts

Once we have begun to lead a person through a process of rewriting their story, ironically, the next step to wholeness and presence is to help them *transcend* their story. I don't wish to underplay the effectiveness of re-authoring the story. It is a powerful practice and for some people that's as far as they want to go (or can go) for the present. It is certainly far healthier to have a positive self-claimed story of who we are than to carry around an unexamined conditioned sense of self. In any case, the newly revised story does not need to be abandoned to be transcended, in fact it can't be unless we withdraw entirely from humanity. We still must live on the level of form, so we need that story, but we do not need to identify with it to derive a sense of self.

What does it mean to transcend the story of who we are? If we live solely from our form identity, we are trapped by our conditioning and conceptual thought. Let me take you back to the beginning where I mentioned the Indian spiritual teacher Ramana Maharshi who set his students the task of meditating on, "Who am I?" It's really a trick question designed to shake up a person's habitual thinking patterns, not unlike a Zen koan. No verbal or conceptual answer to that question is right, because to say, "I am this," or "I am that," divides us into two opposing entities of subject and object, being and doing. The right answer, or at least I should say the one that leads to awareness and presence is simply "I am", in other words "I exist" or "I am being". "I" and "being" are as one rather than two separate concepts: once we learn to rise above thought (to give it no mind), subject and object collapse into one.

What are transcendent humans like? They are firmly rooted in being as are all animals. They are not trapped by their thoughts, worries, emotions and feelings, and they will have made peace with past and future. Thought will not be habitual, undermining and repetitive, but will be used as a useful tool to be activated as needed. Enlightened humans would have form identities related to how they live, with their likes, dislikes, emotions and abilities intact, but they would not view their form identity as essentially who they are. They would live from their soul identity, largely unaffected by the conditioned mind. They would know the soul as the "I am", while at the same time recognizing that they have a form identity with which to function in the human world. They would make peace with the certainty that everything of form identity will eventually fall away, erode, dissolve and die, but they would still allow themselves to enjoy ever-changing forms (including their own) in all their mystery. Form is to be enjoyed, and there is nothing intrinsically wrong with that, but they would derive their meaning and sense of presence from the deeper self of soul identity. They would know that form and spirit (or soul) are yin and yang for each other, that they need each other for as long as they are embodied.

If we are to transcend our personal story then how do we know what is truth and reality? We experience what we call the reality of the (so-called) outside world through our primary five senses, but as I mentioned earlier, our senses and neural processes can't possibly process all the data coming at us. One way to see how we take in information is to consider that all sensations come to our sense organs as energetic touch. Putting it simply, vision is the result of light waves touching our retina that our brain then interprets as a picture. It appears that the picture is "out there" but it's not, it's inside our heads. It's the same with hearing: sound waves touch our eardrums and make them vibrate, which the brain interprets as music, the spoken word or noise. Taste and smell come from the touch of tiny particles in the mouth and nostrils. All these different kinds of touch to our sensory nerves are, at the same time, both particles and energy waves. We know this from Einstein who pointed out that matter is energy, and we also know from metaphysics that there must be an experiencer for there to be an experience and that the mere act of observation changes what we look at. That means that if you train yourself to be the observer of your mind, and if you do nothing more, your mind will change and you will, over time, experience an increase in spaciousness. This is a very important point to remember for it gives us hope that transformation is possible.

Both science and philosophy support the realization that reality is mentally constructed, that there is no such thing as absolute reality for any living being. To the extent that reality exists, *you are it*. Reality is constructed within our brains, our cells and our DNA. How we experience the external world is limited by the available spectra within which our primary senses operate (which is a very narrow bandwidth).[1] A deeper reality is the awareness of being that transcends the ego. This is our soul identity and is a place of *no form*. It is timeless and formless, and is a place we know in the depth of our being the moment thinking subsides.[2] All religions have this understanding, while giving it other names such as Nirvana in Buddhism and the Tao in Taoism. It is what St. Paul called "the peace that surpasses all understanding."[3] The meanings of Peace, Nirvana, Heaven and the Tao cannot be fully captured through words and mental concepts because words are form, whereas the spaciousness of the soul is formless. The very first sentence in the Tao Te Ching is,

"The Tao [the Way] which can be expressed in words is not the eternal Tao."[4] This says that if we think we can precisely define spirituality or soul spaciousness, we are describing something wide of the mark. It can't be done. The Tao, the Soul, the Christ within and Buddha nature, are all names for the same spaciousness that can never be described accurately through concepts. That hasn't stopped many thousands of books being published on these subjects, but along with this book they can only ever point to something formless that has to be experienced to be understood. The wonderful thing about working with horses is that by its very nature it is experiential. Ideas, thoughts and practices help us to get into a frame where we open to deeper experience, but both spiritual experience and the explanation for it resists encapsulation through words. It will always be the peace that surpasses all understanding (Example 7).

FORM TO FORMLESSNESS

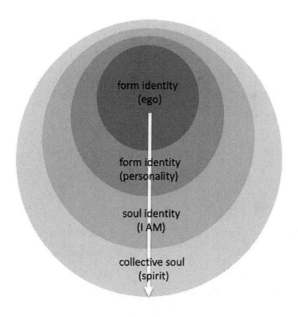

Example 7

When I first became aware of the soul space as felt experience beyond mental concepts, I understood that I had always known it but had never truly recognized that knowing. The closest I can get to a description is that it feels like an eternal deep river running beneath my being and all living things, connecting us all and supporting all of life. I know it as a place of peace underlying everything; I know it as the essence of my being that can be too easily obscured through my own thinking. Even when obscured, even though I get lost in ego and must find my way back, I know that spaciousness cannot be entirely lost or disturbed by anything external. A Zen story encapsulates this:

> During the civil wars in feudal Japan, an invading army would quickly sweep into a town and take control. In one village, everyone fled just before the army arrived, everyone except the Zen master. Curious about this old fellow, the general went to the temple to see for himself what kind of man this master was. When he wasn't treated with the deference and submissiveness to which he was accustomed, the general burst into anger. "You fool," he shouted as he reached for his sword, "don't you realize you are standing before a man who could run you through without blinking an eye!" But despite the threat, the master seemed unmoved. "And do you realize," the master replied calmly, "that you are standing before a man who can be run through without blinking an eye?"[5]

Personally, I am light years away from being that Zen Master, but deep within I know what the story is pointing to. There is an essence of me that cannot be touched by anything physical. It's worth repeating that the soul space is that part of us that never changes and has always been there. It is also the part of me that is not really mine since there is only ever one universal soul, one knowing and one life. As Alan Watts puts it, "You are a function of what the whole universe is doing in the same way that a wave is a function of what the whole ocean is doing."[6] We are not only a part of the ocean, we *are* the ocean.

Be still with your horse and know that you are an expression of the very same life. You, your horse, all flora and fauna, the sea and the sky, reside within one consciousness and are expressions of the one life. We are all connected even though we take on various functions within the one organism, within one being and within one world. We are all manifestations of a single life force. Look into the horse's eyes and see that the light coming from her eyes is the same light in your eyes. Know from the depths of your being that we are all connected, we are all made of the same stuff, we are all ONE.

Footnotes

1. Although this does not account for near-death experiences when the brain is technically not functioning.

2. Eckhart Tolle (2011) *Transcending the Ego: Finding Our Roots in Being.* ASIN: B0068ZSYZO.

3. New Testament, Philippians 4:6, New International Version of the Bible.

4. Translation by Lionel Giles, http://www.bopsecrets.org/gateway/passages/tao-te-ching.htm (Accessed 31 January 2022).

5. As quoted from: https://www.worldclasslearning.com/zen-stories/without-fear-zen-stories.html (Accessed 12 December 2021).

6. Alan Watts, as quoted in: https://surfd.com/2015/08/alan-watts-on-the-ocean-15-08-2015 (Accessed 12 December 2022).

Chapter 32

Conclusion

Everywhere the winged horse Pegasus struck the earth with his hoof, a spring of life-giving water burst forth.[1]

This book offers a way of integrating spirituality into existing methods, models and practices in equine assisted work. Such a spiritual approach is not anti-intellectual but recognizes that experiencing life through mental concepts alone is unlikely to lead to fulfilled and peaceful lives. Spirituality arises naturally within our psyches as a place of inner knowing that we all share and always have done. A desire to explore the soul (or spirit) naturally occurs on the psycho-spiritual continuum but there is no need to regard one end of the continuum as taking precedence over the other. We do not need to make a case for living through mental conceptualization *or* intuition and inner knowing. We have been given both, and we need both for true inner balance. Humans are beings, both intelligent and sensitive, who experience life non-conceptually as well as conceptually. It is natural for someone's exploration of their psychology to lead to questions of spirituality such as "Who am I?" and "What is the purpose of my life?" Like everything within a continuum, these ways of experiencing and knowing are not oppositional. Like hot and cold, good and bad, up and down, yin and yang, they at the same time delineate and support each other.

Finding our way back

We can find the balance between conceptual and non-conceptual being in the same way that a point of balance can be sought between experiencing nature from the outside and the inside. We know nature as something outside of ourselves to experience deeply and mindfully through our five primary senses. We can also know nature from the inside through inner body awareness (sixth sense) and by being the witness of experience (seventh sense). By realizing that we *are* nature instead of just being *in* nature, we have the chance to access our inherent wisdom and to share in the innate wisdom of all other living things. My hope is that you will access the spaciousness within yourself by opening to soul-to-soul connections with horses and other manifestations of nature. Inviting a spiritual dimension into equine work is a choice any practitioner (or equestrian) can make. All that's needed initially is a desire to connect soul to soul as you put your ego to one side. Horses do the rest. There is nothing difficult about doing this, in fact it's more of an *undoing* than a *doing* through the process of stopping (or ignoring) the incessant chatter in our heads, putting to one side our desires for particular outcomes and allowing what is, to be as it is.

Modern humans need spiritual healing through one means or another for the simple reason that we all carry a primary wound. We hold deep unacknowledged grief through our loss of connection with the land, the sky, the ocean and with all of nature. When we are born we come into form derived from elements of this planet and the universe. Clearly, we are not born *into* the world, we are born *out of* the world and it is no coincidence that the Earth as an entity is referred to by ancient and indigenous cultures and world religions as our true Mother or Father. Just as infants go through the pain of separation from their mothers as they develop a sense of individuality through gradual ego development, we also feel the pain of separation from our primary Mother or Father, i.e. planet Earth. The good news is that we can find our way back home through nature itself, whereas reading about it and watching nature programs will never fully suffice. We need to smell the moss and wet humus of the forest; we need to listen to the dawn chorus from a place alive with trees and birds; we need to feel the cool breeze on our skin in the early morning and we need to share space with animals doing no more than being themselves. In this book we have focused on horses (me as writer and you as reader) because they are one of the most generous animals on the planet and because you and I love them. With an open mind, looking through the parted curtains of ego, we are simply asking to walk a little while with horses. We ask them to impart some of their wisdom as we open ourselves to them both conceptually and non-conceptually. The wisdom of animals and nature in general is always there. It never withdraws its generosity. What does change is our willingness to notice it and to recognize the same within ourselves.

Story-making and real connection

Throughout this writing I have put forward two fundamental pathways for making soul-to-soul connections with horses. One is to make *real connection* by approaching them on their terms, by reading their subtle body language to know what they are experiencing, by respecting their point of view and by developing true compassion for them. Real connection is something that I firmly believe every practitioner needs to develop with their own horses before working with clients. We need to know ourselves well, but equally, we must know our horses well if we are to have anything to offer anyone else. Making real connection with a horse is a profound experience for anyone who feels they have lost touch with themselves and others emotionally or spiritually, and that applies to both practitioner and client. When I work with a client along spiritual lines I feel equally moved by the experience as the client. That is when we know it is working. It reminds me of the definition I have for friendship: when two of us have shared time and stories I ask myself afterwards whether I feel as though I have both given and received energy or whether it has flowed in one direction only. Regarding our human and equine friends the experience should be the same, otherwise we need to ask whether there was an element of exploitation or patronization in our "conversation".

The other main pathway to psycho-spiritual wholeness is working with the natural human capacity for *story-making* through allowing, recognizing and encouraging analogy, metaphor and projection. By inviting horses' perspectives on emerging stories, clients find themselves rewriting a narrative free from conditioning, rediscovering the true self they know themselves to be. Story exploration is well suited to clients whose habitual ways of thinking about themselves block their way to wholeness.

Neither the *real connection* nor the *story-making* pathway is better than the other. They simply have different applications and can be used together, but with care since it is usually disruptive when immersed in story-making or re-authoring to draw a client's attention to the real physical/emotional state of the horse (although as a matter of safety I constantly read my horse to know how she is feeling). During story-making processes it is the client's imaginative interpretation more than anything that leads to personal insight, hence I recommend consciously using one pathway at a time. It is often the case too, that a client naturally leans towards either story-making or real connection. However, it is certainly beneficial to lead an individual through both paradigms when working together over a significant period of time.

Accessing the metaphorical mammalian brain

Both horses and humans can access within themselves everything they need to know to thrive. But we don't necessarily believe this to be true. We have largely lost the ability to access or to trust the intuitive knowledge within our own being and, metaphorically speaking, we no longer know how to trust our "mammalian" brain as the center of our emotions. In the Western world we trust cognitively derived knowledge far more than intuitive ways of knowing. There is no need to swing entirely the other way and distrust our cognitive abilities, but when we learn to trust our innate knowing through somatic awareness, spaciousness and mindfulness, we become healthier, happier and whole human beings. Horses are openheartedly willing to model this way of being for us.

Knowing that horses want real engagement

Because horses have an ability to guide us to the spiritual dimension within I have suggested that they *want* to engage with us, soul to soul. I say this because I see that horses are mystified and confused by human brokenness and falseness when they come across it. They expect us to be at home in our skins, just as they are. We need to be, therefore, not horse whisperers but *horse listeners* and *horse observers*. It is not what we want our horses to do for us that is transformative, rather, it is asking how we can be more like them as their brothers and sisters in nature that brings transformation.

Viewing horses as spiritual beings

There is more to life than what we conjure up mentally: the spiritual dimension goes way beyond thought. There is even more to life than what we experience through our primary senses since they are limited by the way they have evolved according to environmental challenges to the organism. But there are ways to experience our inner being as the foundation for all other experience. Horses show us all these aspects of ourselves. They remind us of, and awaken us to, what we used to know thousands of years ago that is still embedded in our

DNA. Spend a day with horses doing nothing and you might agree. There is more to horses than eating grass, procreating and running around, and there is more to us than a constant stream of conditioned thought and busyness. It is up to us to look within and discover just what that is.

Regarding everything as sacred

It is the gift of mindfulness to discover how to value all we do and experience, and to cease to regard what we do as simply a means to an end. We notice our tendencies to devalue much of our experience out of a sense of urgency to meet a goal, to achieve or to "get somewhere". When we are with horses we can practice valuing everything we do with them. Everything is both of value and has its own lesson because absolutely everything in the world has its place, its role and its value in the sacred. My challenge to you is to also value "nothingness". Horses (and all animals) are good at this and it does them no psychological harm at all. Modern humans, however, are uncomfortable with not utilizing time to achieve something. If we can put aside our phones, computers, to-do lists, mental chatter and worries for a while with a horse and simply experience their environment with them, we are better people for it.

Knowing we are not separate beings

True personal transformation comes from rejecting the illusion that we are separate and independent beings. We are not separate entities but are intimately connected to each other in the same way that the billions of cells in our bodies are not separate entities (even if they think they are). We all share the same life, spirit, soul, atman or beingness. Behaving solely as separate individuals is a threat to nature and to human survival. Dr. Gabor Maté suggests in *The Myth of Normal* that, "No hominin species could have survived long enough to evolve had its members seen themselves as atomized individuals, pitted by Nature against their fellow beings."[2] All creatures on the planet, including human beings, are connected in a web of interdependence just as our brains are a complex of 128 billion neural connections within which specialized functions reside. Until us humans see the truth of our interconnectedness and transform societal structures accordingly we are destined to saw off the very branch upon which we are all sitting. We know this now. We see it plainly in the results of climate change and in the dreadful degradation of natural habitat throughout the planet. Horses (and all of nature) want to lead us out of this illusion of separateness that carries with it the burden of alienation and psychological pain.

Including everything

We do not need to go back to the innocence of hunter-gatherer societies (even if we could) and forget everything we have learned through science, agriculture, art, religion and human law. We might have lost our innocence and interconnectedness with nature by overvaluing the fruits of cognition but we do not need to throw everything out and start again. All we need, I believe, is to discover the depth of our own being and to communicate with other humans and nature through that dimension.

Allowing horses to complete us

We were never meant to be creatures separate from nature but that is how most of us view ourselves: as separate from, superior to, and protected from, nature. To know how to live fully we urgently need to open ourselves to the knowledge that comes from the natural world. We can learn these lessons from plants, trees, mountains, deserts, fish and any animal or group of insects. Indigenous peoples have always known this since it is how they survived and how they derived meaning from life.

The concept of horses "completing" humans is, for me, an irresistible metaphor. In the physical sense, if we could put our two species' capacities together as one being we would have the most amazing running, thinking, sensitive and scheming animal on the planet. When a very fine equestrian and an athletic horse work together at top capacity this single entity can indeed be seen as epitomizing such an ideal. It is not surprising that the image of the Centaur as an ancient Greek mythological being, half horse and half human, has endured to the present day.

The nonphysical qualities we identify in the horse are the very qualities that we as humans need to, and want to, reclaim to reconnect within our being. Horses ask us to open to them at the deepest level and they expect us to be like them in this respect. This is palpable when they appreciate us sharing concern for the things they value. They invite us to view the world through their eyes and they expect us to be on the same plane as them, just as humans expect of each other. Horses show us how to rediscover our true selves and to deepen our awareness of that which underlies all of life. Nature completes us, animals complete us, and horses complete us but in the end we are likely to discover that we have travelled full circle as we see that we always have been complete. Just as horses have everything they need to know to be whole, we humans also have everything we need to know to be whole.

Looking into the eyes of a horse

What do I see as I look into the eyes of a horse? I see the generous dark orbs of a beautiful, soulful and sensitive animal. She looks back at me with honesty and trust. There is no fear in her eyes. There is no pretence. Neither is there any desire: she is not asking me for anything but is content with what the present moment has to offer. I linger as we hold our gaze, and my question "Who are you?" merges with "Who am I?"

Without needing to put it into words I feel that I understand this amazing being and she understands me. We no longer feel like two different creatures separate from each other. Together we are one small detail within an enormous and infinite pattern. We know each other from within the timeless place where life is shared. The unchanging in me sees the unchanging in the horse; the unchanging in the horse sees the unchanging in me.

Look deeply into the eyes of a horse with an empty mind and you will sink into softness and know you are looking into her soul. Maintain a state of presence and you might experience the horse sinking into the softness of your eye as she looks deeply into your soul.[3]

Footnotes

1. https://thepegasusinstitute.com (Accessed 31 January 2022).
2. Maté (2022) p. 121.
3. Mutually "seeing" each other is a profound experience but don't *try* to achieve it; it must be effortless. Simply stay open to the possibility while practicing being present and authentic.

References

Baker, W. B. (2004) *Healing Power of Horses: Lessons from the Lakota Indians*. Irvine, California: BowTie Press.

Barrett, L. F. (2017) *How Emotions Are Made: The Secret Life of the Brain*. Boston: Houghton Mifflin Harcourt.

— — — (2020) *Seven and a Half Lessons About the Brain*. Boston: Houghton Mifflin Harcourt.

Boone, J. A. (1954) *Kinship with all Life*. New York: Harper One.

Brannaman, B. (1997) *Groundwork: The First Impression*. Westlake Village, CA: Rancho Deluxe Design.

Budiansky, S. (1997) *The Nature of Horses: Their Evolution, Intelligence and Behaviour*. London: Phoenix.

Chabris, C. & Simons, D. (2010) *The Invisible Gorilla: How Our Intuitions Deceive Us*. New York: Harper Collins.

Cohen, M. J. (2007) *Reconnecting With Nature: Finding Wellness Through Restoring Your Bond with the Earth*. Minnesota: Eco Press.

Dass, R. (2014) *Polishing the Mirror: How to Live from Your Spiritual Heart*. Louisville, CO: Sounds True.

— — — "Cultivating the Witness" [online]. Available at: https://www.ramdass.org/cultivating-witness/ (Accessed 1 April 2023).

de Waal, F. (2019) *Mama's Last Hug: Animal Emotions and What They Teach Us about Ourselves*. London: Granta.

di Nicola, V. (2018) "'Take Your Time': The Seven Pillars of a Slow Thought Manifesto". *Aeon Magazine* [online]. Available at: https://www.academia.edu/36033149/_Take_Your_Time_The_Seven_Pillars_of_a_Slow_Thought_Manifesto (Accessed 1 April 2023).

Dürckheim, K. G. (1956) *Hara: The Vital Center of Man*. Rochester: Inner Traditions.

Earley, J. & Weiss, B. (2013) *Freedom from your Inner Critic: A Self-Therapy Approach*. Louisville, CO: Sounds True.

Ecker, S. & Lykins, A. (2019) "Effects of Short-Term Human-Horse Interactions on Human Heart Rate Variability: A Multiple Single Case Study". *People and Animals: The International Journal of Research and Practice*, Vol. 2, Issue 1, Article 2 [online]. Available at: https://docs.lib.purdue.edu/paij/vol2/iss1/2 (Accessed 10 October 2022).

Frankl, V. E. (1959/2006) *Man's Search for Meaning*. Boston, MA: Beacon Press.

Grandin, T. (2006) *Animals in Translation: Using the Mysteries of Autism to Decode Animals*. London: Bloomsbury Publishing.

— — — (2010) *Animals Make Us Human: Creating the Best Life for Animals*. New York: First Mariner Books.

Hallberg, L. (2008) *Walking the Way of the Horse*. Bloomington, IN: iUniverse.

— — — (2017) *The Clinical Practice of Equine-Assisted Therapy: Including Horses in Human Healthcare*. London & New York: Routledge.

Hamilton, A. J. (2011) *Zen Mind, Zen Horse: The Science and Spirituality of Working with Horses*. North Adams, MA: Storey Publishing.

— — — (2016) *Lead with Your Heart: Lessons from a Life with Horses*. North Adams, MA: Storey Publishing.

Holman, P. (2018) *Living Space: Openness and Freedom through Spatial Awareness*. Winchester, UK: O-Books.

Honoré, C. (2005) *In Praise of Slowness*. New York: Harper Collins.

Jackson, J. (2014) *Paddock Paradise: A Guide to Natural Horse Boarding*. Arkansas: Star Ridge Publishing.

Jones, J. (2020) *Horse Brain, Human Brain: The Neuroscience of Horsemanship*. Vermont: Trafalgar Square Books.

Kalsched, D. (2013) *Trauma and the Soul: A psycho-spiritual approach to human development and its interruption*. New York: Routledge.

Kimmerer, R. W. (2013) *Braiding Sweetgrass: Indigenous Wisdom, Scientific Knowledge, and the Teachings of Plants*. Minneapolis: Milkweed.

Kirby, M. (2016) *An Introduction to Equine Assisted Psychotherapy*. Bloomington, IN: Balboa Press.

Kohanov, L. (2007) *The Tao of Equus*. Novato, CA: New World Library.

— — — (2016) *The Five Roles of a Master Herder: A Revolutionary Model for Socially Intelligent Leadership*. Novato, CA: New World Library.

Kowalski, Gary (1991/2007) *The Souls of Animals*. Novato, CA: New World Library.

Kutsch, A. (2021) (English translation). *From the Horse's Point of View: Beyond Natural Horsemanship: Horse Training's New Frontier*. Vermont: Trafalgar Square Books.

Lakoff, G. & Johnson, M. (1980) *Metaphors We Live By*. Chicago: University of Chicago Press.

Levine, G. et al. (2013) "Pet Ownership and Cardiovascular Risk". *Circulation*, Vol. 127, Issue 23, 11 June 2013.

Liefooghe, A. (2020) *Equine-Assisted Psychotherapy and Coaching: An Evidence-Based Framework*. London & New York: Routledge.

Lilly, J. (1972/2001) *The Center of the Cyclone: An Autobiography of Inner Space*. London: Marion Boyars Publishers.

Masson, J. M. (1995) *When Elephants Weep: The Emotional Lives of Animals*. New York: Delta.

Maté, G. with Maté, D. (2022) *The Myth of Normal: Trauma, Illness & Healing in a Toxic Culture*. London: Vermilion.

McBane, S. (2012) *Horse Senses*. London & New York: Routledge.

McCarthy, M. (2016) *The Moth Snowstorm: Nature and Joy*. London: John Murray.

McCormick, A. & M. D. (1997) *Horse Sense and the Human Heart*. Deerfield Beach, FL: Health Communications.

McGilchrist, I. (2009) *The Master and his Emissary: The Divided Brain and the Making of the Western World*. New Haven & London: Yale University Press.

Mehrabian, A. & Ferris, S. R. (1967) "Inference of attitudes from nonverbal communication in two channels". *Journal of Consulting Psychology*, Vol. 31, Issue 3, 248–252. Accessible at: https://doi.org/10.1037/h0024648

Miller, R. (1999) *Understanding the Ancient Secrets of the Horse's Mind*. Neenah, WI: Russell Meerdink.

— — — (2007) *Natural Horsemanship Explained: From Heart to Hands*. CA: Robert M. Miller Communications.

Milner, M. (1934/2011) *A Life of One's Own*. London & New York: Routledge.

Morgan, A. (2000) *What is narrative therapy? An easy-to-read introduction*. Adelaide: Dulwich Centre Publications.

Morgan, M. H. (1962) *Xenophon: The Art of Horsemanship*. London: J. A. Allen.

Olmert, M. D. (2009) *Made for Each Other: The Biology of the Human-Animal Bond*. Cambridge, MA: Da Capo Press.

Palmer, P. J. (2009) *A Hidden Wholeness: The Journey Toward an Undivided Life*. Hoboken, NJ: Jossey-Bass.

Panksepp, J. (1998) *Affective Neuroscience: The Foundations of Human and Animal Emotions*. New York: Oxford University Press.

Pert, C. (1997) *Molecules of Emotion: The Science Behind Mind-Body Medicine*. New York: Scribner.

Pony Boy, G. (1998) *Horse, Follow Closely: Native American Horsemanship*. Mount Joy, PA: Fox Chapel Publishing.

Rashid, M. (2015) *Horses Never Lie*. New York: Skyhorse Publishing.

Russell, T. (2015) *Mindfulness in Motion: a happier, healthier life through body-centred meditation*. London: Watkins Publishing.

Scott, B. D. & Martin, M. (2016) "Understanding vital life signs in horses" [PDF]. Available at: https://texashelp.tamu.edu/wp-content/uploads/2016/02/understanding-vital-life-signs-in-horses.pdf (Accessed 1 December 2022).

Seth, A. (2021) *Being You: A New Science of Consciousness*. London: Faber & Faber.

Sewell, A. (1877/1994) *Black Beauty*. London: Puffin Books.

Sheade, H. (2021) *Equine-Assisted Counseling and Psychotherapy: Healing Through Horses*. London & New York: Routledge.

Shields, J. "Why Didn't Evolution Give Us the Ability to Smell Fresh Water?" *How Stuff Works* [online]. Available at: https://science.howstuffworks.com/life/evolution/humans-smell-fresh-water-evolution.htm?srch_tag=cl35wo6ghmuwvtk7zo7bkuanzwvc3ebs (Accessed 10 December 2021).

Shipman, P. (2021) *Our Oldest Companions: The Story of the First Dogs*. Cambridge, MA: Harvard University Press.

Siegel, D. (2011) *Mindsight: The New Science of Personal Transformation*. New York: Bantam.

Sullivan, W. (1972) "The Einstein Papers. A Man of Many Parts". *The New York Times*, March 29, 1972.

Tabernaberri, C. (2007) *Through the Eyes of the Horse—Common Ground, Common Goals*. Footscray, VIC: Moonrise Media.

Tolle, E. (2004) *The Power of Now*. Sydney: Hodder Australia.

— — — (2005) *A New Earth: Create a Better Life*. New York: Penguin.

Watts, A. (1991) *Nature, Man and Woman*. New York: Random House.

——— "Love of Waters" [online]. Available at: https://alanwatts. org/transcripts/love-of-waters/ (Accessed 10 October 2022).

White, M. & Epston, D. (1990) *Narrative Means to Therapeutic Ends*. New York: W. W. Norton & Company Inc.

Wilsie, S. (2017) *Horse Speak: An Equine-Human Translation Guide: Conversations with Horses in Their Language*. Vermont: Trafalgar Square Books.

——— (2018) *Horses in Translation: Essential Lessons in Horse Speak: Learn to "Listen" and "Talk" in Their Language*. Vermont: Trafalgar Square Books.

Wolynn, M. (2017) *It Didn't Start with You: How Inherited Family Trauma Shapes Who We Are and How to End the Cycle*. London: Penguin.

Yong, E. (2022) *An Immense World: How Animal Senses Reveal the Hidden Realms Around Us*. New York: Random House.

Websites accessed

Adyashanti: https://www.soundstrue.com/collections/ shop?q=adyashanti

Cherokee parable: https://medium.com/@EdwigeRobinson/the- wolf-you-feed-7095a0cd7586

Chinese parable: https://bremeracosta.medium.com/parable-of- the-chinese-farmer-f012db83694d

Dass: https://www.ramdass.org/cultivating-witness/

di Nicola article: https://www.academia.edu/36033149/

Ecker & Lykins article: https://docs.lib.purdue.edu/paij/vol2/ iss1/2

Kirby: https://www.equinepsychotherapy.net.au

Lindblom: https://www.nadinelindblom.com

Nhat Hahn: https://plumvillage.org/articles/love-letter-to-the- earth-2

Royal article: http://www.TeAra.govt.nz/en/kaitiakitanga- guardianship-and-conservation/page-1

Schlote: https://naturallifemanship.com/can-animals-consent; https://equusoma.com/connection-before-concepts

Scott & Martin article: https://texashelp.tamu.edu/wp-content/uploads/2016/02/understanding-vital-life-signs-in-horses.pdf

Shields article: https://science.howstuffworks.com/life/evolution/humans-smell-fresh-water-evolution.htm?srch_tag=cl35wo6ghmuwvtk7zo7bkuanzwvc3ebs

Sinclair: https://www.tamingwild.com

Spira: https://www.scienceandnonduality.com/video/our-unborn-undying-nature; https://www.youtube.com/watch?v=Thl6kNVBiio

Tolle: https://eckharttolle.com

Watts: https://alanwatts.org/transcripts/love-of-waters

Wikipedia articles: Pech Merle; Stanislav Petrov

About the Author

Suzanne Court, PhD, is a qualified equine assisted therapist and mental health practitioner with over 30 years' horse experience and ten years' experience working professionally with horses in the mental healing and spiritual space. She teaches group and individual courses and gives lectures on Equine Assisted Therapy. She comes from a musical and academic background, having been a performing classical guitarist and a professor of music. She has published widely in historical musicology, and this book is her first regarding horses. She shares the equine therapy work with seven beautiful horses and her partner on their small farm in Waikato, New Zealand. She can be reached on https://earthhorse.co.nz.

O-BOOKS

SPIRITUALITY

O is a symbol of the world, of oneness and unity; this eye
represents knowledge and insight. We publish titles on general
spirituality and living a spiritual life. We aim to inform and
help you on your own journey in this life.
If you have enjoyed this book, why not tell other readers
by posting a review on your preferred book site?

Recent bestsellers from O-Books are:

Heart of Tantric Sex
Diana Richardson
Revealing Eastern secrets of deep love and intimacy
to Western couples.
Paperback: 978-1-90381-637-0 ebook: 978-1-84694-637-0

Crystal Prescriptions
The A-Z guide to over 1,200 symptoms and their healing crystals
Judy Hall
The first in the popular series of eight books, this handy little
guide is packed as tight as a pill bottle with crystal remedies
for ailments.
Paperback: 978-1-90504-740-6 ebook: 978-1-84694-629-5

Shine On
David Ditchfield and J S Jones
What if the aftereffects of a near-death experience were undeniable? What if a person could suddenly produce high-quality paintings of the afterlife, or if they acquired the ability to compose classical symphonies? Meet: David Ditchfield.
Paperback: 978-1-78904-365-5 ebook: 978-1-78904-366-2

The Way of Reiki
The Inner Teachings of Mikao Usui
Frans Stiene
The roadmap for deepening your understanding of the system of Reiki and rediscovering your True Self.
Paperback: 978-1-78535-665-0 ebook: 978-1-78535-744-2

You Are Not Your Thoughts
Frances Trussell
The journey to a mindful way of being, for those who want to truly know the power of mindfulness.
Paperback: 978-1-78535-816-6 ebook: 978-1-78535-817-3

The Mysteries of the Twelfth Astrological House
Fallen Angels
Carmen Turner-Schott, MSW, LISW
Everyone wants to know more about the most misunderstood house in astrology — the twelfth astrological house.
Paperback: 978-1-78099-343-0 ebook: 978-1-78099-344-7

WhatsApps from Heaven
Louise Hamlin
An account of a bereavement and the extraordinary
signs — including WhatsApps — that a retired
law lecturer received from her deceased husband.
Paperback: 978-1-78904-947-3 ebook: 978-1-78904-948-0

The Holistic Guide to Your Health
& Wellbeing Today
Oliver Rolfe
A holistic guide to improving your complete health,
both inside and out.
Paperback: 978-1-78535-392-5 ebook: 978-1-78535-393-2

Cool Sex
Diana Richardson and Wendy Doeleman
For deeply satisfying sex, the real secret is to reduce the heat,
to cool down. Discover the empowerment and fulfilment
of sex with loving mindfulness.
Paperback: 978-1-78904-351-8 ebook: 978-1-78904-352-5

Creating Real Happiness A to Z
Stephani Grace
Creating Real Happiness A to Z will help you understand
the truth that you are not your ego
(conditioned self).
Paperback: 978-1-78904-951-0 ebook: 978-1-78904-952-7

A Colourful Dose of Optimism
Jules Standish
It's time for us to look on the bright side, by boosting
our mood and lifting our spirit, both in our interiors,
as well as in our closet.
Paperback: 978-1-78904-927-5 ebook: 978-1-78904-928-2

Readers of ebooks can buy or view any of these bestsellers by
clicking on the live link in the title. Most titles are published
in paperback and as an ebook. Paperbacks are available in
traditional bookshops. Both print and ebook formats are
available online.

Find more titles and sign up to our readers' newsletter at
www.o-books.com

Follow O books on Facebook at **O-books**

For video content, author interviews and more, please subscribe to our YouTube channel:

O-BOOKS Presents

Follow us on social media for book news, promotions and more:

Facebook: O-Books

Instagram: @o_books_mbs

Twitter: @obooks

Tik Tok: @ObooksMBS

www.o-books.com